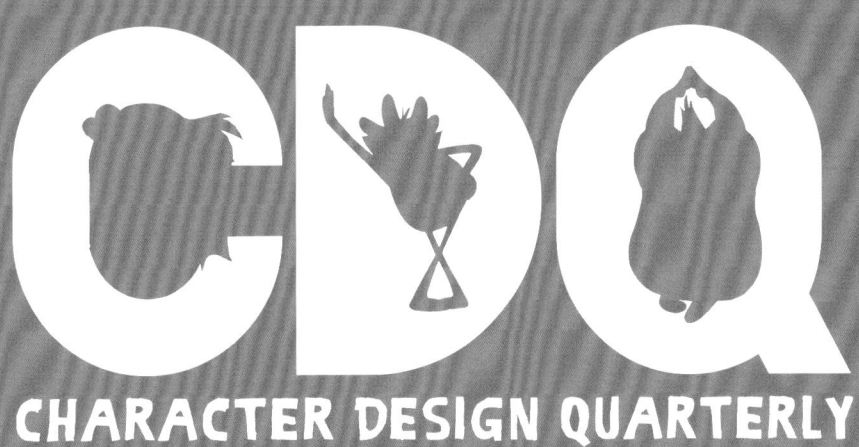

CHARACTER DESIGN QUARTERLY

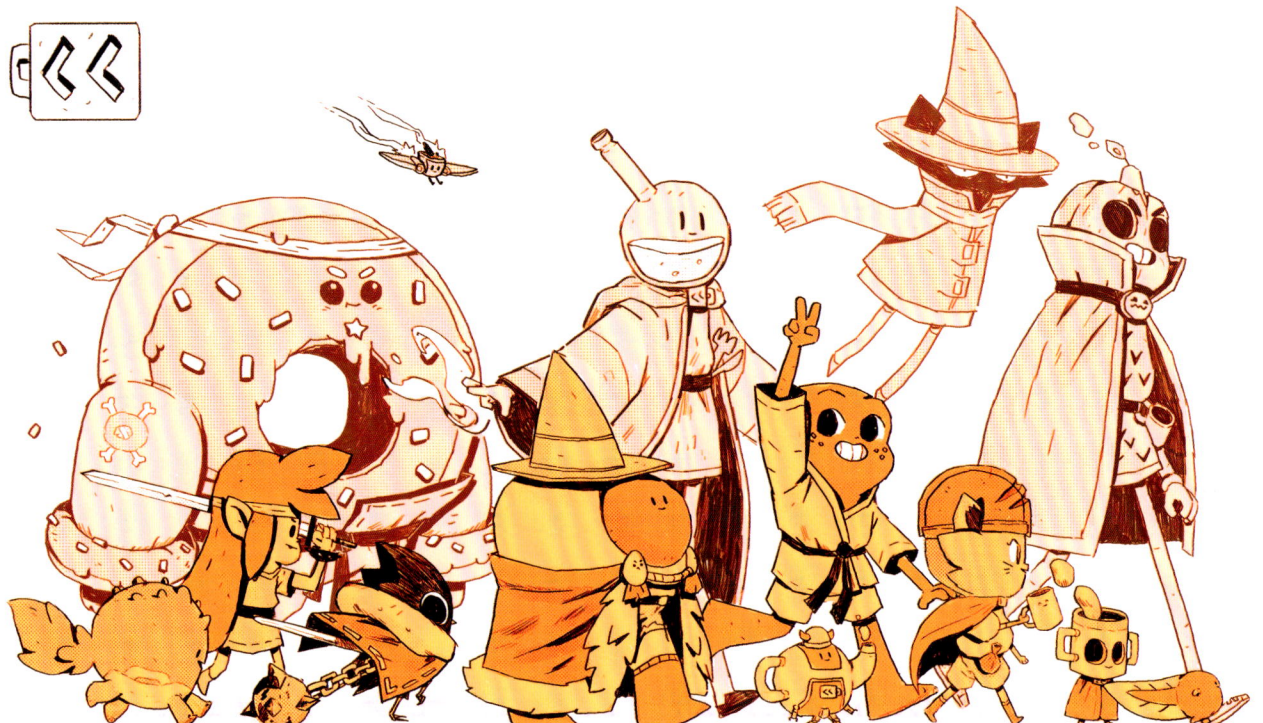

Image © Trudi Castle

CONTENTS

WELCOME TO *CHARACTER DESIGN QUARTERLY 28*

Creating unique, interesting character designs is a challenge, no matter your level of experience. In this issue, we feature several artists who suffer setbacks with their first ideas for a design, and who show us how they overcome bumps in the road to still create complete and original characters.

Our cover artwork this month is by the wonderfully talented Jackie Droujko. As well as speaking to us about her career and art development, Jackie shares how she struggled to make her idea for the cover work, refining her ideas to overcome her anxieties and create a memorable mermaid character.

Thomas Campi also explores how connecting with a prompt can sometimes be a challenge, as he creates a romantic moment between two characters. Elsewhere in the issue, Noor Sofi gives us a detailed look at how costume design can contribute to creating memorable characters, and Trudi Castle and Julia Korner share fascinating insights into their process and experiences in the industry.

So, if you're struggling with your own ideas, this fresh mix of imaginative character tutorials, interviews, and gallery art is sure to inspire you to keep going.

SAM DRAPER
EDITOR

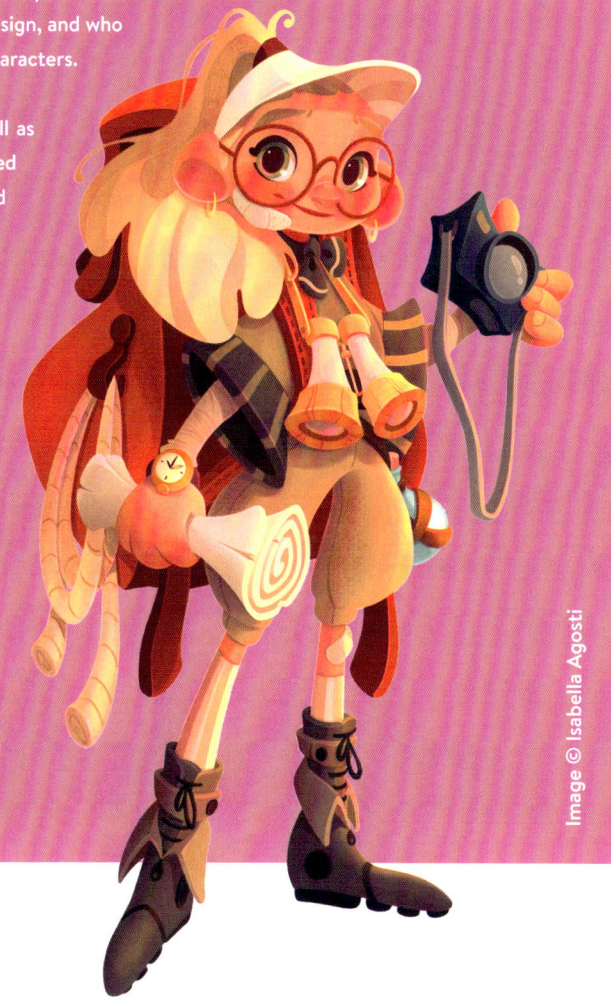

Image © Isabella Agosti

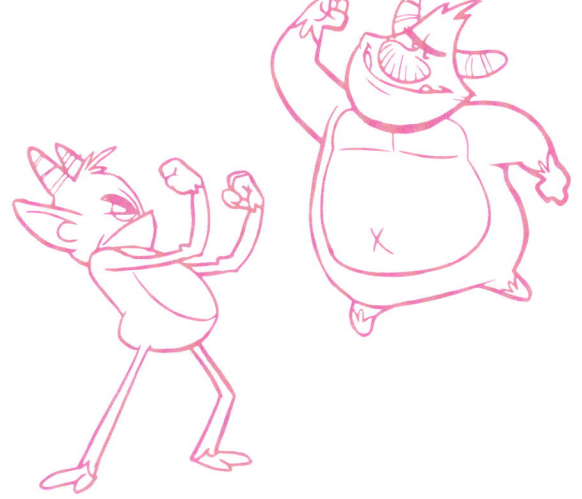

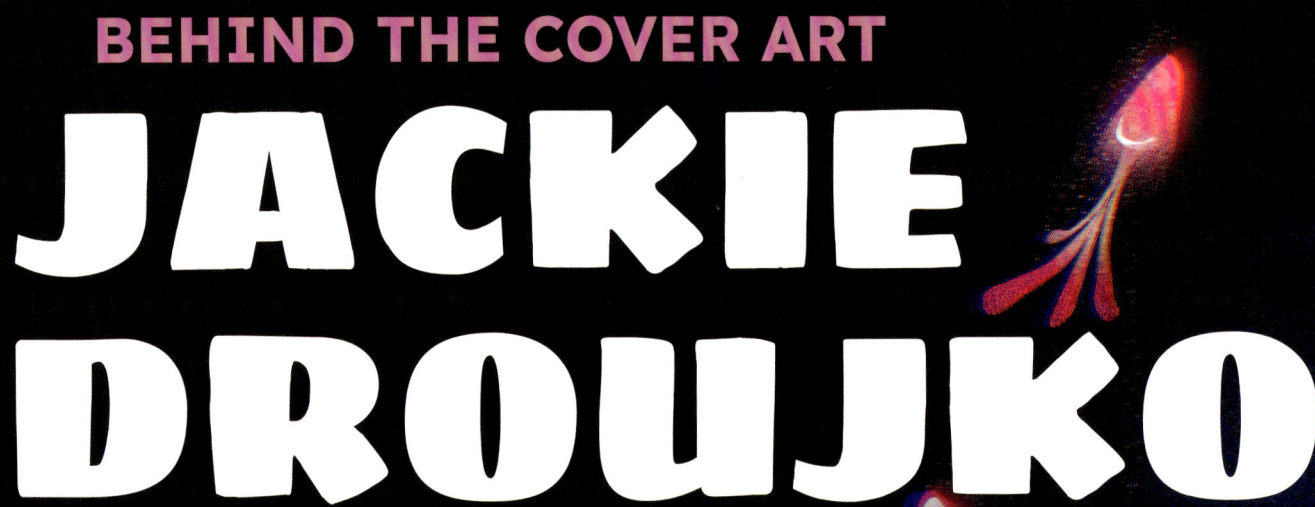

JACKIE DROUJKO

Jackie Droujko is a professional character designer and film-maker. Her vibrant, appealing designs have earned her a legion of fans on social media, and led to work with Netflix and Disney. We spoke to Jackie about her design principles, and the challenges of creating character work for animation, and she shows us how the striking cover art came together.

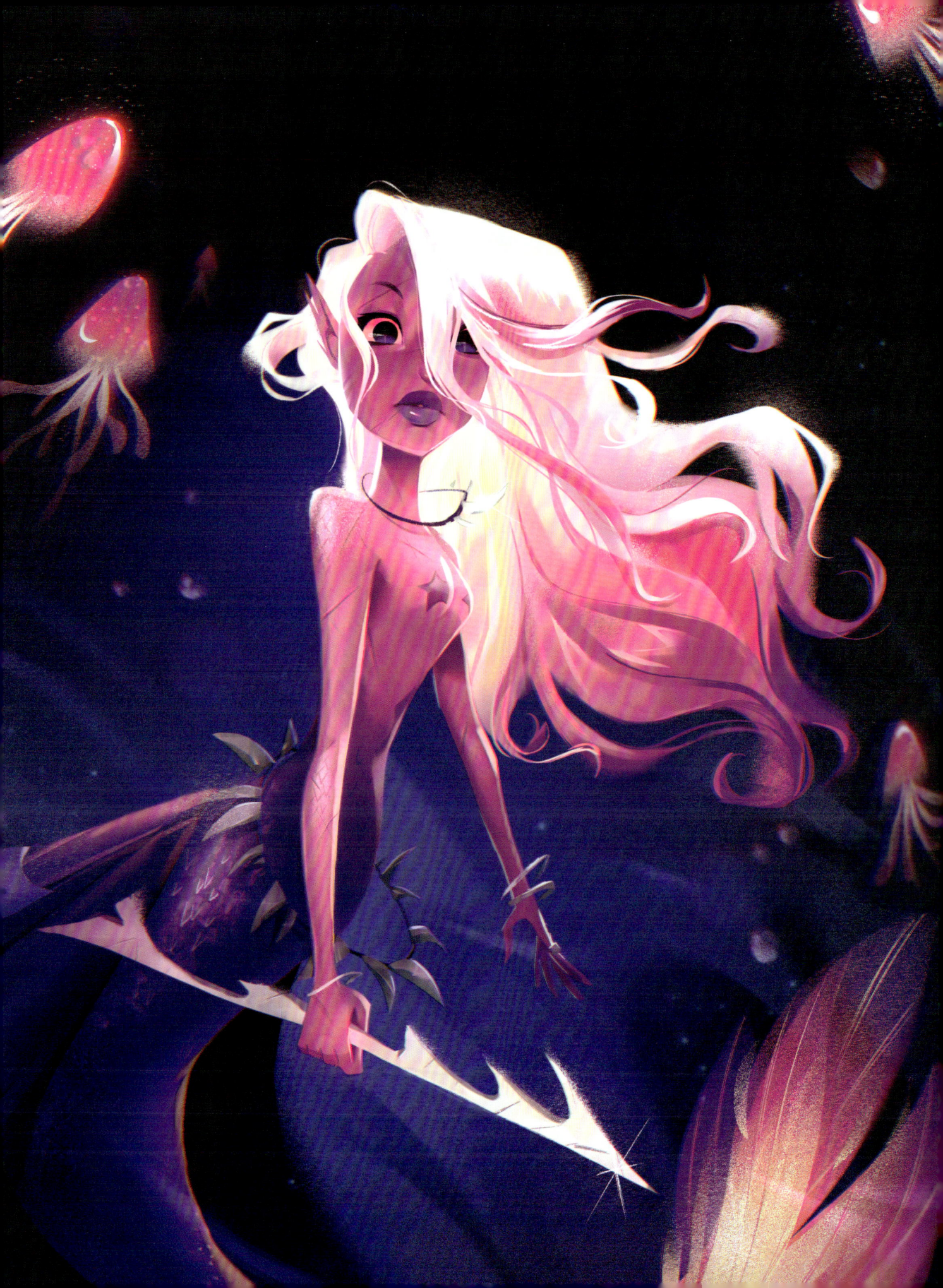

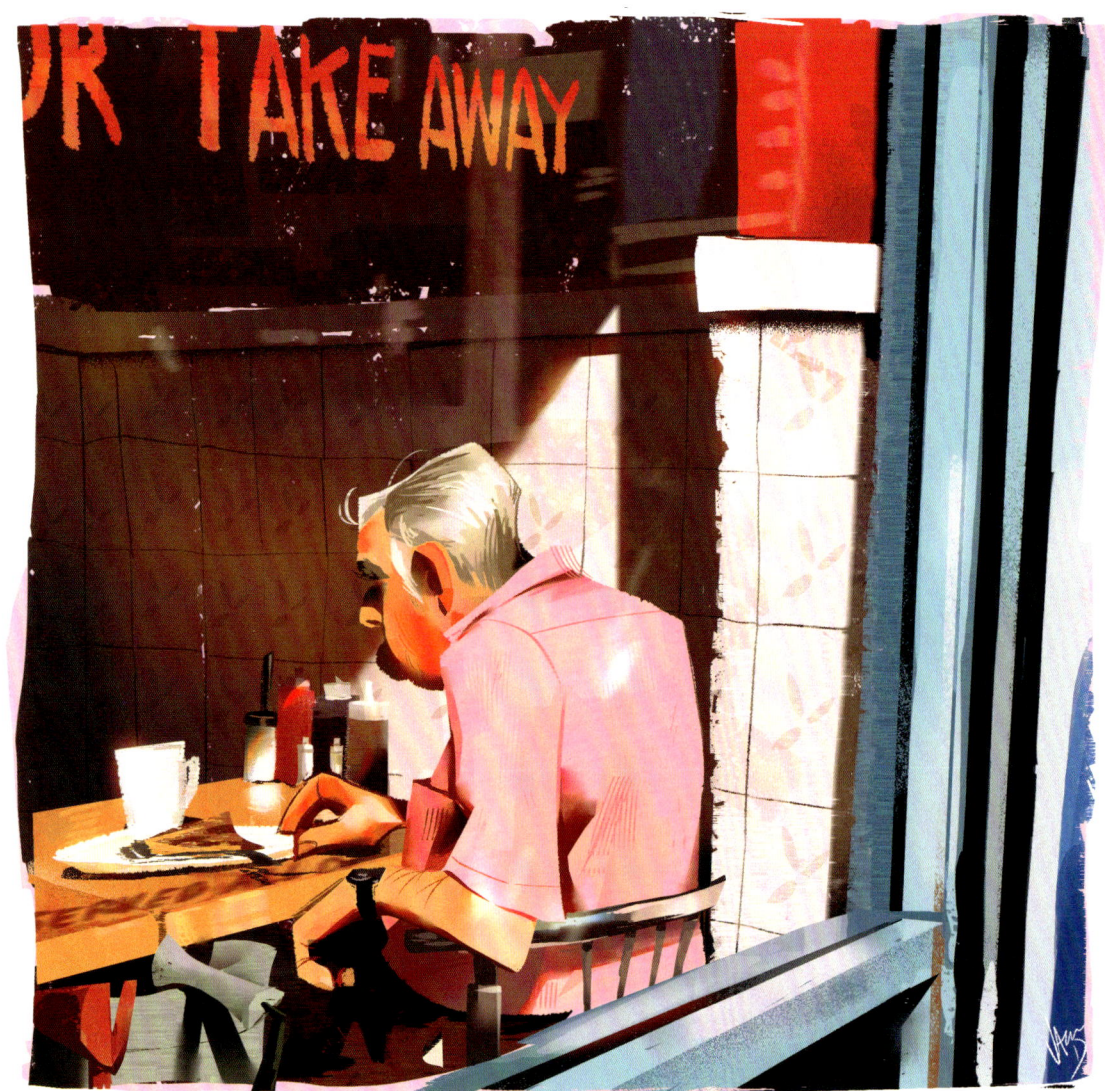

This page:
A stylization study
from a photo

Opposite page:
A portrait study
from a photo

Hi Jackie, welcome back to *CDQ*! Could you catch us up on your career so far, for our readers who aren't familiar with your work?

Hi *CDQ*! Thanks for having me back. I'm a character designer at Disney TVA, currently working on *The Proud Family: Louder and Prouder*. Before this, I was at Netflix for a few years, working on features, and I also spent some time on projects at Nickelodeon and Warner Bros. I love making short films in my spare time and released an animated short, *Mismatched*, at the end of 2022, which was a big feat since I made it all by myself while working full time. I also have a YouTube channel and TikTok, where I share my art process and give advice to up-and-coming character designers.

How has your art style evolved over the years?

My style evolves as my interests evolve. When I was into anime and grunge in high school, you could see that reflected in my art: I drew lots of moody, emo characters with spiky hair. In college, I was influenced by my peers at Sheridan (I took my bachelor of animation there) and my style became flat and cartoony as I was being prepared for the animation industry. Now, my style can generally be summed up with words like vibrant, shape heavy, and dynamic. But I like to experiment and hope that my style is ever evolving. Sometimes, I like to create really sketchy illustrations with exaggerated proportions, other times I'll try realistic lighting with a very polished final look. I hope in a few years I'll be able to give you a completely different answer as I continue to grow as an artist.

'MY STYLE CAN GENERALLY BE SUMMED UP WITH WORDS LIKE VIBRANT, SHAPE HEAVY, AND DYNAMIC'

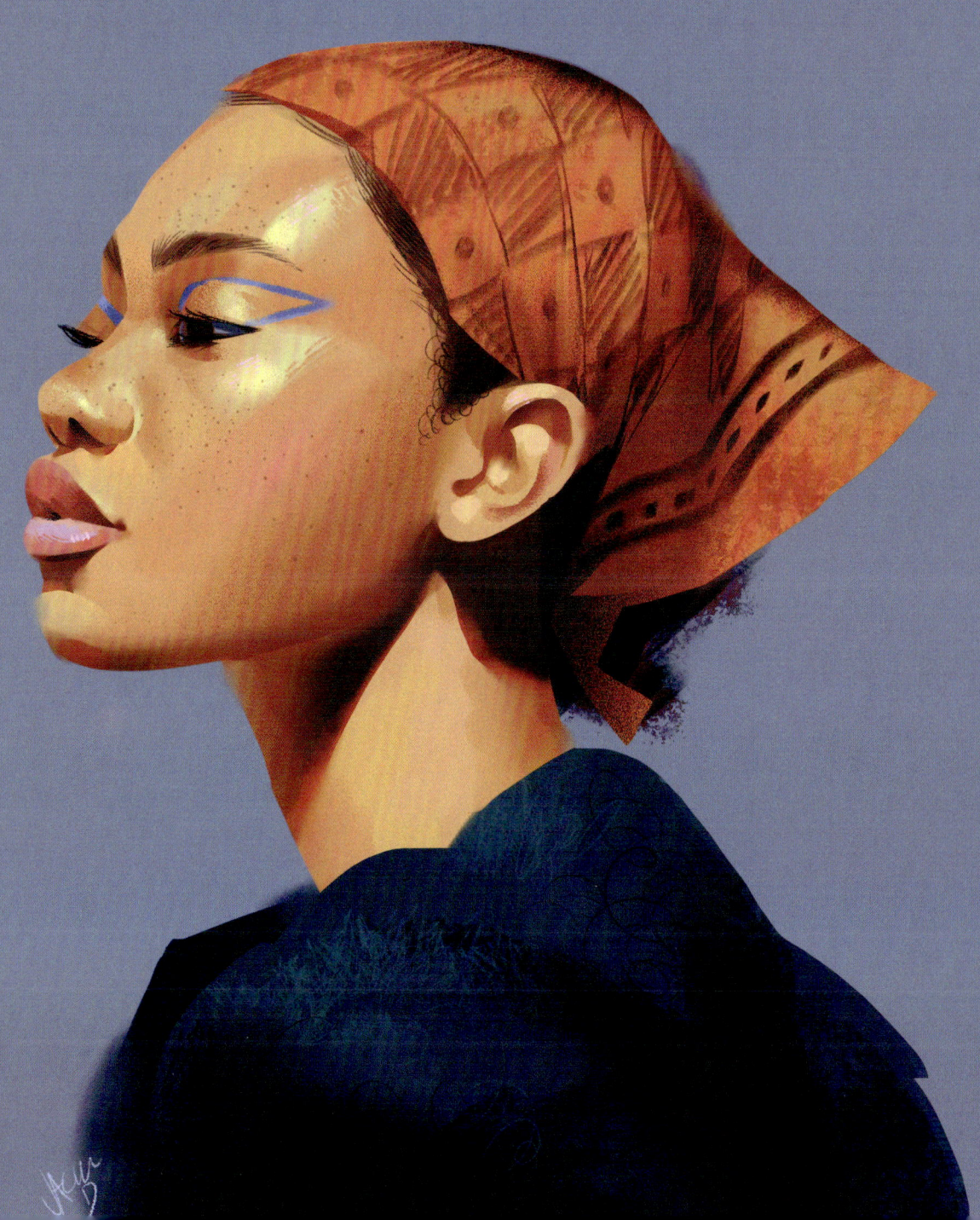

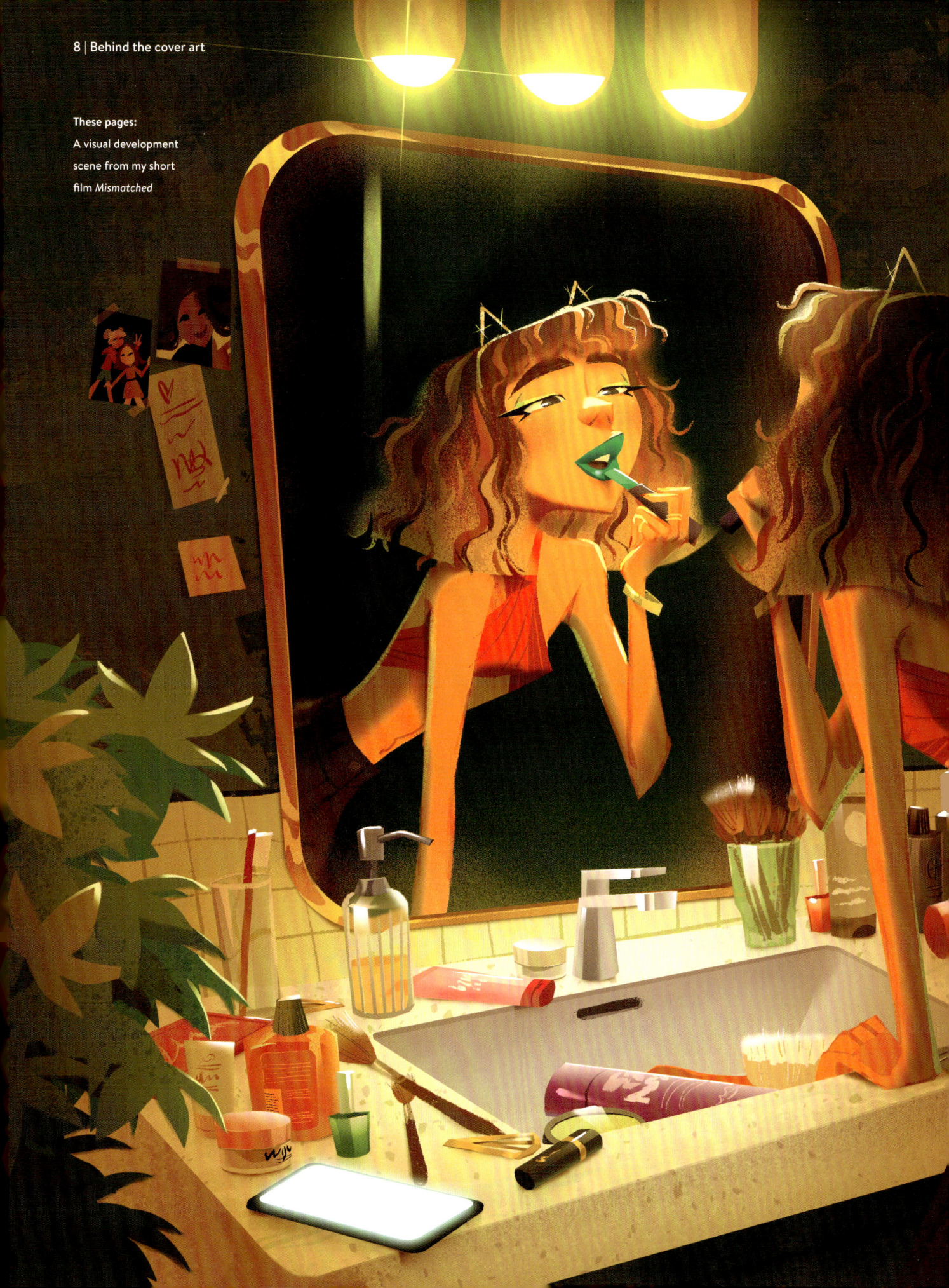

These pages:
A visual development
scene from my short
film *Mismatched*

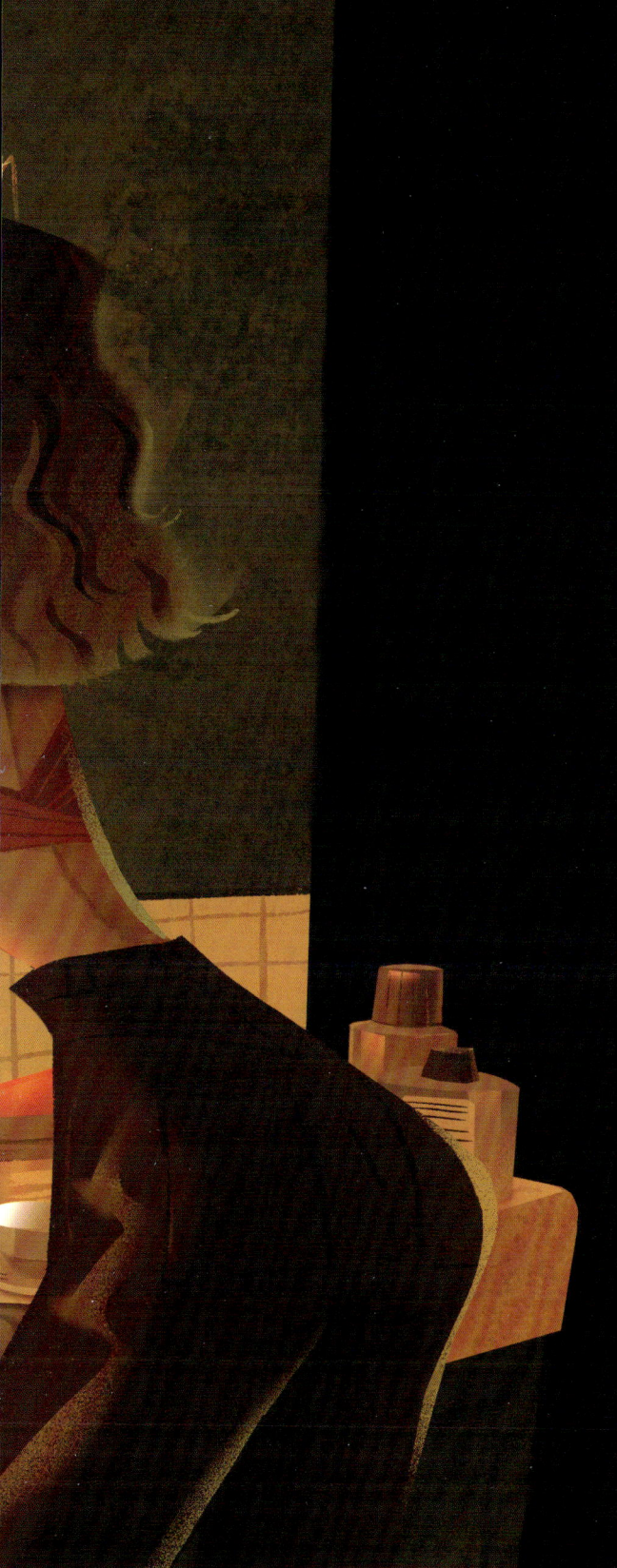

'EVERY DESIGN PRINCIPLE IS JUST A DIFFERENT WAY OF CONTRASTING ELEMENTS'

What do you think are the key elements of good character design?

The most important element of design is storytelling. Without storytelling, these are just lines on a page. Once the audience connects to the character, then it becomes a real person. In terms of technical design, my most essential technique is contrast. Every design principle is just a different way of contrasting elements. Straights versus curves? That's contrast. Differences in scale? Contrast! By creating contrast in each line of your drawing, you create interest.

What are the different challenges when designing static characters versus those for animation?

Oh, good question! When designing for animation, there's a lot to think about. If it's for 2D animation, you have to consider if the character is simple enough to draw over and over. If your project works with 2D rigs, you need to think about where you place lines – for instance, you shouldn't put a sleeve end right at a character's elbow because that's where the puppet bends and it'll create complications.

For 3D, you might think 'Oh, it's just a rig, you can make it as complicated as you want', but in reality, there's lots to consider: the budget of the project, if things move as secondary actions (this will cost more), and the textures of your design. When I draw static characters for myself, I still try to think of the principle of simplification. How can you break down your character into its most essential elements? Anything after that is just an accessory.

What do you find most enjoyable about the character design process?

I love starting off with no idea what I want to draw, and as I sketch out nothingness, I start to imagine how my lines feel and the mood I'm trying to convey – this is where a character usually forms. I seek out their personality, their emotions, and what I want to convey to my audience. And then, when I add colour, everything starts to come together. The shapes, colours, and energy of the character are what move me forward – I think these elements are the most powerful.

Finally, do you have anything coming up soon we should look out for?

I've had a crazy year with self-publishing my new art book, *Rhythm & Line* (check it out on my site!), working at the convention Lightbox selling my art, doing lots of secret projects for some cool companies, and managing to create consistent YouTube videos. In the near future, I want to be kind to myself and allow myself some rest. It's hard to say no when opportunities come, but I'm starting to feel burnt out and definitely need to spend time recharging!

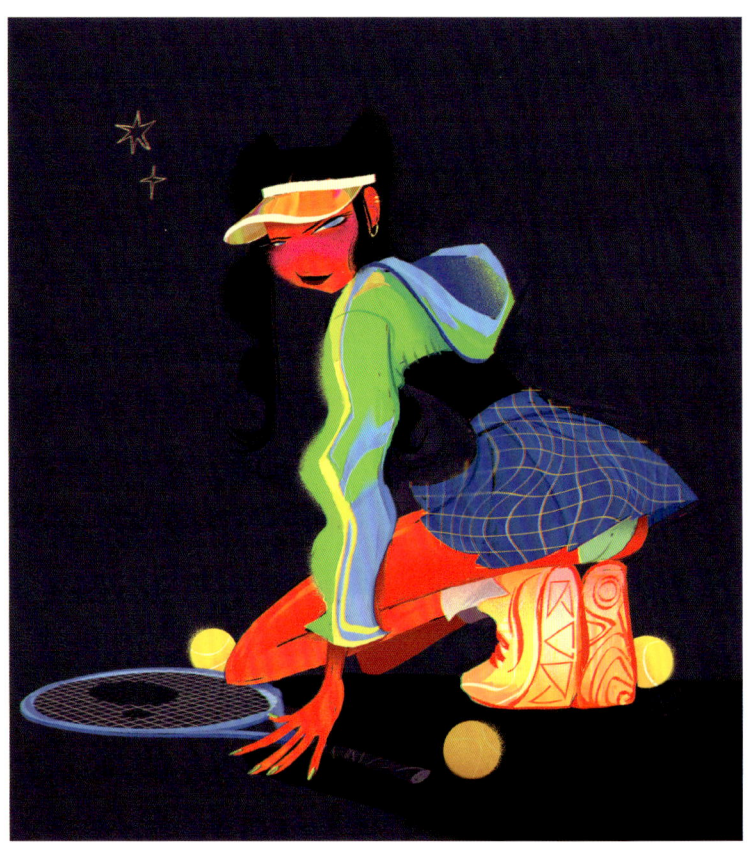

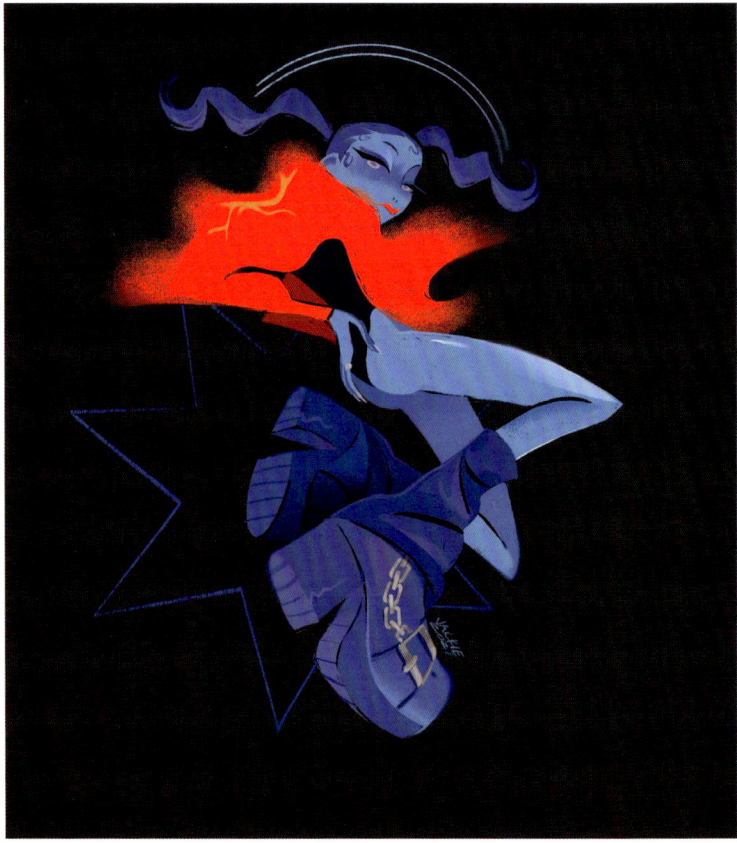

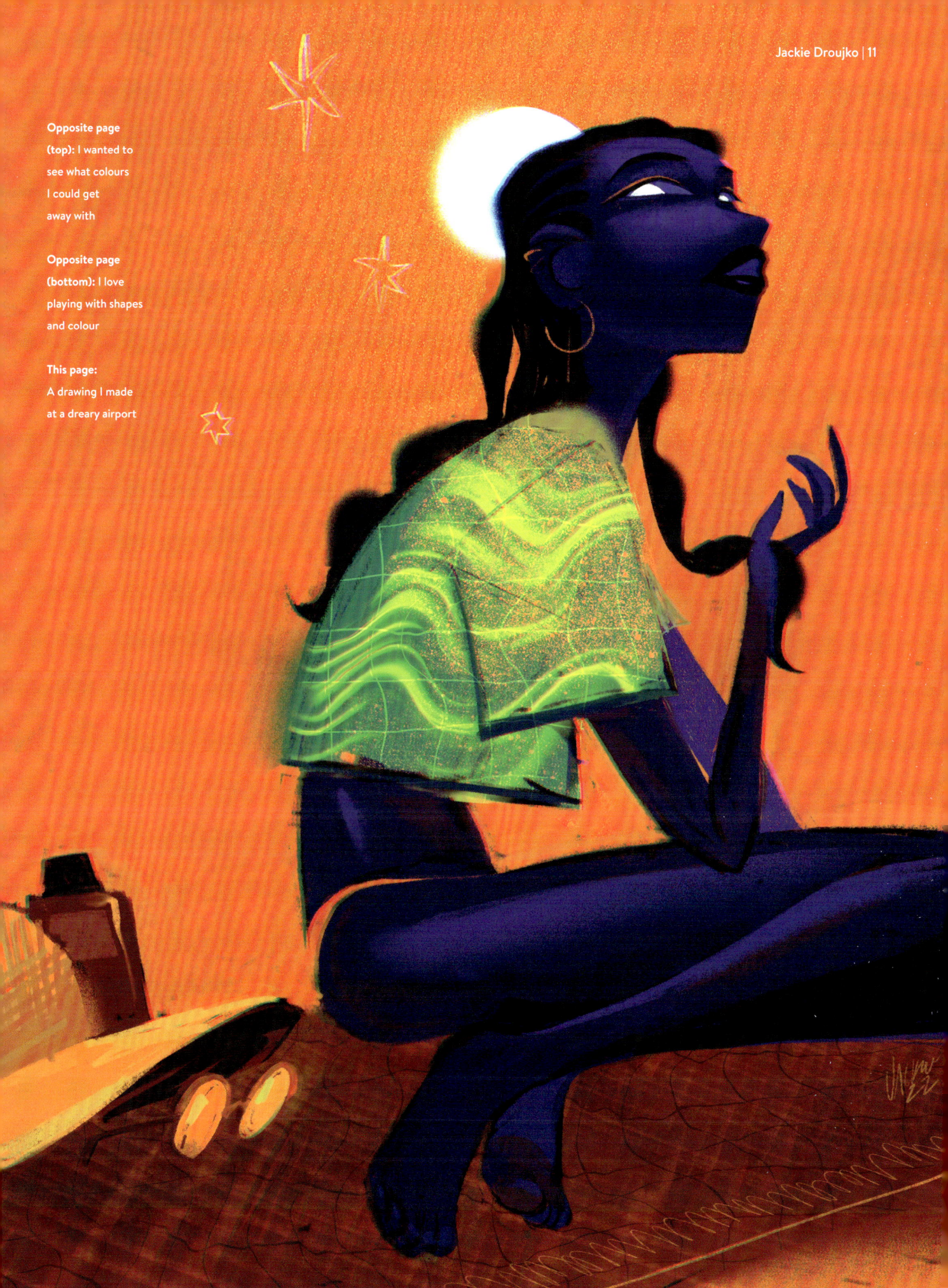

Opposite page (top): I wanted to see what colours I could get away with

Opposite page (bottom): I love playing with shapes and colour

This page: A drawing I made at a dreary airport

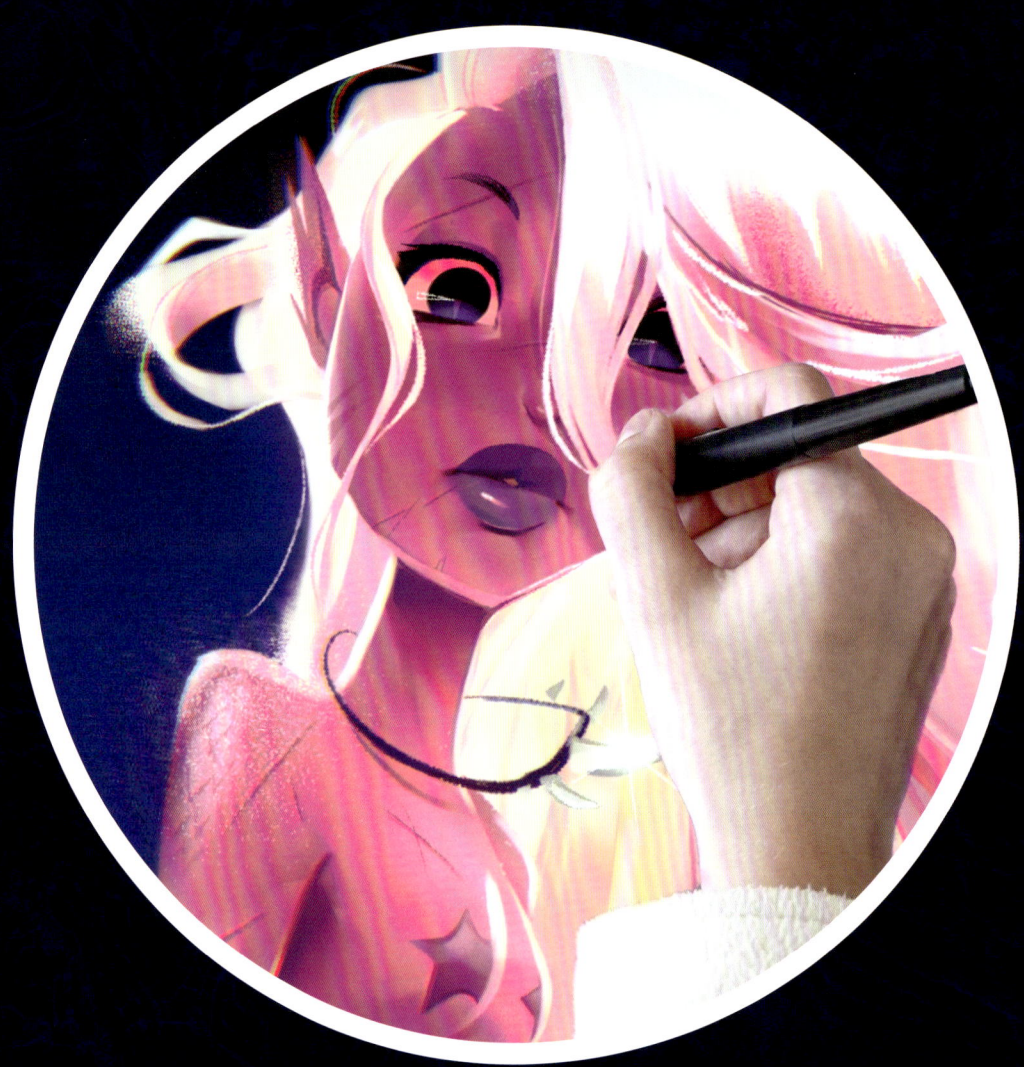

CRAFTING
THE COVER

This tutorial covers my process of creating a digital character illustration using Photoshop. I use a newer technique of rendering with realistic lighting in this piece, which proves to be a challenge. I also struggle with the concept of this character halfway through, trying different ideas to save the piece and bring it back to its original intention.

START WITH A SKETCH!

I always start my pieces with a loose sketch. I draw roughly at this stage because this allows me to use my imagination to see between the lines and visualize what the piece needs. I feel like this mermaid character has a striking look, hooking the viewer into her world. I imagine a dynamic background, my character surrounded with jellyfish, bubbles, and movement.

CHOOSING COLOUR

I tighten the lines a bit after deciding how I want to render this piece. My goal is to create a lot of volume and realism in the way I render, so the piece will be lineless. This is a pretty new technique for me, so I cross my fingers and hope I can figure it out. I settle on these colours after testing a few variations. My colour palettes are usually very vibrant. Because this piece is for print, I toggle between CMYK and RGB settings to be sure my colours are accurate. I also flip my canvas to black and white to be sure the tones work together and have enough contrast.

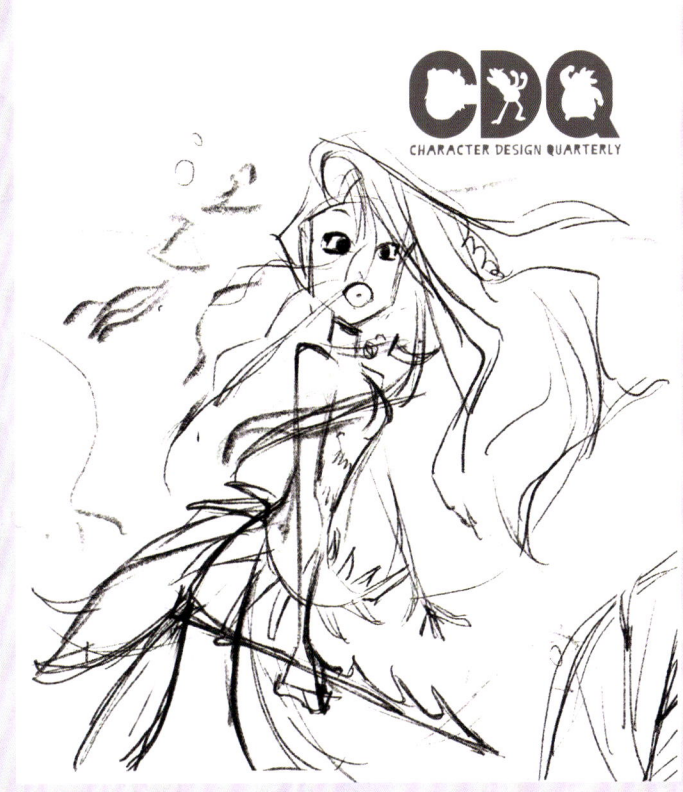

This page (top): A rough and non-committal sketch helps visualize the piece

This page (bottom): Blocking in colours to further understand the tone

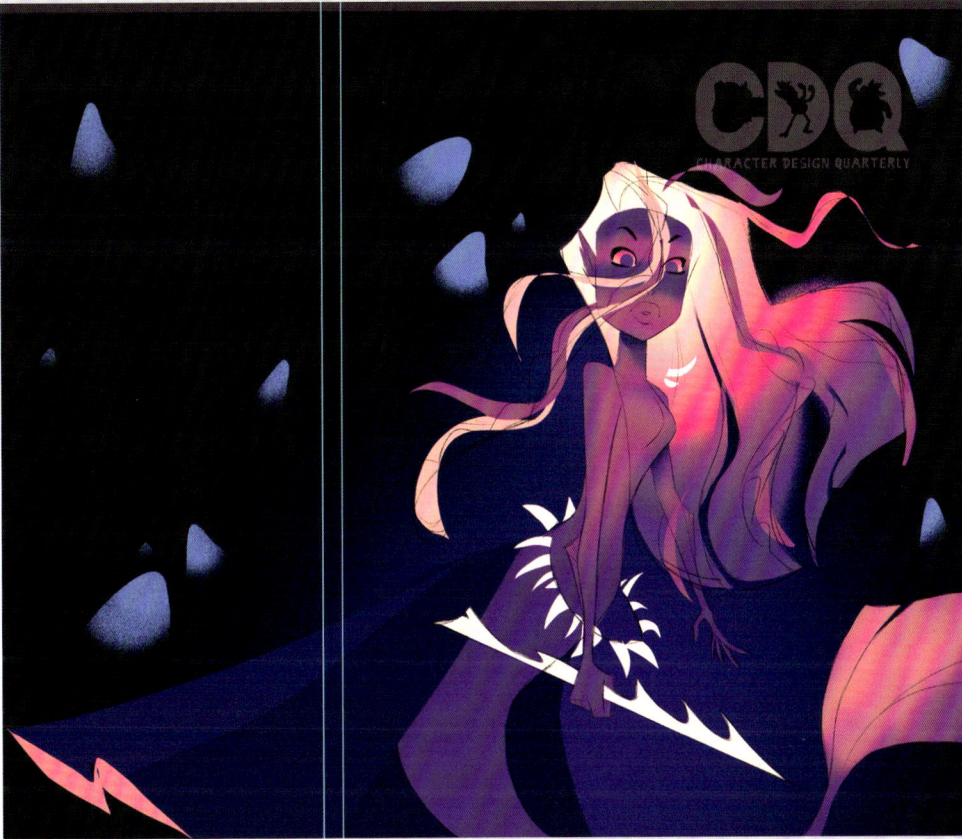

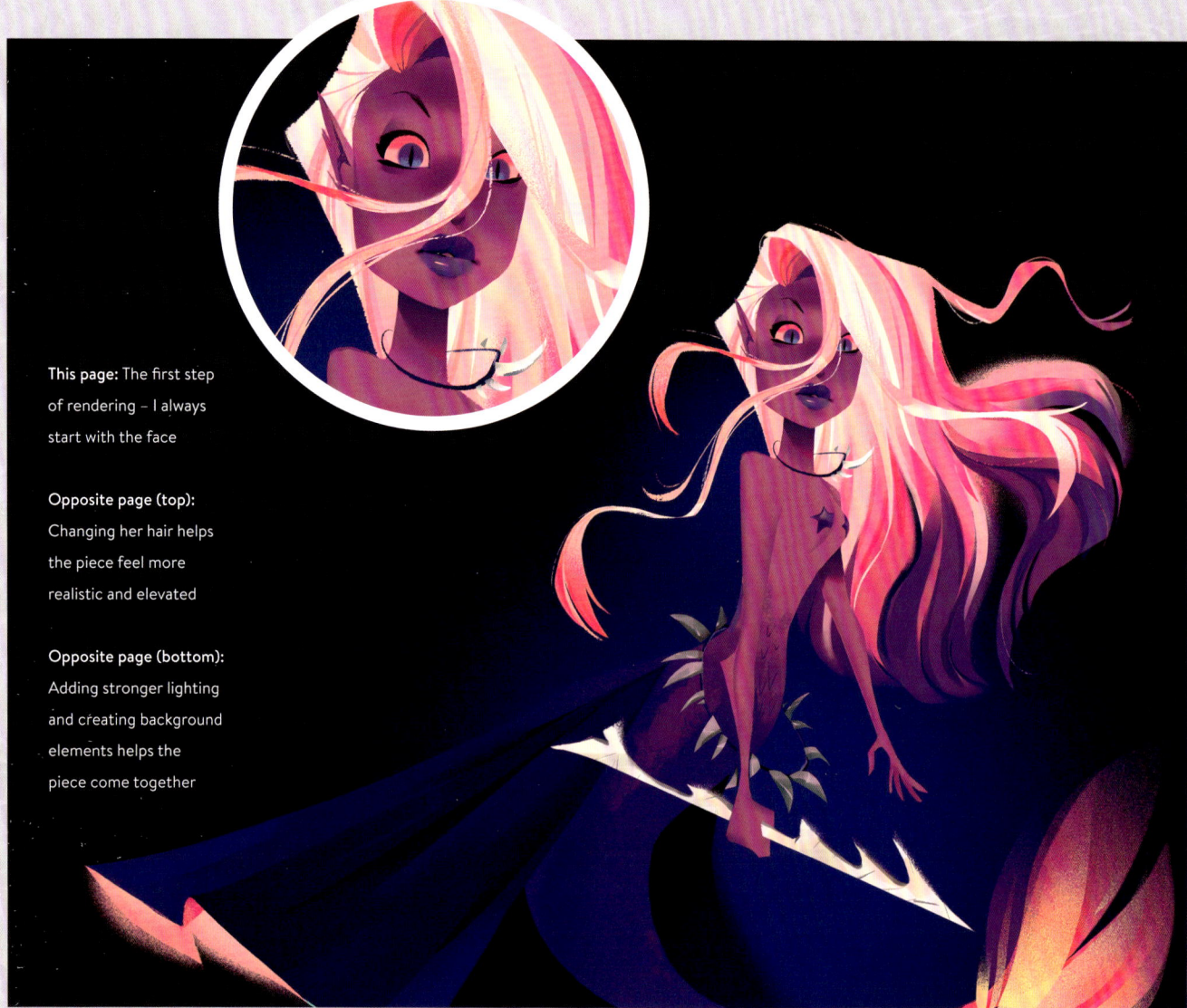

This page: The first step of rendering – I always start with the face

Opposite page (top): Changing her hair helps the piece feel more realistic and elevated

Opposite page (bottom): Adding stronger lighting and creating background elements helps the piece come together

BEGIN RENDERING

I start by rendering the character, creating dimension in the base of the character with a minimal amount of shading. I always begin with the face, since it's the focal point of the piece. I also work on creating an interesting composition with the hair and the ombré colouring. The more I look at the hair, the more unhappy I am with it. It feels childish, with vibrant colours for no reason, so I'll need to revisit it later on. I focus on some of her accessories and make sure things work tonally before I move on to the next step.

CHANGING COURSE

I'm struggling to work out why I don't like the piece so far. I think it's because I want to create a striking and badass piece but it currently feels juvenile and young, because of the mermaid concept and bright colours. I redo the hair with several subtle colour changes and a more natural composition. These changes help to elevate the piece. I add a light source to illuminate the hair and shadows to create volume. I carve out some subtle anatomy to add a touch of realism.

ADDING DETAILS

I add background elements like jellyfish, bubbles, and waves, and final details to the character, like scratches, scales, and accessories. I complete final lighting passes to push her tail into the background, while brightening her upper body to lead the viewers' eye to the focal point. However, I still can't tell what's wrong with the piece. Is it too monochromatic? Is it over rendered? Is it too childish? For my first *CDQ* cover I want to impress and the pressure's getting to me! I don't have time to restart, so I'll put my best foot forward and see how I can edit this piece until I'm satisfied.

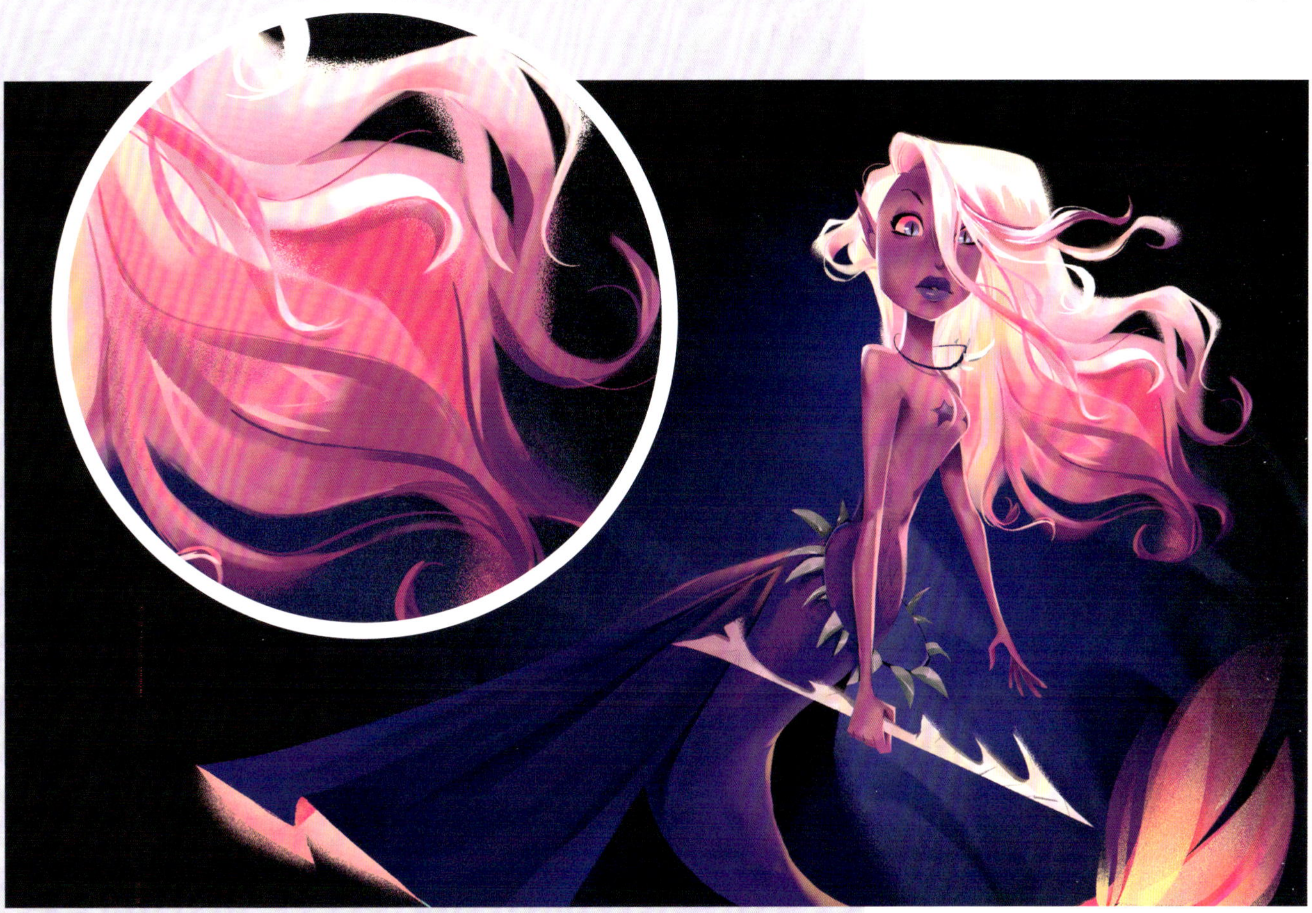

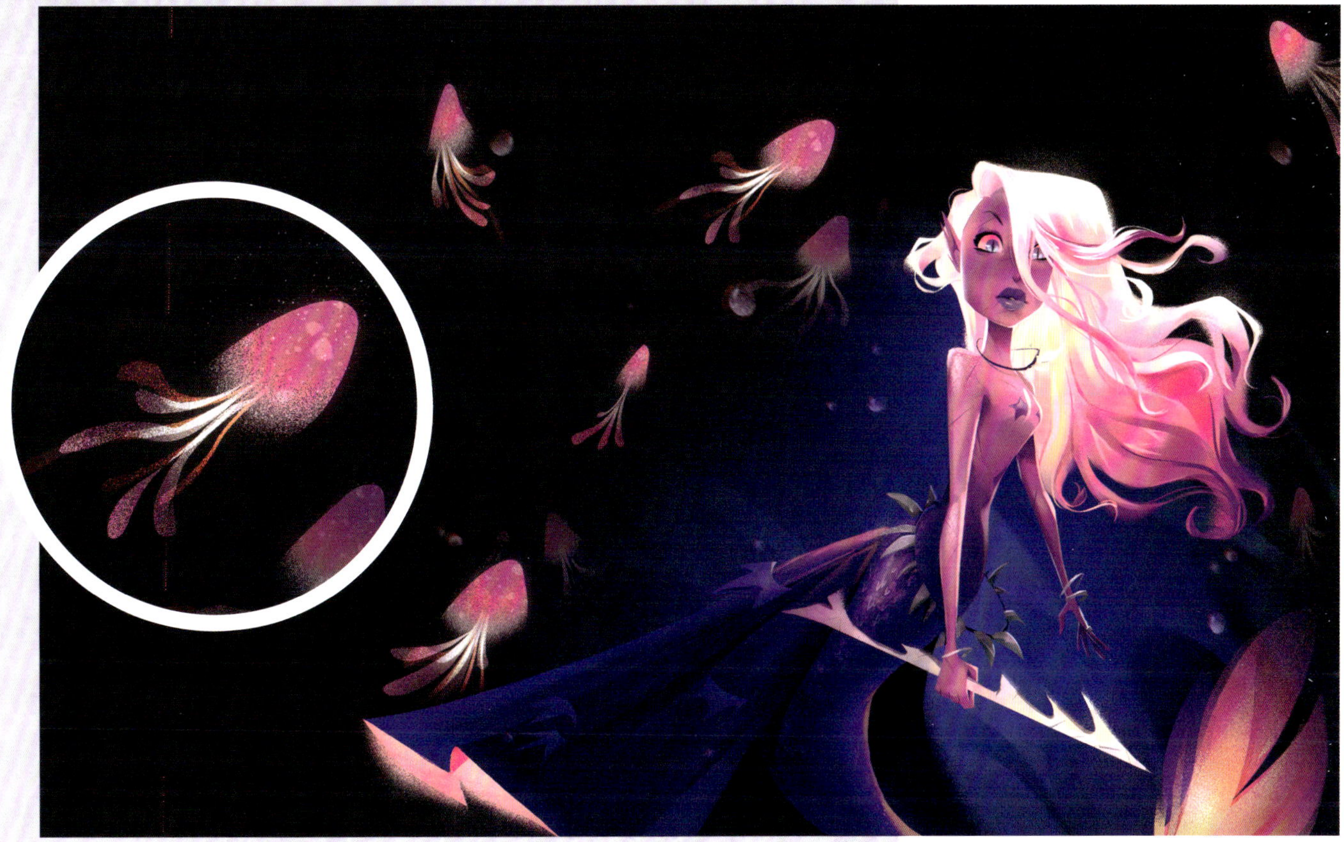

SWITCHING IT UP FOR THE BETTER

I look back at my initial sketch and feel like I'm missing something in her expression. I use the Liquify tool to change her facial proportions as I feel it's unclear which direction her head is tilting. I make her irises black, which adds better contrast to her face. I also add my favourite RGB split for fun and a few other final touches that make the piece pop, like overlays, and more background elements.

I believe that whatever you learn from your artwork will help to improve your next piece – I'm glad to have learned a lot creating this character.

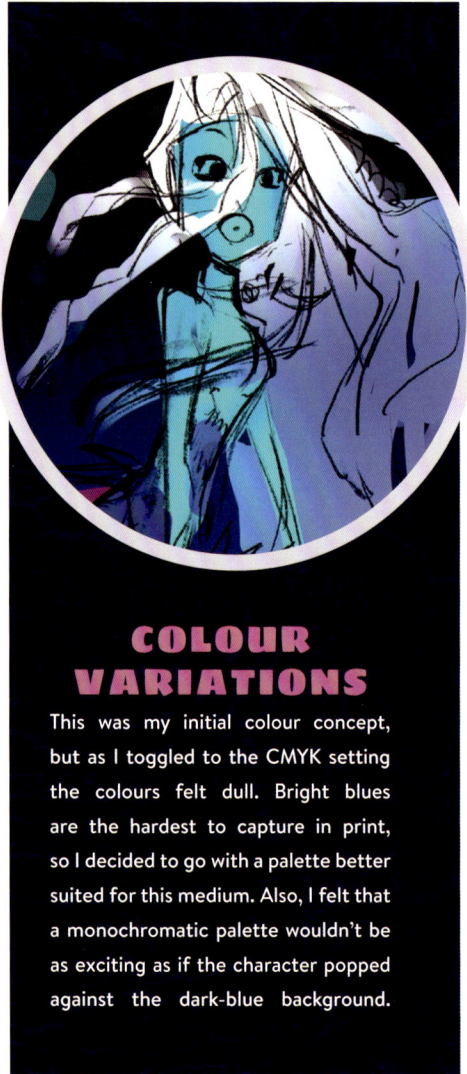

COLOUR VARIATIONS

This was my initial colour concept, but as I toggled to the CMYK setting the colours felt dull. Bright blues are the hardest to capture in print, so I decided to go with a palette better suited for this medium. Also, I felt that a monochromatic palette wouldn't be as exciting as if the character popped against the dark-blue background.

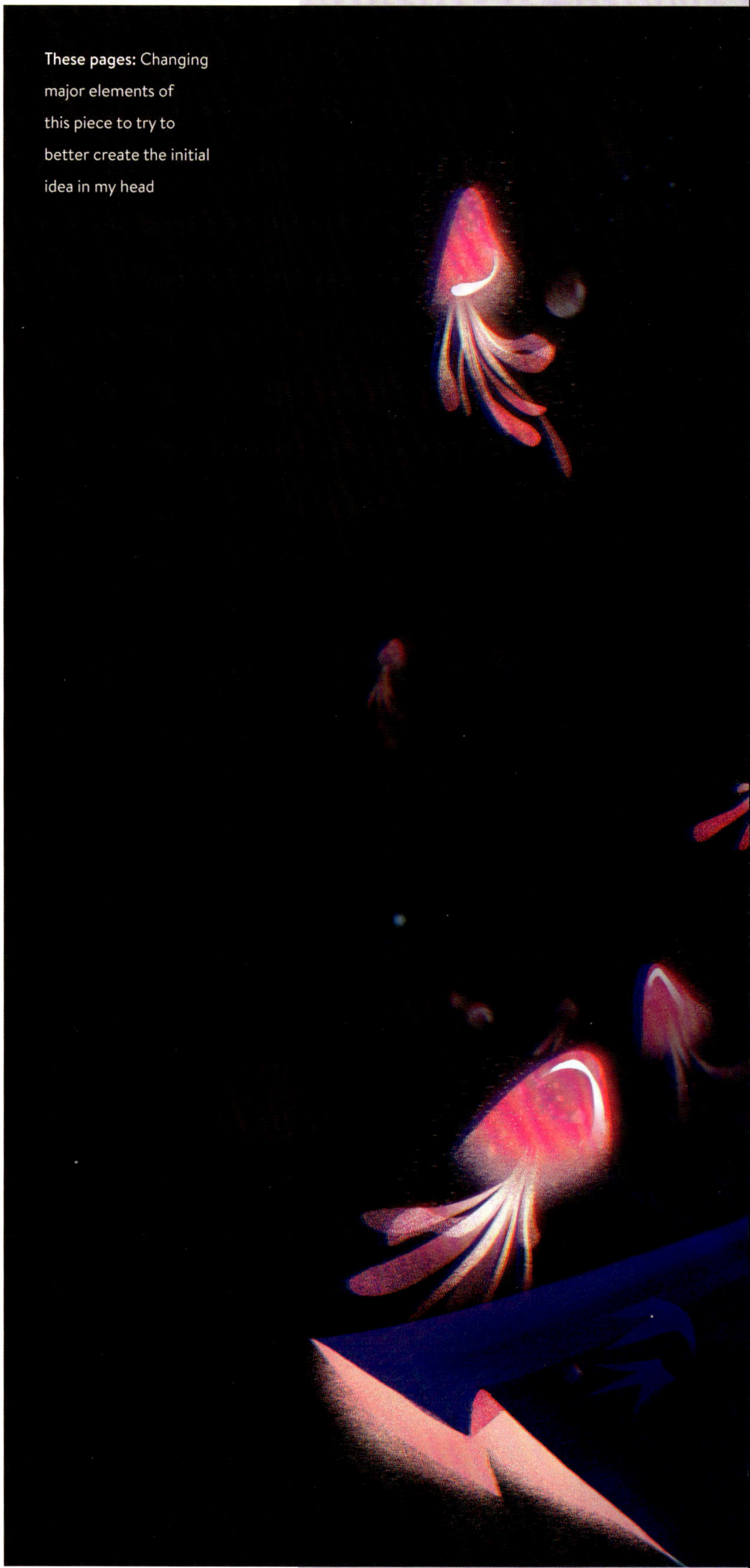

These pages: Changing major elements of this piece to try to better create the initial idea in my head

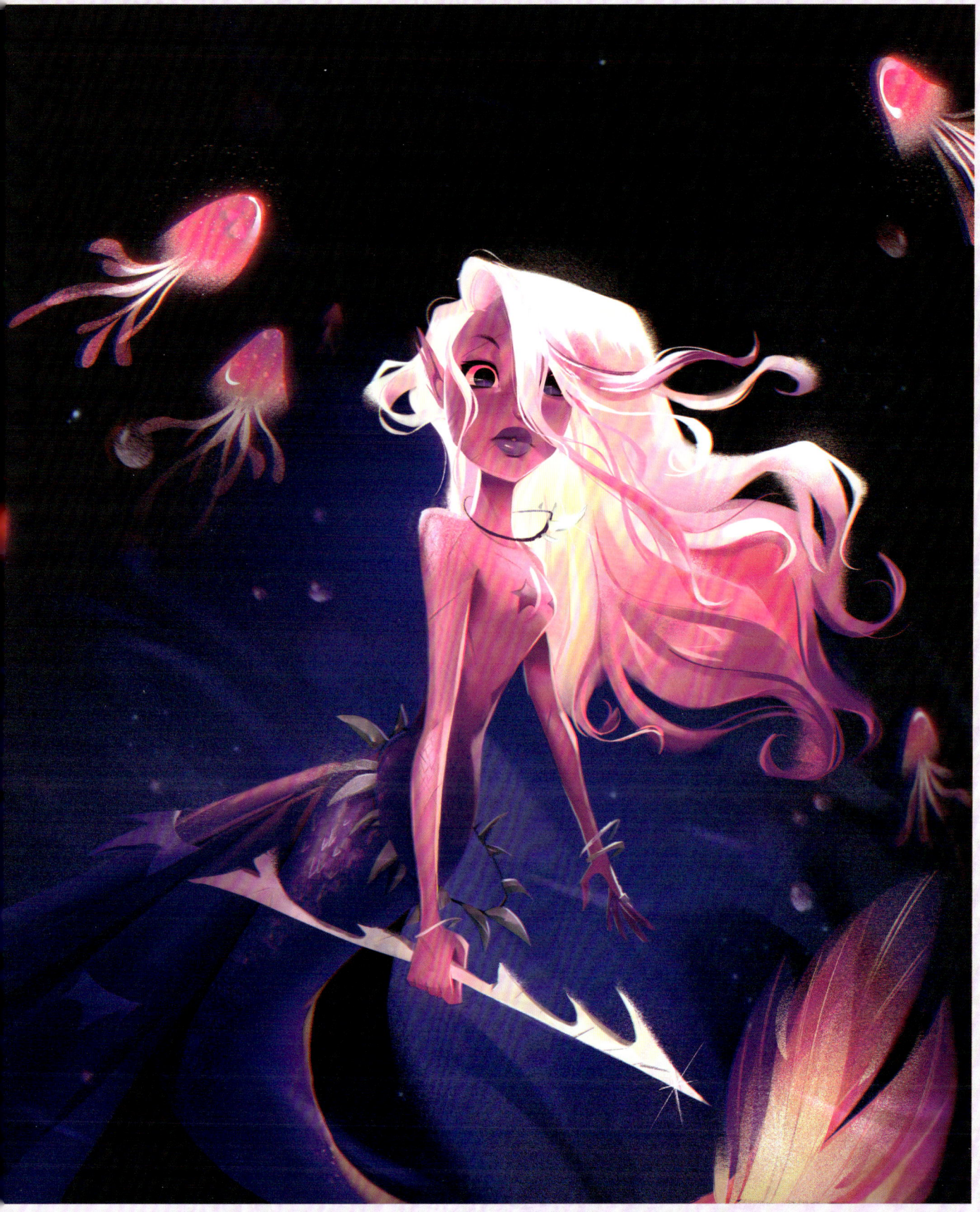

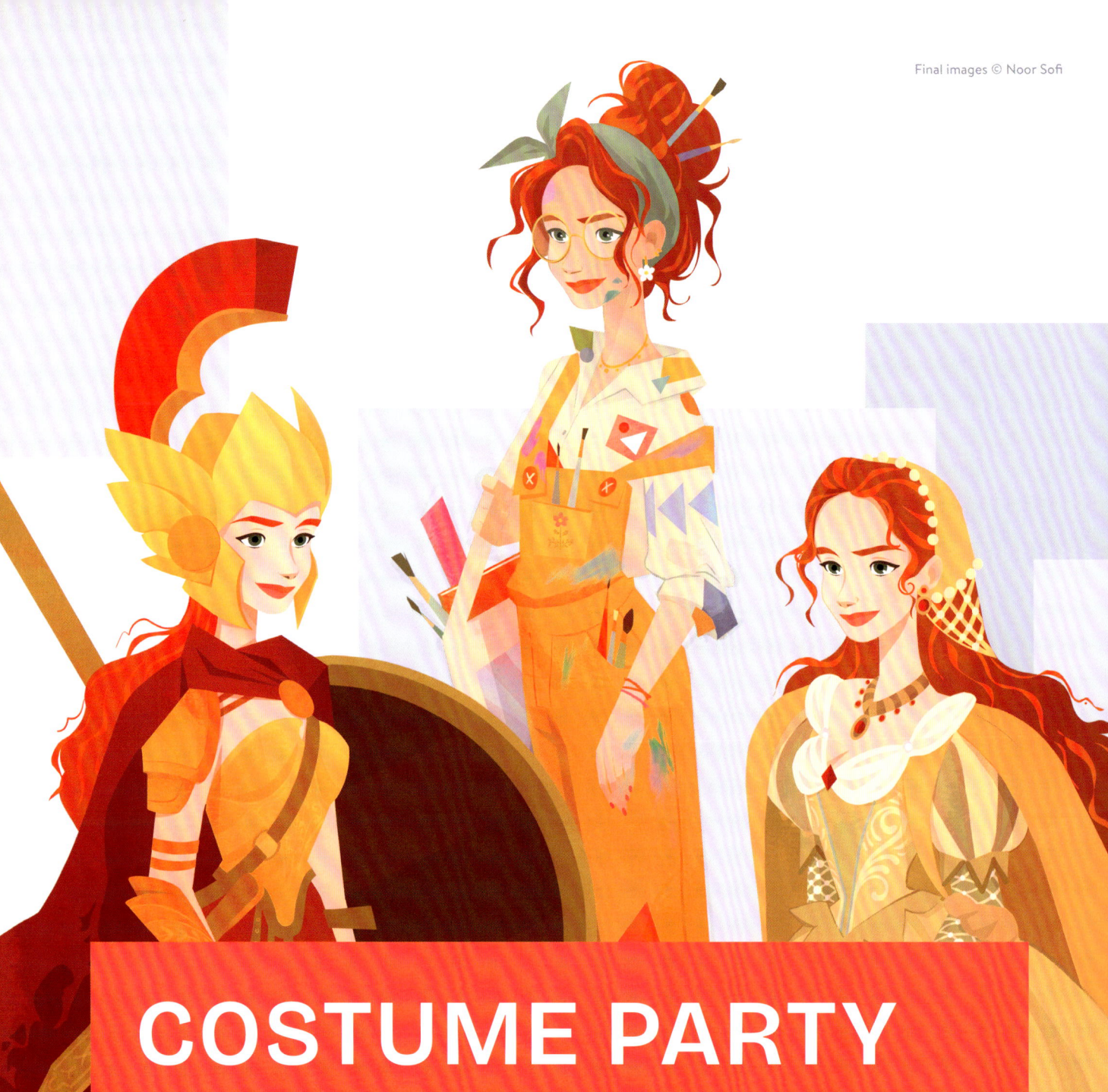

COSTUME PARTY
NOOR SOFI

Costume design is an art form that transcends the boundaries of mere clothing and plays a pivotal role in shaping a character's identity on screen or stage. It is a powerful tool in the hands of skilled designers, capable of breathing life into fictional personas and bringing them closer to reality. Through careful consideration of colours, fabrics, styles, and symbolic elements, costume designers can artfully convey a character's evolution, inner conflicts, and diverse facets, ultimately enhancing the narrative, and enriching the audience's understanding and connection to the story. In this regard, costume design stands as an indispensable ally to the storyteller, as it wields the potential to transform an actor into a living embodiment of the character they portray. In this tutorial we will cover the thought process that goes into designing an eye-catching costume for a specific character.

BRAINSTORMING

The initial step in the costume design process involves a brainstorming session to determine the characters we will craft ensembles for. From this exercise, three distinctive personas emerge, each exuding a unique aura and essence. First and foremost, a Renaissance queen embodies regal elegance and refinement, adorned in opulent fabrics, ornate accessories, and intricate details that befit her majestic stature. Secondly, an artist beckons with a bohemian spirit, her costume a crafted mess of paint stains, bold colours, and mismatched patterns, reflecting her scattered yet inspired mind. Lastly, a formidable Roman warrior, clad in battle-worn armour, symbolizing strength, valour, and an indomitable will to conquer. Each of these designs possesses a distinct personality, promising to breathe life into these characters and transport them across epochs, captivating audiences with their varied and compelling presences.

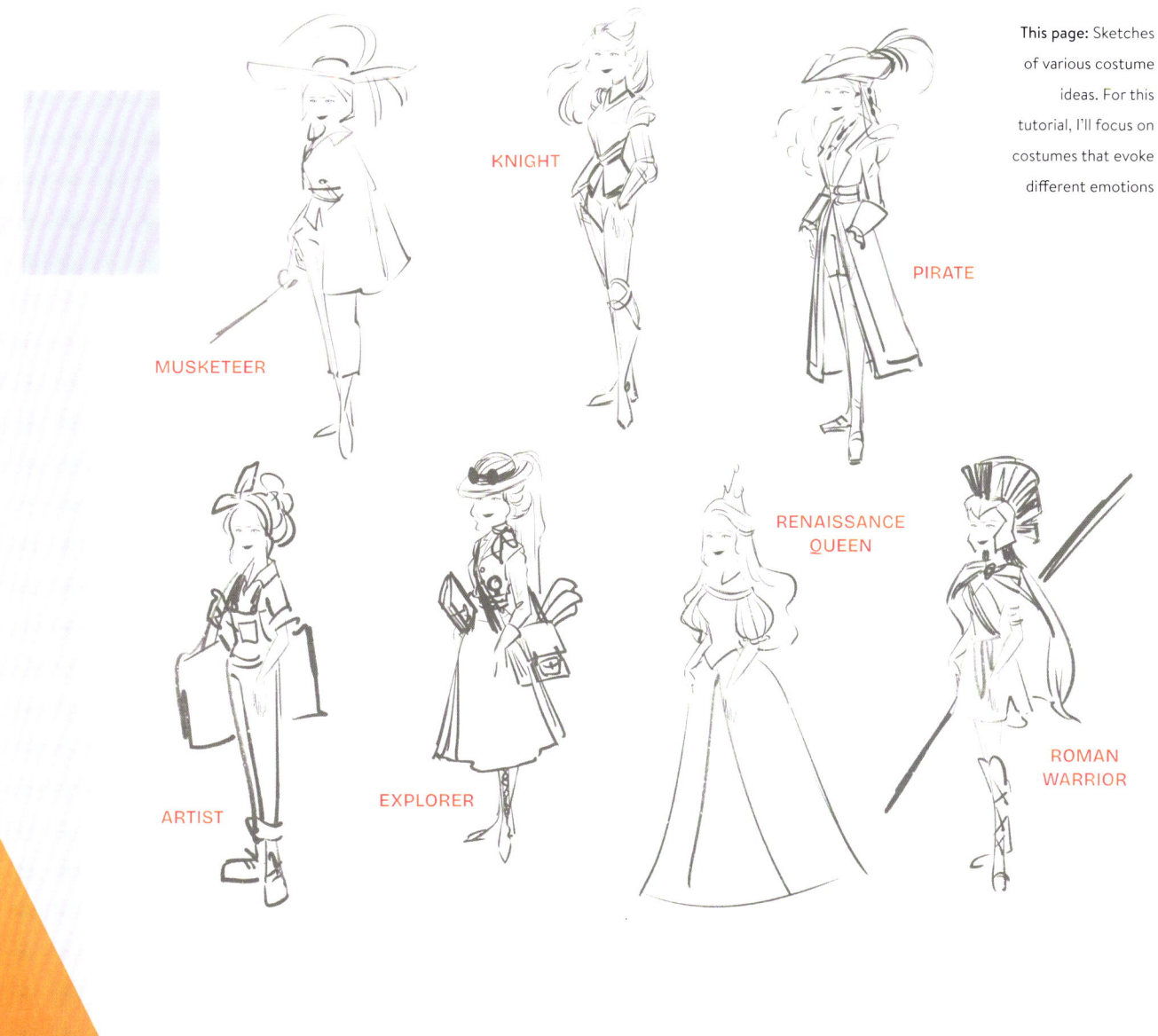

This page: Sketches of various costume ideas. For this tutorial, I'll focus on costumes that evoke different emotions

KNIGHT

PIRATE

MUSKETEER

ARTIST

EXPLORER

RENAISSANCE QUEEN

ROMAN WARRIOR

ORDINARY PEOPLE

I made the decision to forgo the musketeer, knight, pirate, and explorer design ideas due to their lack of visual interest. While each concept had its merits, they ultimately fell short in terms of captivating visual appeal. The designs felt somewhat ordinary and failed to evoke the excitement and intrigue we were seeking for this project.

THE RENAISSANCE QUEEN

A ROYAL REVERIE

With the captivating trio of characters selected and their distinct personas taking shape, the next step is to embark on a quest for reference images to inspire the regal attire of the Renaissance queen. This critical phase calls for an in-depth exploration of historical artworks, royal portraits, and period fashion, as well as a keen eye for contemporary reinterpretations that add a fresh perspective. The aim is to capture the essence of opulence and grace, drawing inspiration from the ornate detailing of elaborate gowns, sumptuous fabrics fit for nobility, and exquisite accessories that adorn royalty. Each image serves as a guiding star, leading the costume designer through a mesmerizing tapestry of centuries past, fusing tradition with contemporary appeal. Through this visual treasure hunt, the character of the Renaissance queen is infused with authenticity and grandeur, ensuring that her presence commands attention and radiates timeless majesty on the stage or screen.

SHAPE AND EMOTION

The next step of our design journey is creating silhouette thumbnails for the Renaissance queen. These thumbnails focus solely on the character's shape, free from any intricate details. What makes this process truly fascinating is the array of emotions each shape can evoke. Discover the square-shaped silhouette, radiating sturdiness and unwavering strength, a perfect match for a ruler who exudes stability. Observe the circle, a joyous and seamless curve that infuses the queen with an infectious sense of joviality and warmth, spreading cheer to all around her. Finally, there's the triangle, its pointed elegance embodying regal dignity and nobility, a reflection of her majestic bearing. These silhouette thumbnails will become a guide leading you towards the perfect embodiment of the Renaissance queen's character, one simple shape at a time.

This page (top): Collect a variety of reference images to help inform your costume

This page (bottom): Different silhouettes offer different vibes for our queen character. The silhouette can determine how your audience perceives your character

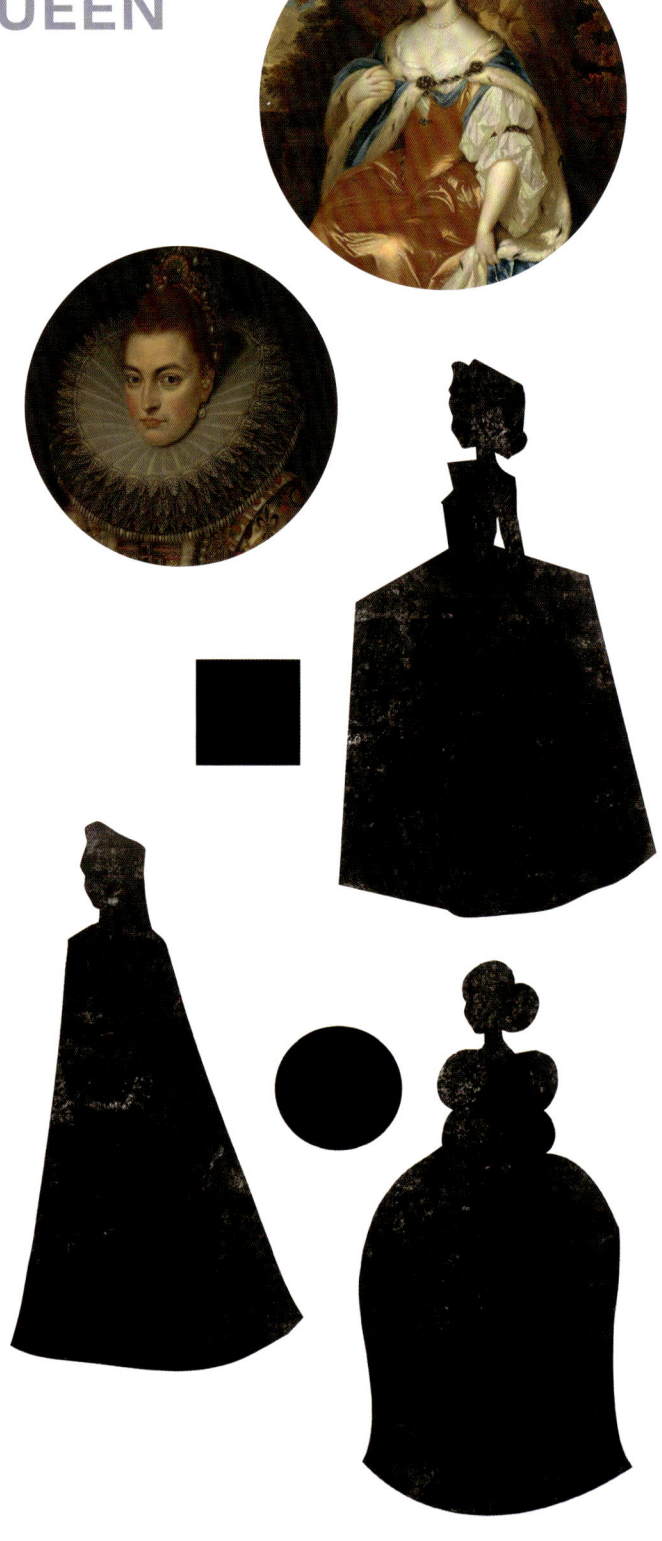

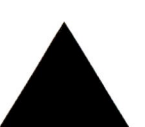

DESIGN BASED ON SHAPES

When trying to imagine varying designs for one character, start by dedicating the design to one shape. Let that one shape dominate the character and you'll be able to get a variety of designs that will give you options to choose from! Different shapes evoke different emotions for people, such as a circle seeming bouncy and happy, a triangle seeming hierarchical, and a square seeming stubborn or strong. Having so many choices will help you decide on a direction for your character.

FROM SILHOUETTE TO SKETCH

With a triangle-based thumbnail as a guide, the costume-design process takes a thoughtful turn as I create a detailed sketch based on this regal shape. Drawing inspiration from the reference images I've gathered, I infuse the sketch with elements that best capture the essence of the Renaissance queen's character. The dignified appeal of the triangle translates into flowing lines that shape a gown fit for her majestic presence. Referencing historical royal portraits and period fashion, I add embellishments and details that symbolize her elevated status. Through this collaborative effort between the chosen silhouette and the reference images, the Renaissance queen's costume design starts to take on a tangible form, ready to enchant the audience and bring her regal presence to life.

CROWNING HER MAJESTY

In the final step of the costume design process, I bring the sketch of the Renaissance queen to life with paint and colour. Inspired by the vision of a queen representing enlightenment and wisdom, I use rich and lustrous golden hues to symbolize her grace and prosperity. The gown glimmers with opulence and intricate patterns are delicately highlighted, reflecting her noble and virtuous character. The golden accents add a touch of brilliance, representing her benevolence and insight as a leader. As the painting takes shape, the costume design becomes a beautiful expression of art and symbolism, portraying the Renaissance queen as a majestic figure, ready to inspire and captivate all who see her stunning attire.

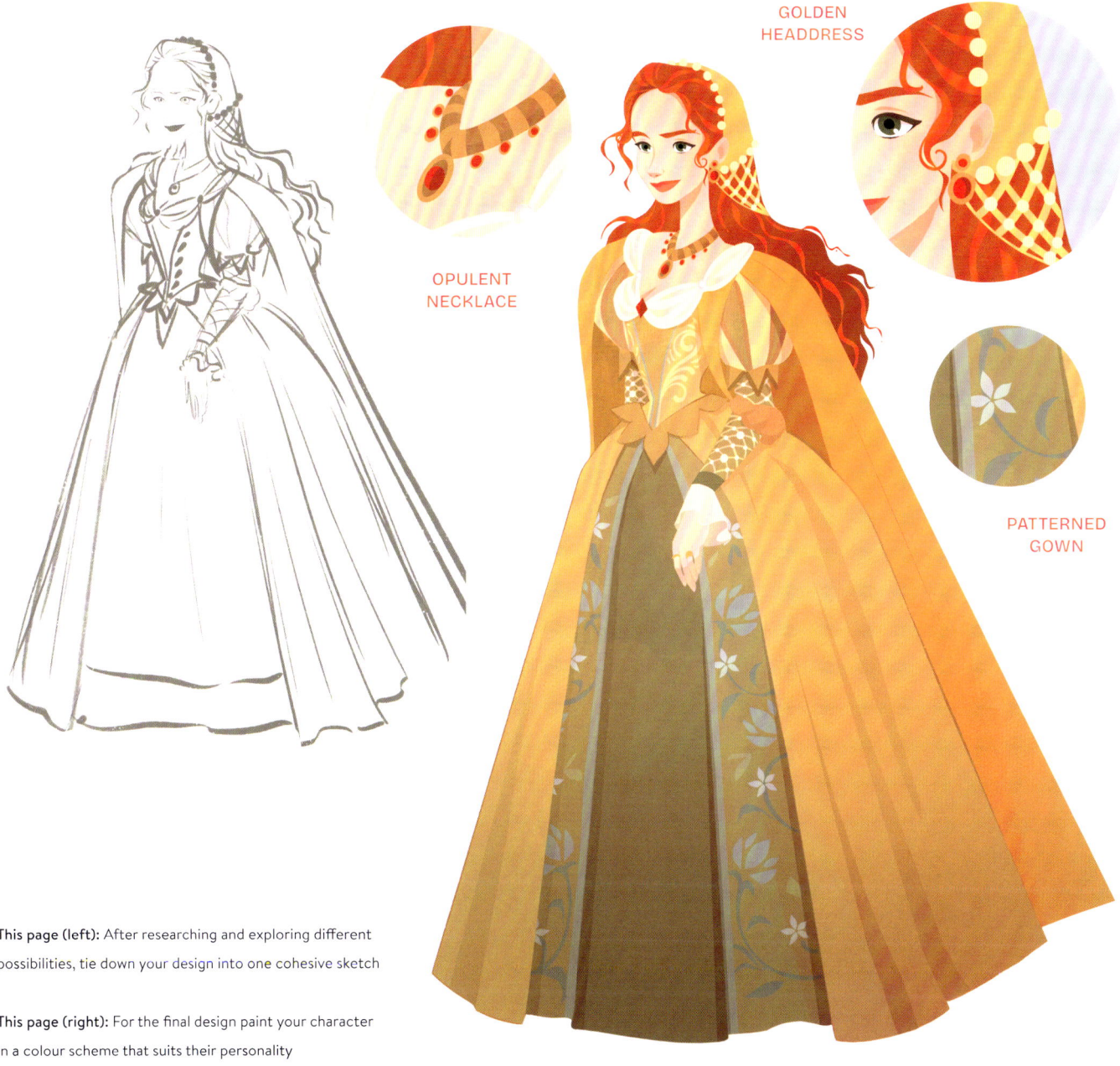

OPULENT NECKLACE

GOLDEN HEADDRESS

PATTERNED GOWN

This page (left): After researching and exploring different possibilities, tie down your design into one cohesive sketch

This page (right): For the final design paint your character in a colour scheme that suits their personality

THE ARTIST

EMBRACE THE BOHEMIAN SPIRIT

Now we move on to designing a character representing a messy artist, searching for reference photos to capture the essence of their bohemian spirit. With a quick browse through art forums, galleries, and everyday snapshots, I find images of hands covered in paint splatters, artists donning comfortable overalls, and carrying an assortment of art supplies. Among these references, we also discover pictures of artists with tousled hair, revealing their carefree nature. These snapshots offer visual inspiration to craft a character who exudes a passionate and creative spirit, unbound by the constraints of tidiness. Armed with these reference photos, I look forward to bringing the essence of the messy artist to life in our design, embracing the charm of delightful disarray in their artistic world.

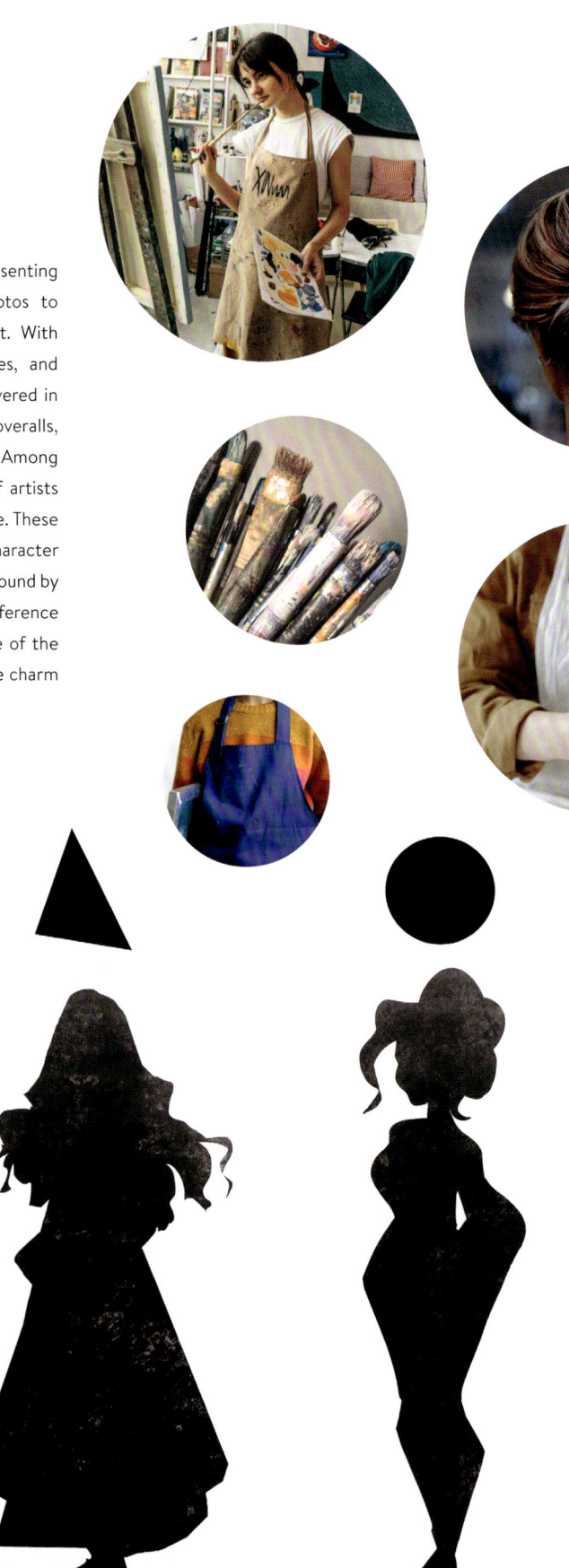

This page (top):
I find references to help design a free-spirited artist

This page (bottom:
Create a variety of silhouettes to explore the different possibilities for your character

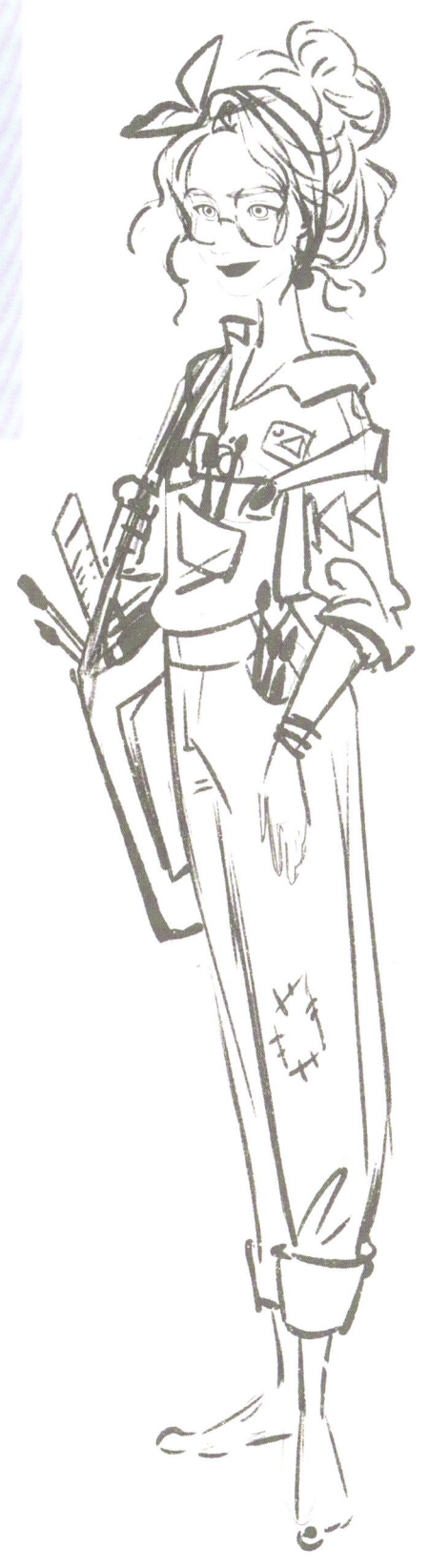

'PROPS WILL ADD DEPTH AND AUTHENTICITY TO THE CHARACTER'

UNLEASH YOUR ARTISTIC FLAIR

In the next step of designing the artist character, we explore a variety of silhouette shapes to find the strongest visual representation. Through a playful process of sketching, we experiment with different forms, from flowing curves to angular lines. Each shape offers a unique perspective, allowing us to see how the character's bohemian spirit can be best captured visually. In the end, I decide on the square-shaped silhouette, as it has a distinct quirkiness reminiscent of an artist. This exploration helps us uncover the perfect silhouette that brings our messy character to life, celebrating their unique and unapologetic artistic flair.

CHARACTER THROUGH PROPS

When designing the bohemian artist character, the choice of props will be a significant part of defining who she is. Each prop tells a part of her story and reveals her personality. I envision her wearing a pair of quirky earrings and stylish glasses that reflect her unique perspective. She carries a practical tote bag filled with art supplies, with her trusty paintbrushes peeking out the top. To emphasize her creative spirit, I add smears of paint to her clothing, showing her constant involvement in her artistic endeavours. These props will add depth and authenticity to the character, giving a glimpse into her vibrant world of imagination and artistry.

This page: Use what you've learned
in the silhouette and prop stages
to inform your final sketch

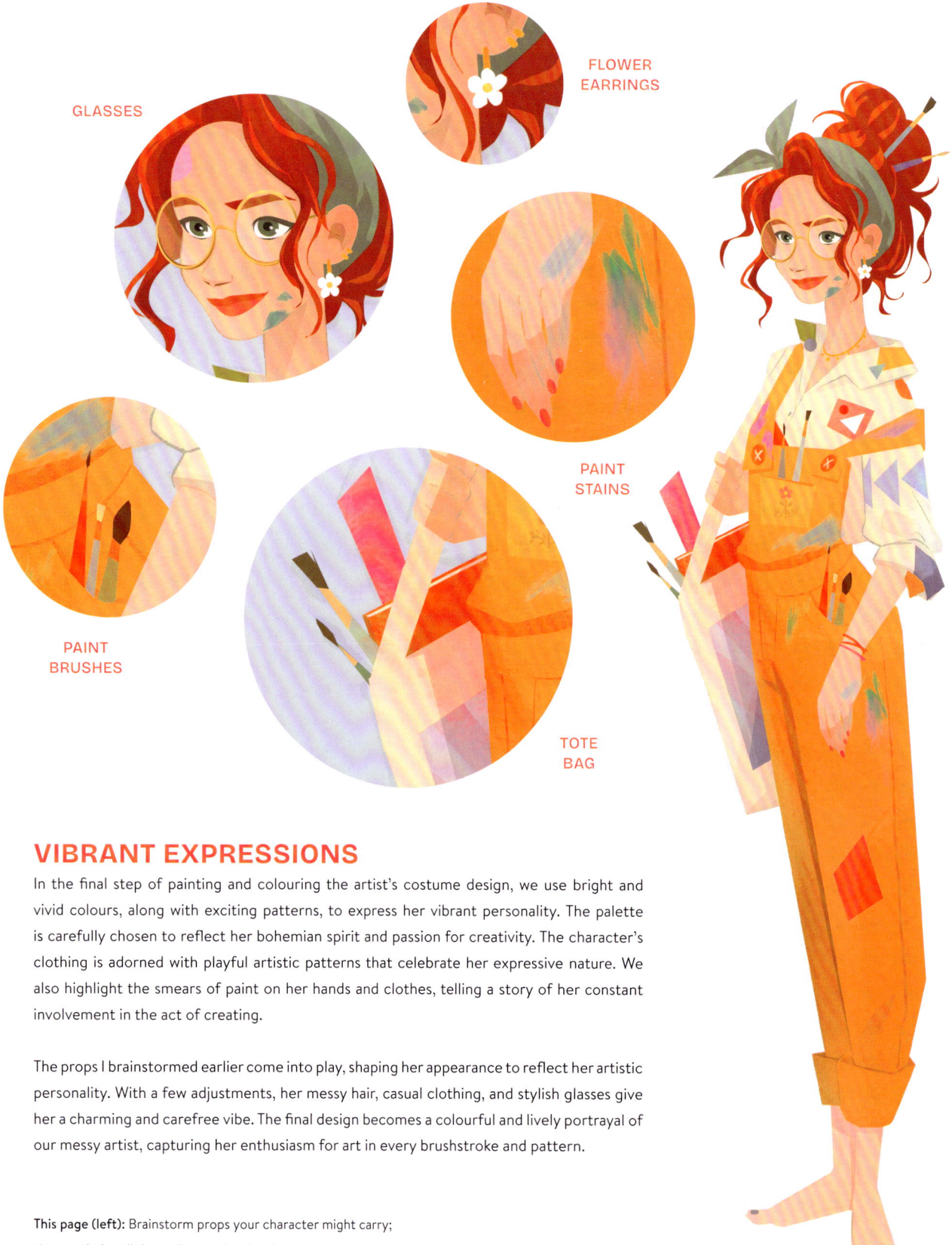

GLASSES

FLOWER
EARRINGS

PAINT
STAINS

PAINT
BRUSHES

TOTE
BAG

VIBRANT EXPRESSIONS

In the final step of painting and colouring the artist's costume design, we use bright and vivid colours, along with exciting patterns, to express her vibrant personality. The palette is carefully chosen to reflect her bohemian spirit and passion for creativity. The character's clothing is adorned with playful artistic patterns that celebrate her expressive nature. We also highlight the smears of paint on her hands and clothes, telling a story of her constant involvement in the act of creating.

The props I brainstormed earlier come into play, shaping her appearance to reflect her artistic personality. With a few adjustments, her messy hair, casual clothing, and stylish glasses give her a charming and carefree vibe. The final design becomes a colourful and lively portrayal of our messy artist, capturing her enthusiasm for art in every brushstroke and pattern.

This page (left): Brainstorm props your character might carry;
they can help tell the audience who the character is

This page (right): Paint the character in a colour
scheme that befits their character

THE ROMAN WARRIOR

AN EMPOWERING PRESENCE

To begin the process of designing a Roman warrior costume, I search for reference photos that showcase warriors wearing armour, displaying strength and power in their attire. My research involves exploring historical artworks to find warriors who exude a commanding presence. The reference photos provide valuable insights into battle-ready armour, protective pieces, and meticulous craftsmanship. With this visual inspiration, I aim to create a Roman warrior costume that reflects the resilience and grace of these historical heroes, presenting a powerful and captivating character.

FORMIDABLE SILHOUETTES

In the next step of designing the Roman warrior costume, I explore various silhouette shape thumbnails to find the most appealing design. I aim to create a look that feels strong, powerful, and fast, embodying the spirit of a formidable warrior. As I sketch different shapes, some emphasize a solid and commanding stance, while others convey a sense of agility and speed. Among the options, I'm drawn to the silhouette inspired by the circle shape. Its unique design suggests a seamless flow of power and strength, making it a perfect fit for my warrior character. With this choice, I've found a silhouette that captures the essence of a Roman warrior who commands respect and radiates a sense of fierce readiness.

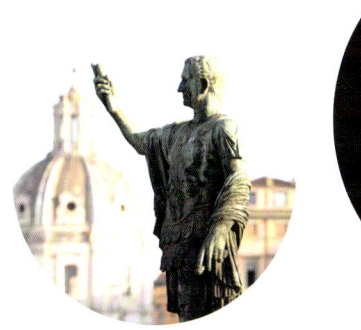
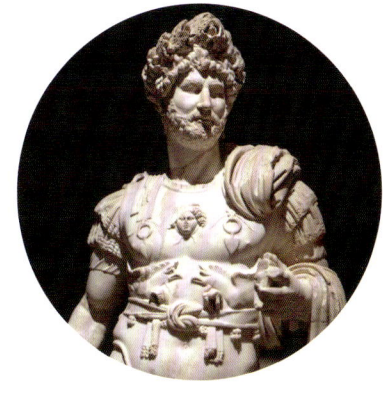

This page (top):
I look at references
of ancient statues
for inspiration

This page (bottom):
Explore different
silhouette shapes
to find the best
one to use for
the next costume
that conveys your
character's presence

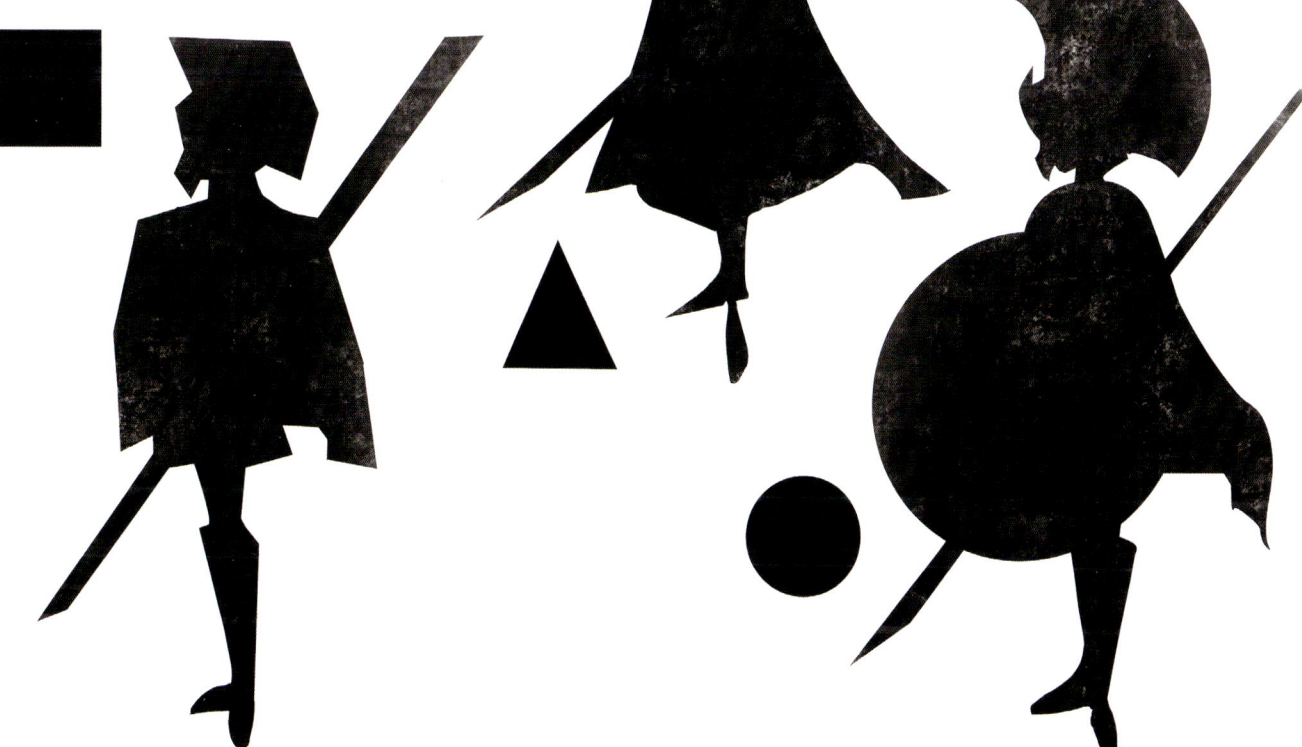

STRENGTH, POWER, AND PROPS

In this next crucial step of costume design, I meticulously plan out the props that will accompany the Roman warrior character, as they play a pivotal role in expressing her personality. My focus is on selecting props that convey strength and power, embodying the formidable nature of this warrior. I envision her wielding an imposing and finely crafted weapon, symbolizing her skill and prowess in battle. A battle-worn shield will rest firmly on her arm, representing her courage and determination to protect and defend. Additionally, a sturdy and intricately designed helmet will crown her head, showcasing her authoritative presence on the battlefield. Each chosen prop serves as a visual testament to the warrior's commanding spirit, enhancing her character's depth, and ensuring she stands as a force to be reckoned with in her quest for triumph and valour.

DYNAMIC DESIGN

In the next step of sketching the Roman warrior character, I merge the chosen circle-inspired silhouette with the carefully planned props. The circular shape lends a dynamic and agile feel to the character, while the props, including the imposing weapon, battle-worn shield, gleaming armour, and intricate helmet, add depth and strength to the design. As we sketch, the character takes form, emanating a commanding presence that reflects her powerful and valourous nature as a warrior. The combination of the silhouette and props creates a captivating and formidable Roman warrior, ready to embark on her heroic journey.

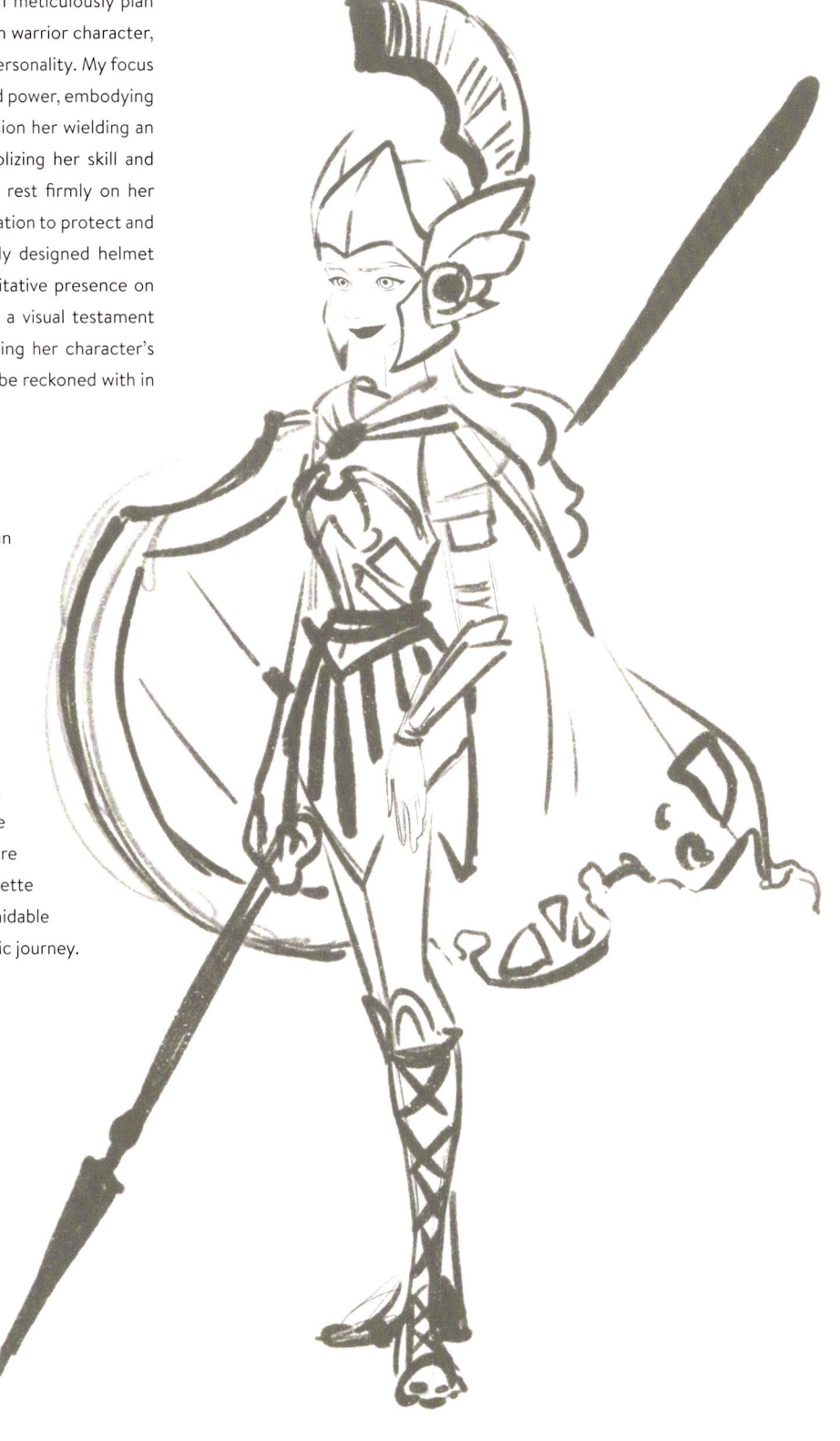

This page: After finding a shape and props that will accentuate the character, I move on to the sketch stage

Opposite page (left): Conceptualize ideas for props that your character might carry

Opposite page (right): I paint the warrior in gleaming colours that represent their path of heroism and glory

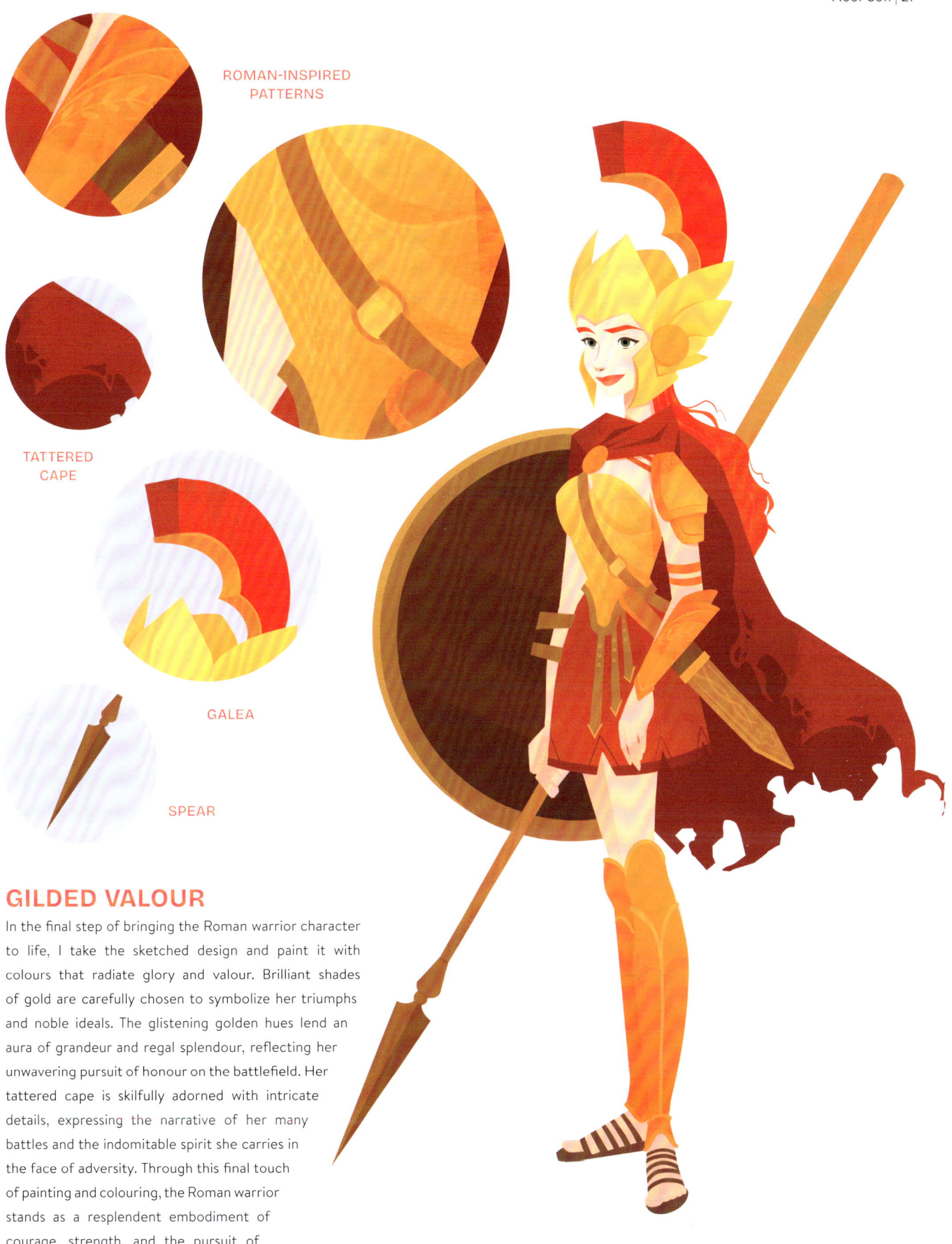

ROMAN-INSPIRED
PATTERNS

TATTERED
CAPE

GALEA

SPEAR

GILDED VALOUR

In the final step of bringing the Roman warrior character to life, I take the sketched design and paint it with colours that radiate glory and valour. Brilliant shades of gold are carefully chosen to symbolize her triumphs and noble ideals. The glistening golden hues lend an aura of grandeur and regal splendour, reflecting her unwavering pursuit of honour on the battlefield. Her tattered cape is skilfully adorned with intricate details, expressing the narrative of her many battles and the indomitable spirit she carries in the face of adversity. Through this final touch of painting and colouring, the Roman warrior stands as a resplendent embodiment of courage, strength, and the pursuit of glory on her heroic journey.

ANGELIC AVIATION

KEVIN HONG

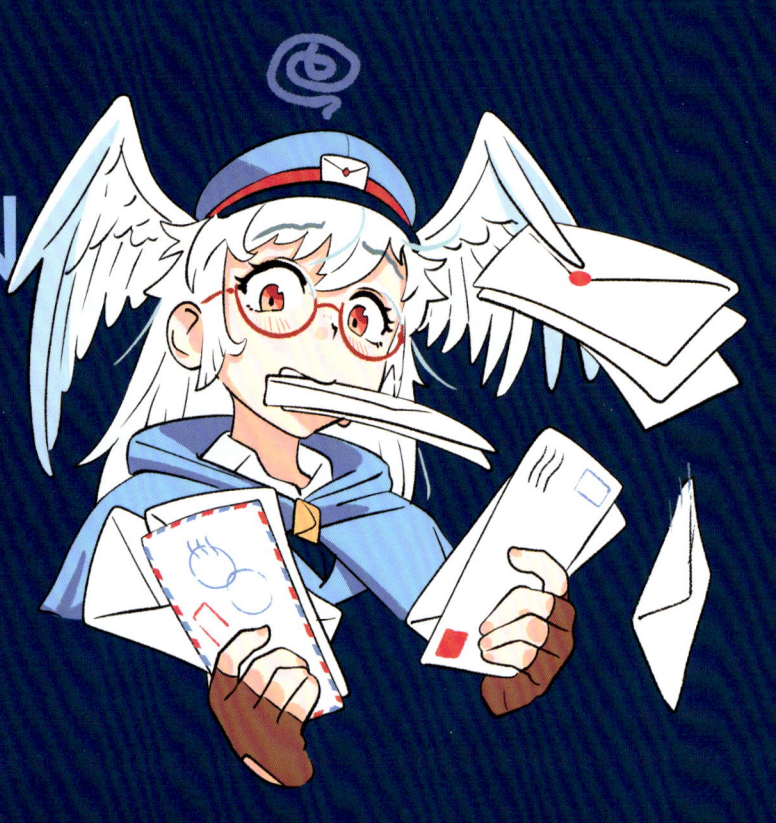

Character design is a multifaceted discipline, requiring unique considerations from the artist depending on the style, medium, and framework they're working within. Nonetheless, there exists universal principles that artists use to craft compelling characters with distinct personalities. With some of these principles in mind, I'll take you through my process of creating a new character for a fantasy world where a magical courier company operates. This character's design will be closely tied to their role and experiences within this setting. I hope that by following along, you'll be able to gain some insight into my method of designing characters, and apply these insights to your own creative process!

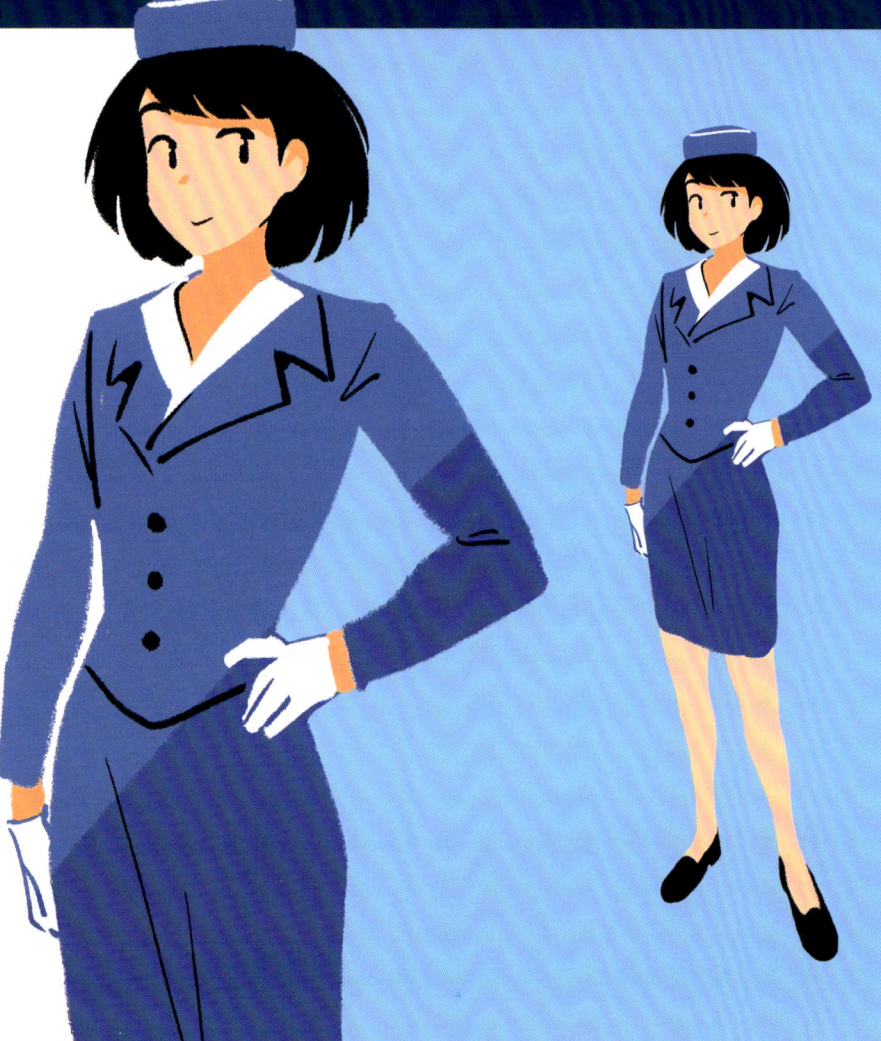

GATHERING REFERENCES

As with any design or illustration, it's helpful to collect ample references and inspiration to work from when coalescing ideas for designs. Creating mood boards will help you to picture your character outside of your head, filling in the details that are missing from your mind's eye. For this character, I knew I wanted her outfit to be the uniform of the courier company she joins. Collecting references of letter-carrier uniforms and aviation uniforms (like the iconic Pan Am flight attendant uniforms) help to define her appearance early on in the process.

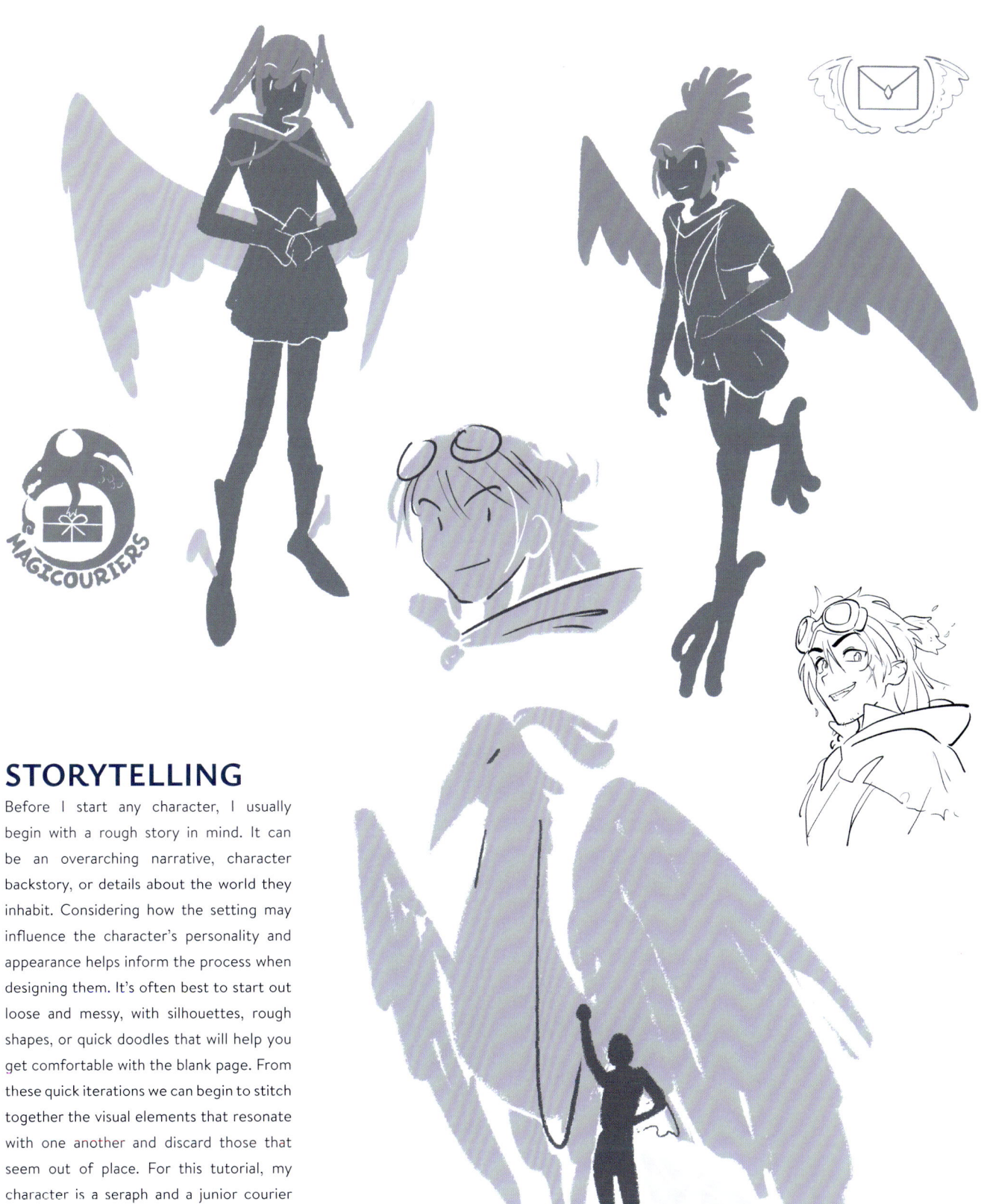

STORYTELLING

Before I start any character, I usually begin with a rough story in mind. It can be an overarching narrative, character backstory, or details about the world they inhabit. Considering how the setting may influence the character's personality and appearance helps inform the process when designing them. It's often best to start out loose and messy, with silhouettes, rough shapes, or quick doodles that will help you get comfortable with the blank page. From these quick iterations we can begin to stitch together the visual elements that resonate with one another and discard those that seem out of place. For this tutorial, my character is a seraph and a junior courier who joins the delivery company near the beginning of her story.

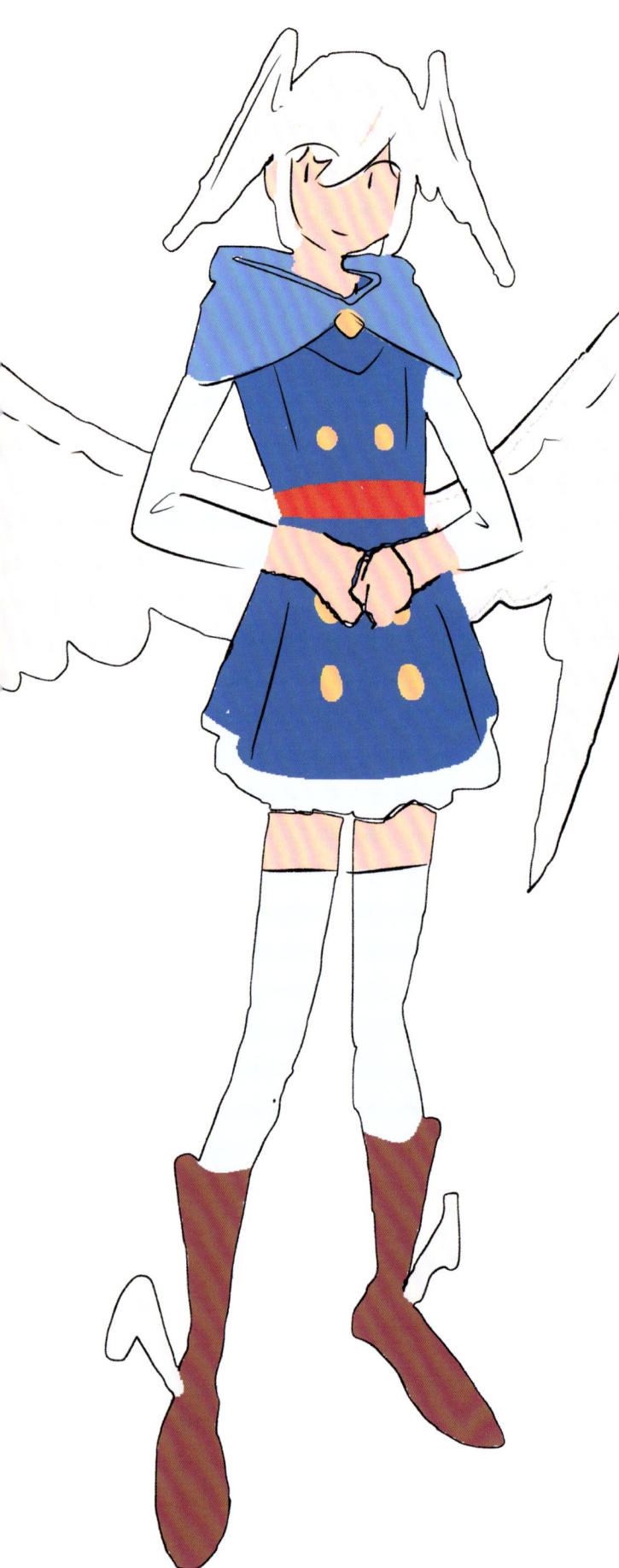

COLOURS AND ACCENTS

After defining some silhouettes, start blocking in colours to get a sense of what their palette may look like. Adding accents and splashes of colour can help you get a feel for the visual flow of your character's appearance, even without a specific costume in mind yet. I sometimes use this method to then decide on what accessories can be added and where, like belts, buttons, and other ornaments.

VIGNETTES

Once your character starts to come into focus, begin refining the concepts to align more with their personality. Experiment with different features, accessories, hairstyles, and poses. Try doodling close ups and facial expressions. To better understand who they are, it helps to imagine simple scenarios or vignettes of them interacting with other characters, objects, or their environment. With this character, I want to accentuate that she's a novice and still a bit clumsy – giving her frizzy hair and having her fumble through letters could help illustrate that!

LOCKING IN LINEART

Now it's time to start finalizing a rough! Because my style is drawing focused, I refine rough concepts using clean line art. However, this stage should be relevant to your own particular process. There's no one right way or approach to finalizing a design, and often you will need to stay within the style and framework of whatever project you are working on. For some of you, your roughs may be the final style you want to aim for.

ALWAYS RECYCLE!

Try not to delete or erase sketches that you think might not be working. After concepting and iterating, keep all your rejected sketches tucked away in another folder. When stuck or in a rut (maybe when designing other characters) sift through these old sketches again and see if they generate any new ideas for you.

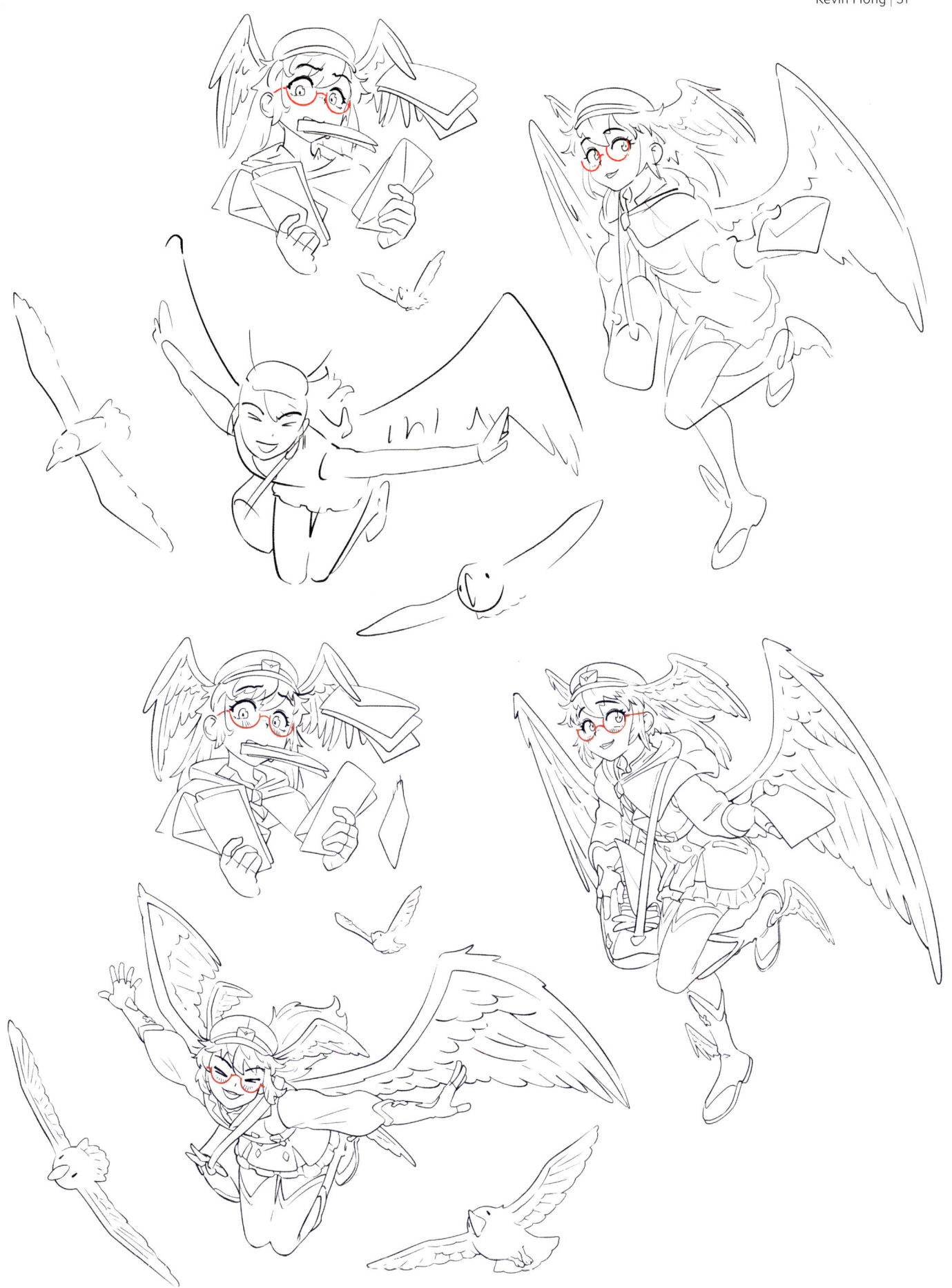

'I LIKE TO ADD SOME FINISHING TOUCHES BY COLOURING IN THE LINE ART IN SELECT REGIONS'

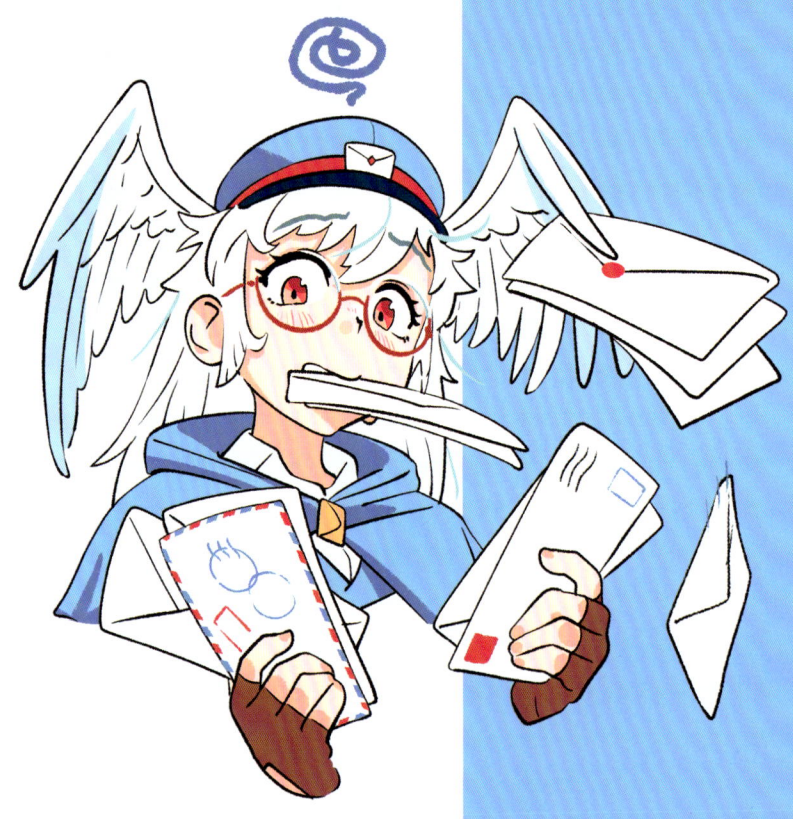

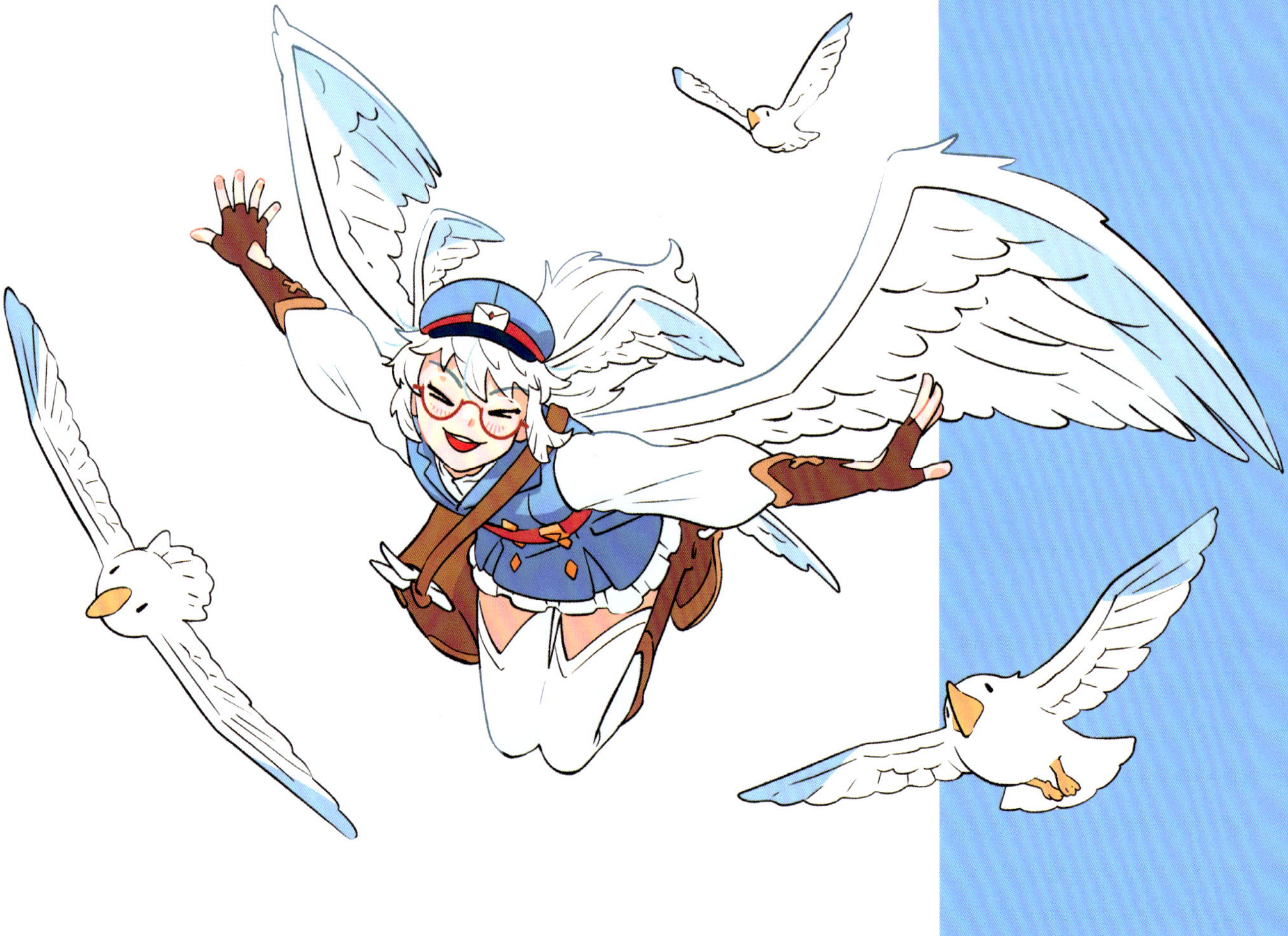

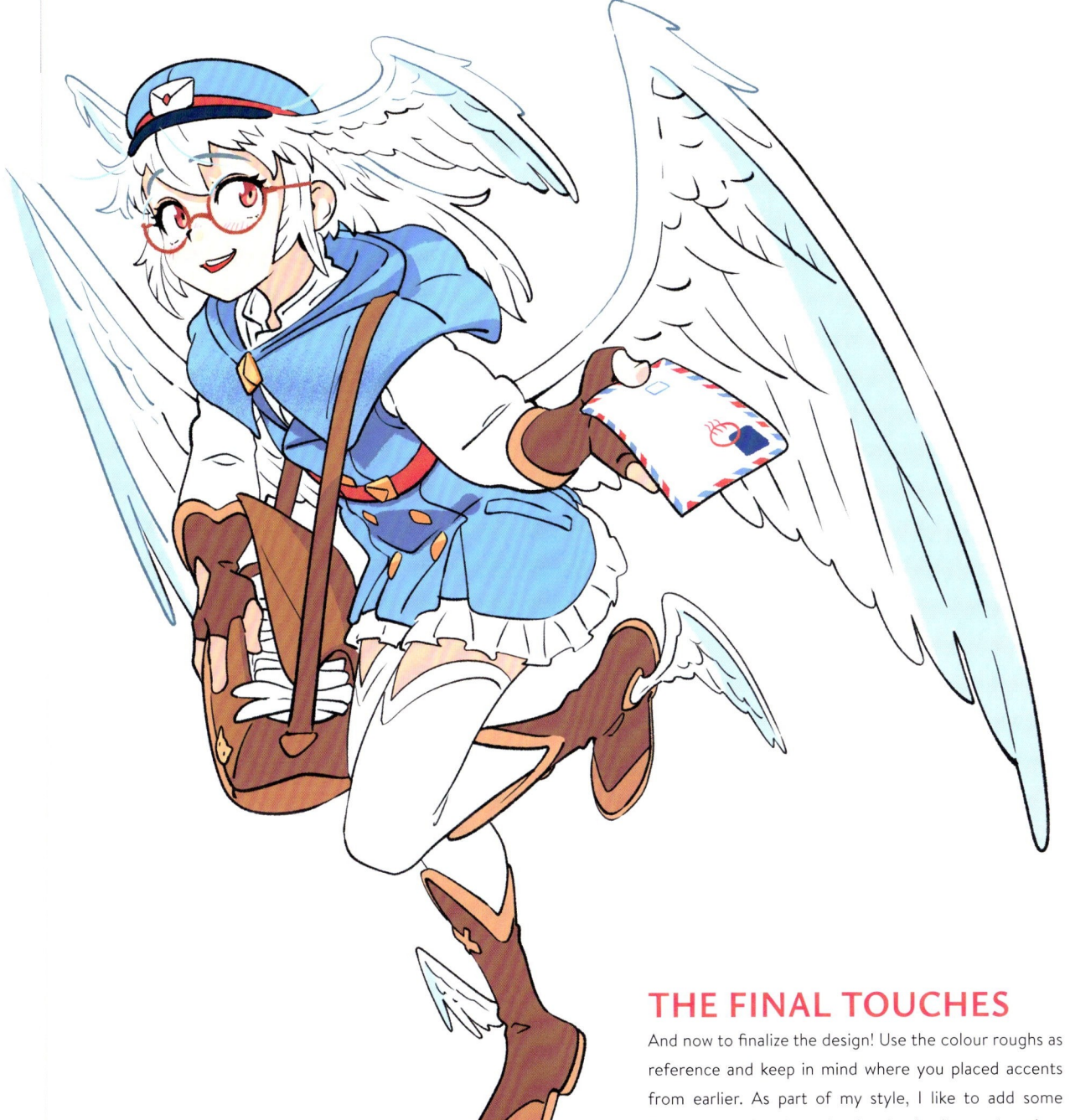

THE FINAL TOUCHES

And now to finalize the design! Use the colour roughs as reference and keep in mind where you placed accents from earlier. As part of my style, I like to add some finishing touches by colouring in the lineart in select regions, softening edges, and adding an impression of highlights and glow. This stage is where you commit to solving the visual challenge of who your character is. Hopefully, through following some of these methods, the design will resonate and speak to who you are as a character designer.

DESIGNING CHARACTERS FOR
ANIMATION
MAOR SHARVIT

Drawing animated characters is not an easy task. There is a lot to think about: anatomy, volume, shapes, proportions – it can all become a bit overwhelming! My approach is to start with big, simple ideas, and let the story and personality lead me in the right direction. Let me show you three characters in two different poses and share some tips for creating the building blocks behind these designs.

THE LINE OF ACTION

Before getting into the detail of the design and pose, I try to think of the whole character as a simplified directional idea, usually a curved line. This helps create poses that are simple and read fast.

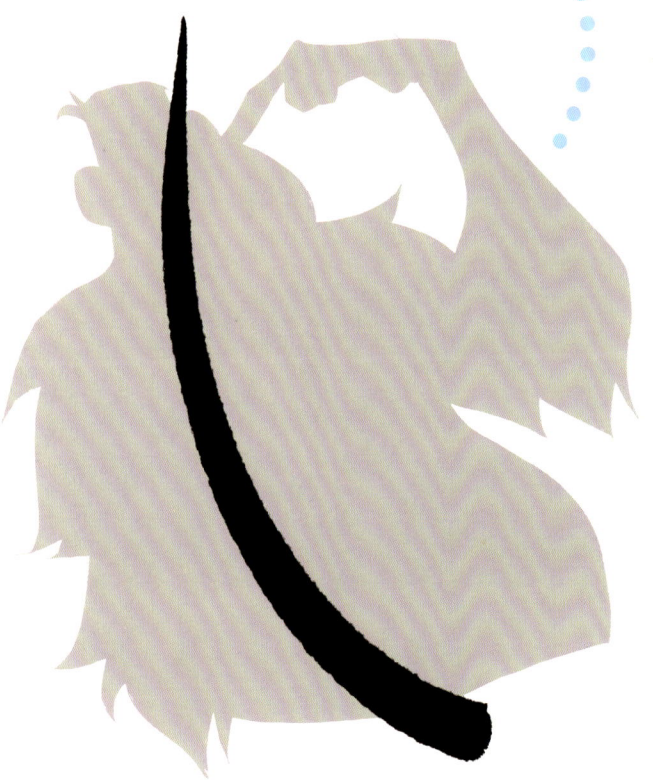

'I TRY TO THINK OF THE WHOLE CHARACTER AS A SIMPLIFIED DIRECTIONAL IDEA'

ONE SPECIAL THING

Every person is special and has a unique way of expressing their emotions. I always try to imagine the inner world of my characters, and find gestures that don't just reflect their emotion, but also their specific personality. Try to look for what is unique about your character and what will make them stand out from other designs. It could be a physical feature, their body language, or even just a memorable hat!

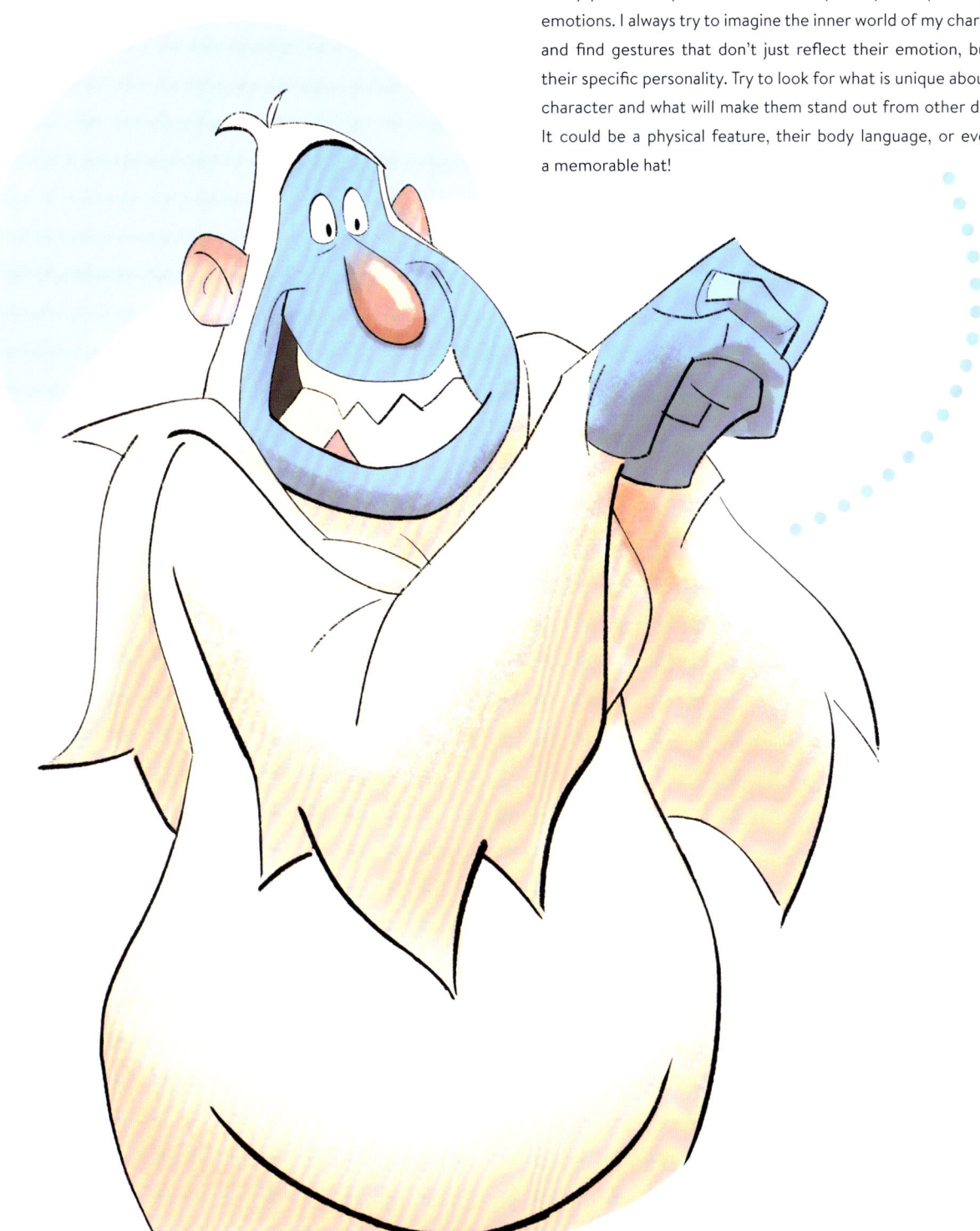

IN THE SHADOWS

As humans, we are very sensitive to graphic ideas, so it's important to make sure that your design and emotion read well as a flat shape. I design this witch so that even in silhouette the idea of a motionless, bored character comes through.

EVEN WITHOUT DETAILS, THE IDEA STILL READS

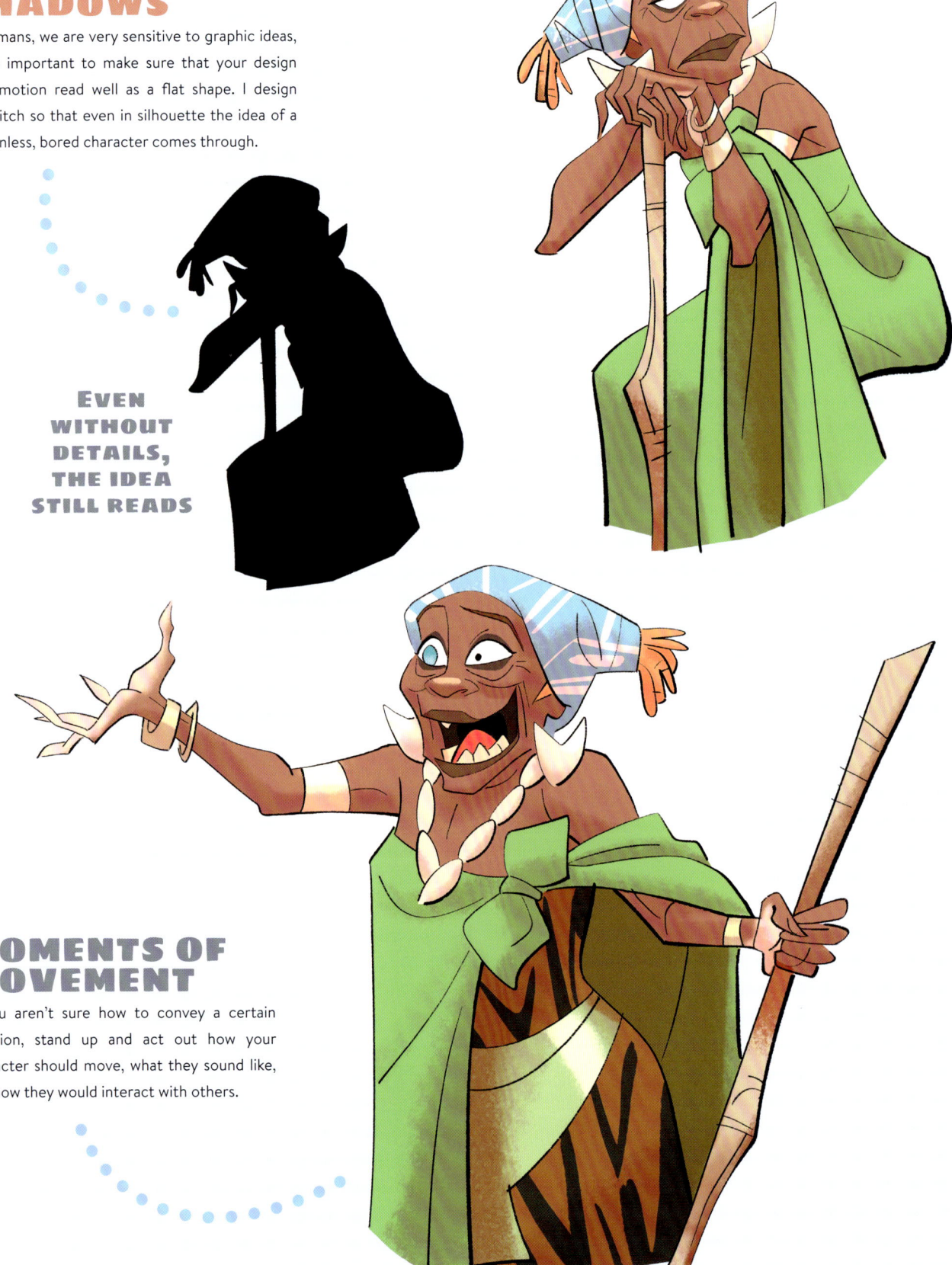

MOMENTS OF MOVEMENT

If you aren't sure how to convey a certain emotion, stand up and act out how your character should move, what they sound like, and how they would interact with others.

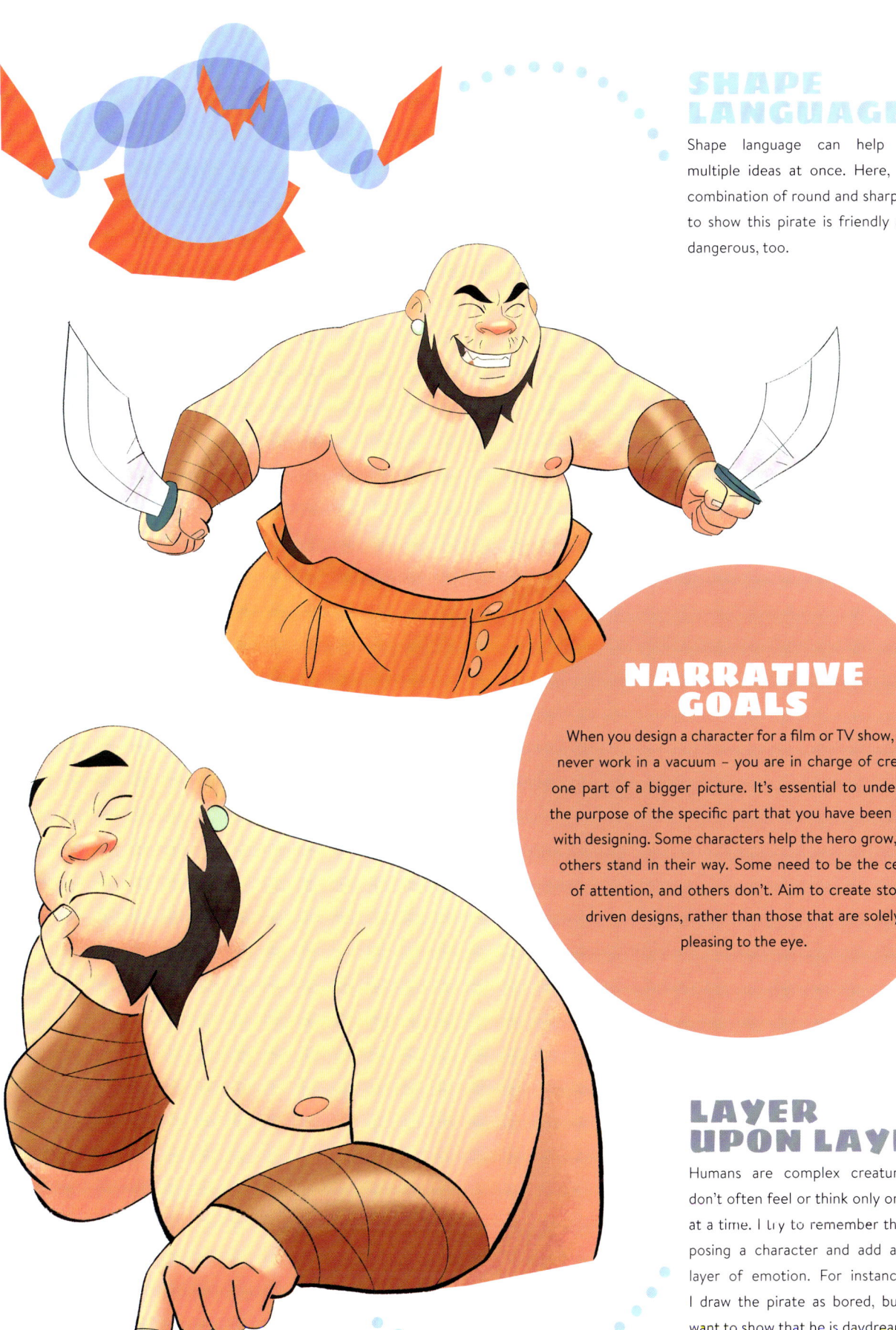

SHAPE LANGUAGE

Shape language can help convey multiple ideas at once. Here, I use a combination of round and sharp shapes to show this pirate is friendly and yet dangerous, too.

NARRATIVE GOALS

When you design a character for a film or TV show, you never work in a vacuum – you are in charge of creating one part of a bigger picture. It's essential to understand the purpose of the specific part that you have been tasked with designing. Some characters help the hero grow, while others stand in their way. Some need to be the centre of attention, and others don't. Aim to create story-driven designs, rather than those that are solely pleasing to the eye.

LAYER UPON LAYER

Humans are complex creatures and don't often feel or think only one thing at a time. I try to remember this when posing a character and add an extra layer of emotion. For instance, here I draw the pirate as bored, but I also want to show that he is daydreaming.

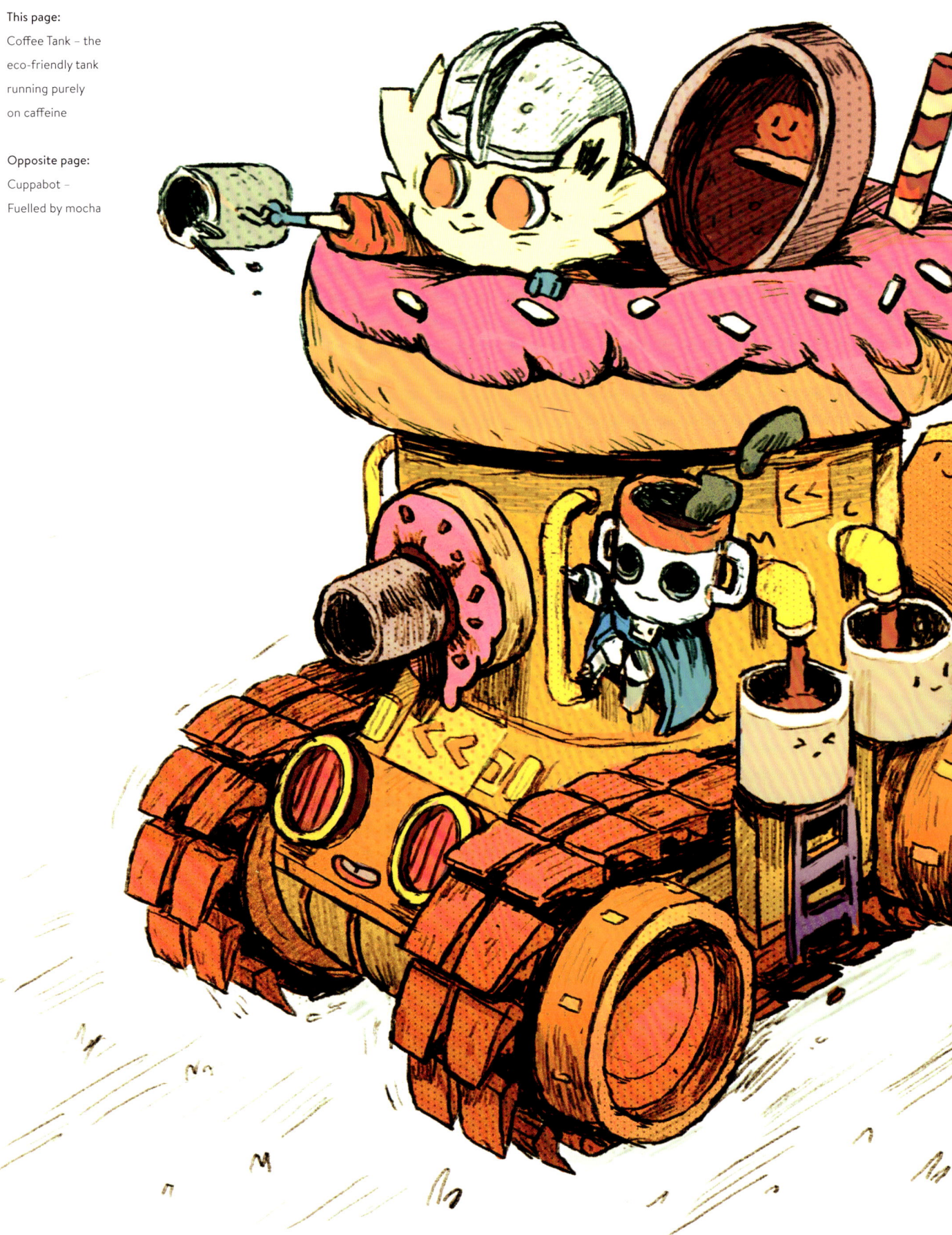

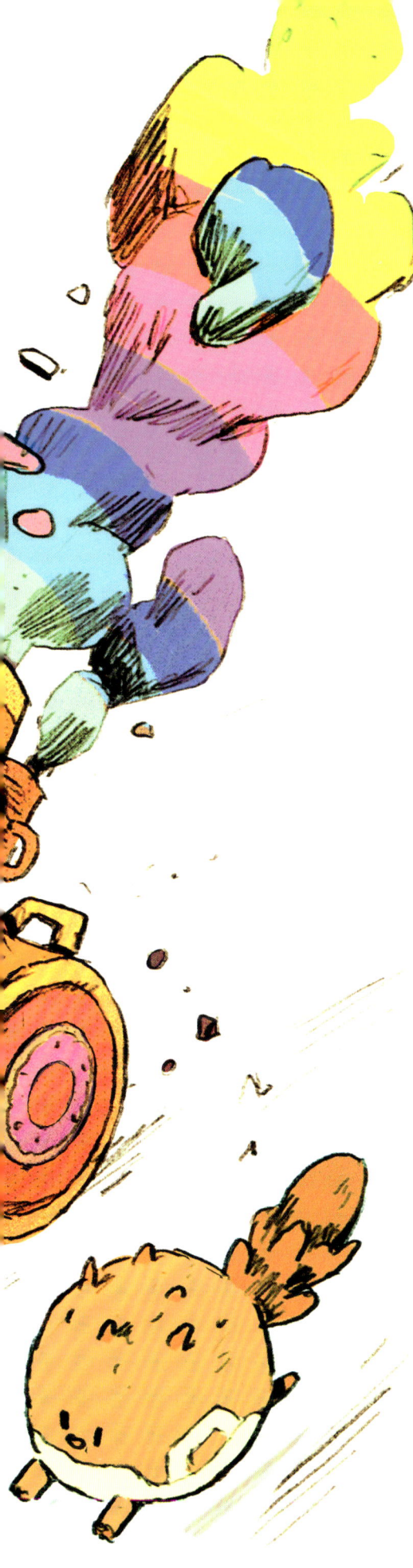

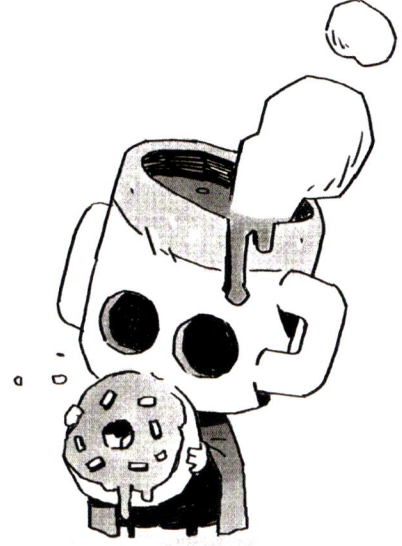

TRUDI CASTLE

Trudi Castle is a concept artist and illustrator who has been working in the games industry for nearly 20 years. Currently, she's an Associate Art Director at Red Hook Studios, where she recently worked on the critically acclaimed game *Darkest Dungeon 2*. We welcomed Trudi back to CDQ to discuss the specifics of character design for games, and to hear her advice on how to follow in her footsteps.

Hi Trudi, welcome back to *CDQ*! Can you let our readers know a bit about your career so far?

Thank you so much for having me back, it's a great honour to be a part of your magazine and community! Here's a brief rundown: I have a degree in illustration, but couldn't find work initially, so I worked in Quality Assurance (QA) in games for a couple of years after graduating. From there, I slowly worked my way up to storyboarding and concepting at various types of game studios, from AAA publishers to mobile, to an indie studio, which is where I work currently, and is also my favourite of the three. In the past year I became an Associate Art Director. If you could go back in time and tell younger me, with only a single toe in the door, that this would happen, then I would be wildly surprised!

What are the unique challenges that arise when creating characters for video games?

Video games have always been a huge passion of mine, even if I can't play as many as I'd like anymore. It can be an incredibly creative industry, full of equally passionate people. Creating characters for games can bring up many issues. Firstly, what medium is the game being viewed on? A mobile phone, handheld device, a giant 4K screen, a monitor – or sometimes even all of the above? Then we have to think about the angle the audience will be looking at our characters from, be it top down, behind the shoulder, even first person – and maybe this perspective can even change throughout the game. All of this will impact the design, the style you choose (realistic, cartoony, and so on), the silhouette, and colours, all aiming for maximum, clear readability. Having so much to consider is what keeps video-game work forever challenging and fun for me!

This page:
Bread Stick –
Cookie on her
usual mode of
transport

Opposite page:
Egg Suit –
A fried-egg
explorer

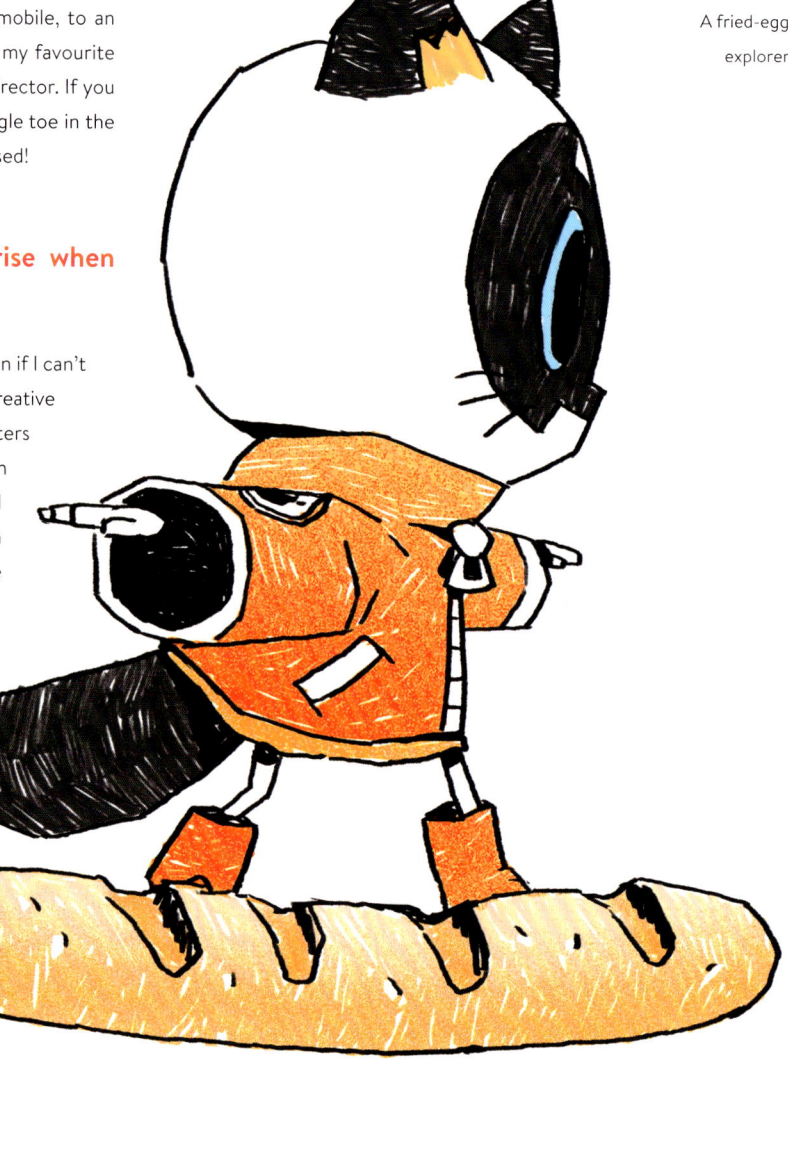

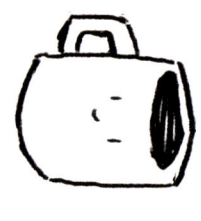

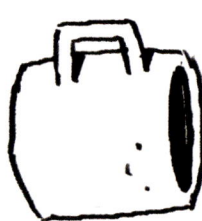

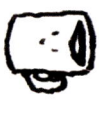

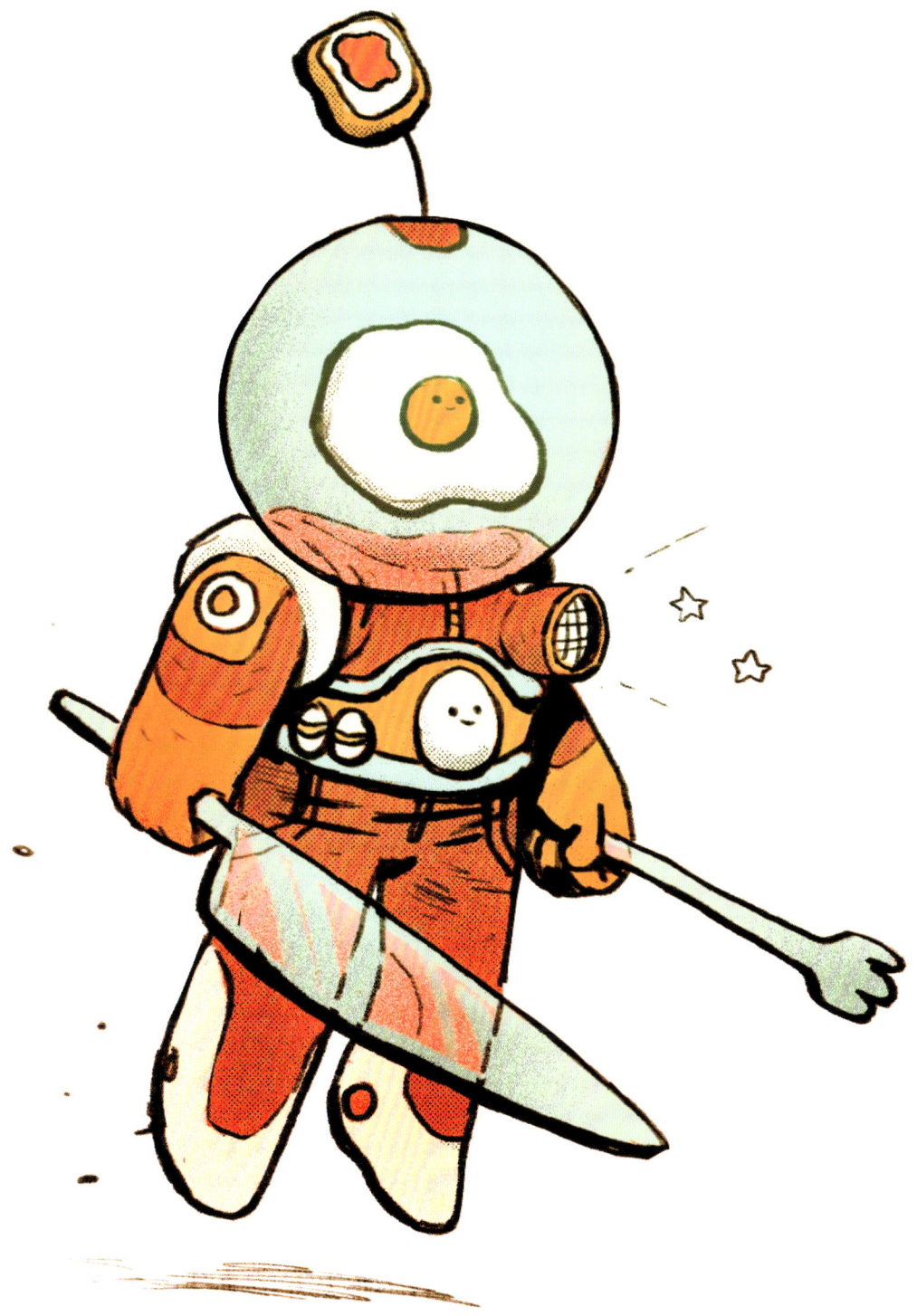

'Video games have always been a huge passion of mine, even if I can't play as many as I'd like anymore'

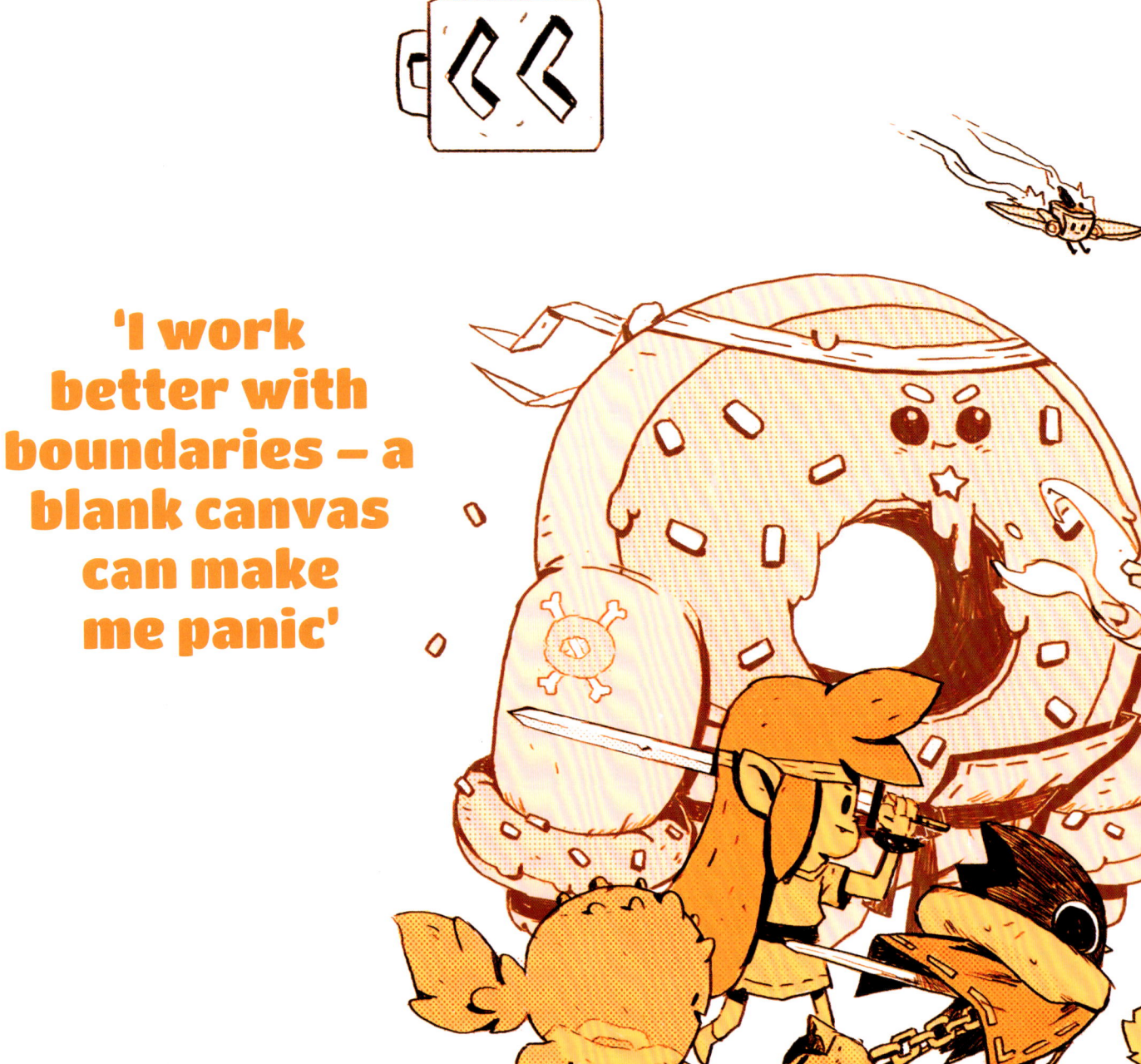

'I work better with boundaries – a blank canvas can make me panic'

What does the day-to-day of your current role at Red Hook Studios entail?

My workday at Red Hook Studios is quite varied! Depending on what the project needs (*Darkest Dungeon 2* currently) I might spend a few weeks on concept art for a whole new level of the game. Once this is agreed upon with the main art director and designer, I create rendered, cleaned-up, and coloured textures, while talking to the 3D modellers about the best approach for putting my ideas into the game. Once the characters are in-game and the sets are decorated, I provide paint-overs of screenshots, and object placement suggestions: whether to move, shrink, enlarge assets, colour adjustments – the list goes on! It's a fun process. Other days, I might be working on icon concepts and clean-up, or drawing corpses, or maybe creating weapon skins. I appreciate the variety!

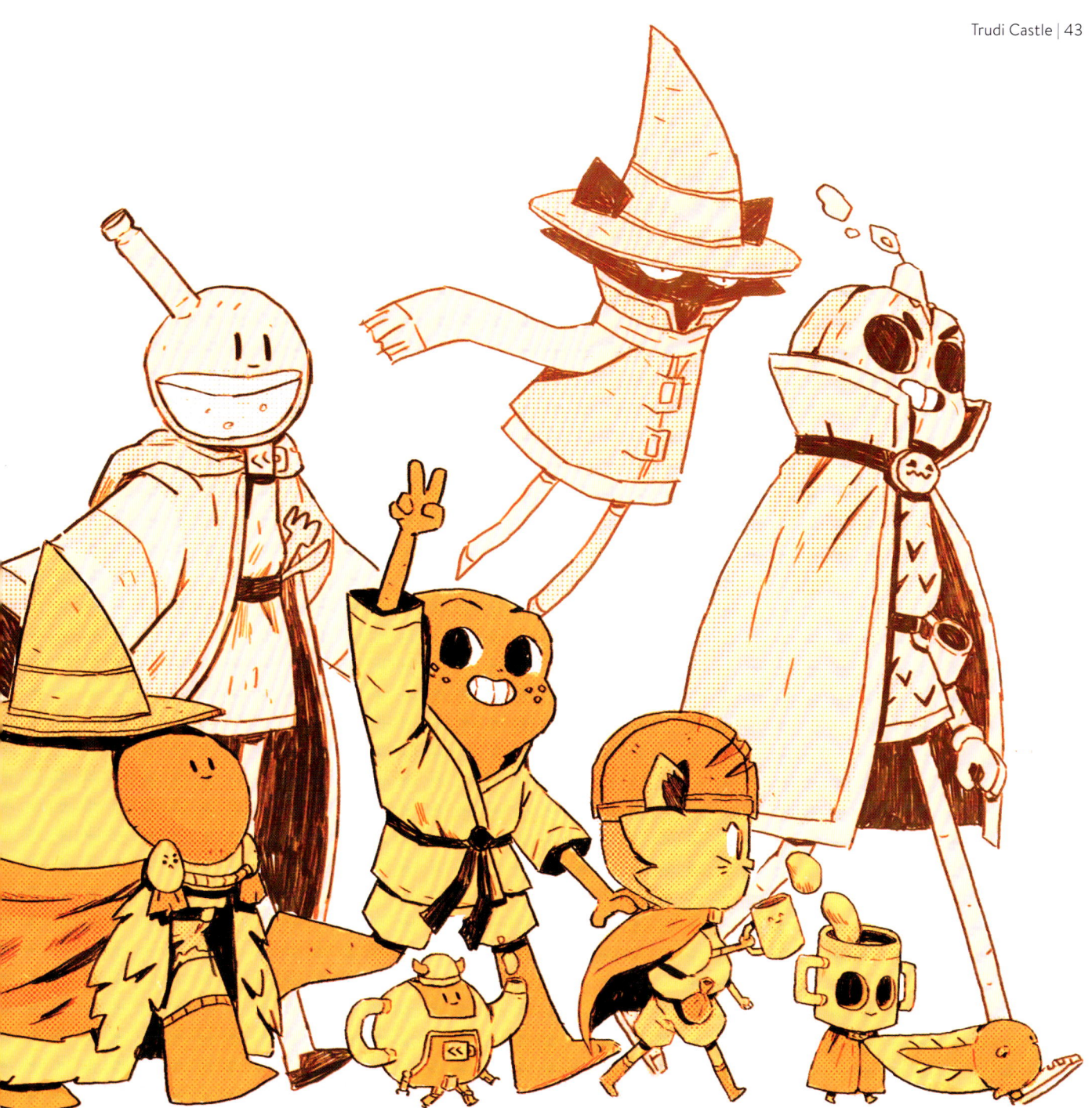

What's been your favourite project to work on, and why?

My favourite project has of course been *Darkest Dungeon 2*! I was given a lot of responsibility, helping to create whole new biomes for the sequel, and we had a great time coming up with the various levels. I think one of the most fun parts was deciding on the time of day and weather for each level – maybe it's because I'm British, but I could talk about the weather all day long – I find it endlessly fascinating. Taking the original game's look and 'growing it up' slightly, while keeping true to the original's art style was a fun restriction to work within. Personally, I work better with boundaries – a blank canvas can make me panic.

These pages: The Coffee Crew –
The gang's all here

This page: Coffee Mage –
A magical caffeine-
powered wizard

Opposite page (left):
Halloween Ghost –
A reptile ghost who
just loves pumpkins!

Opposite page (right):
Cookie – A bread-
loving cat

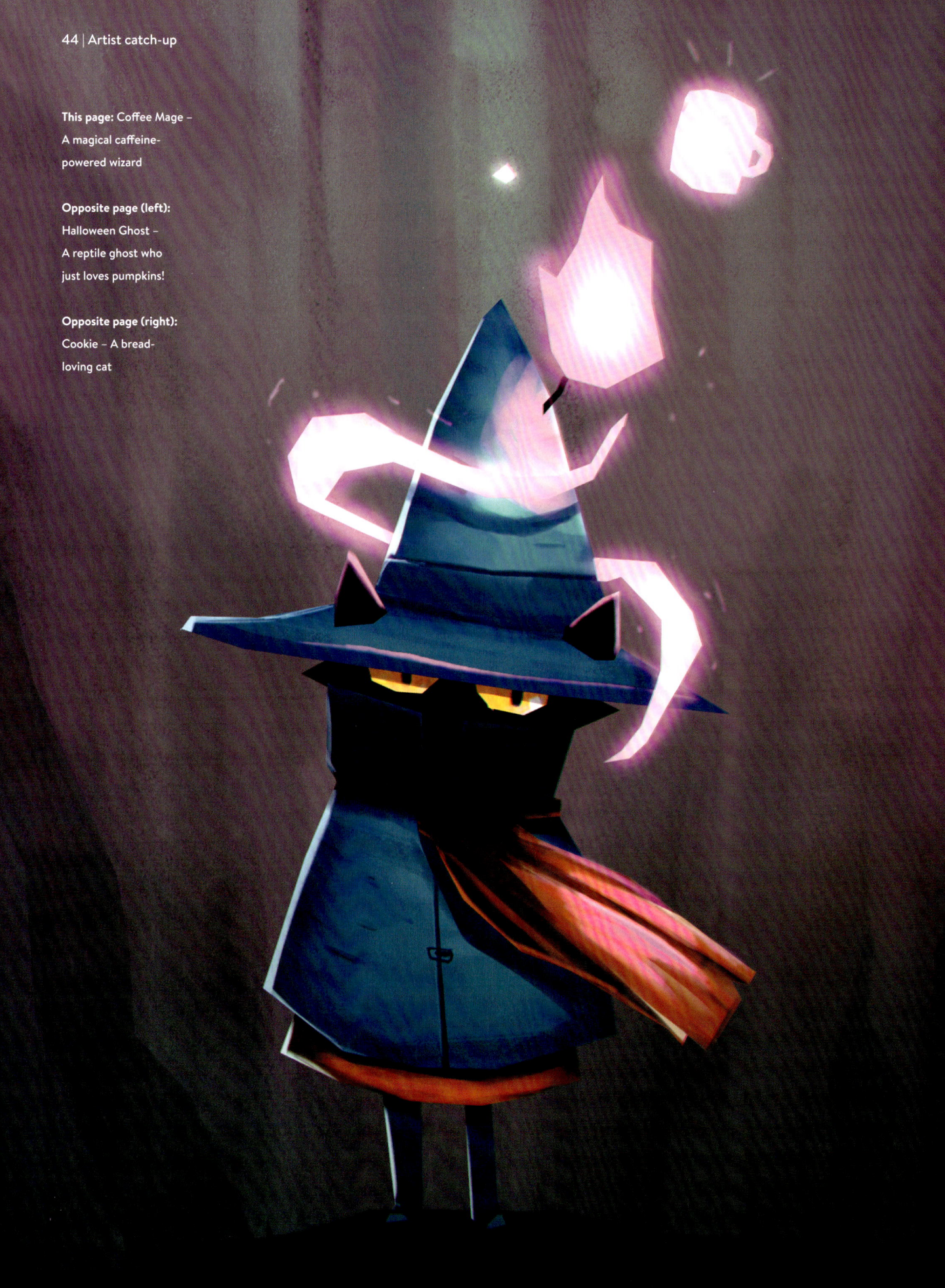

'I would always advise to look outside of your chosen field for inspiration'

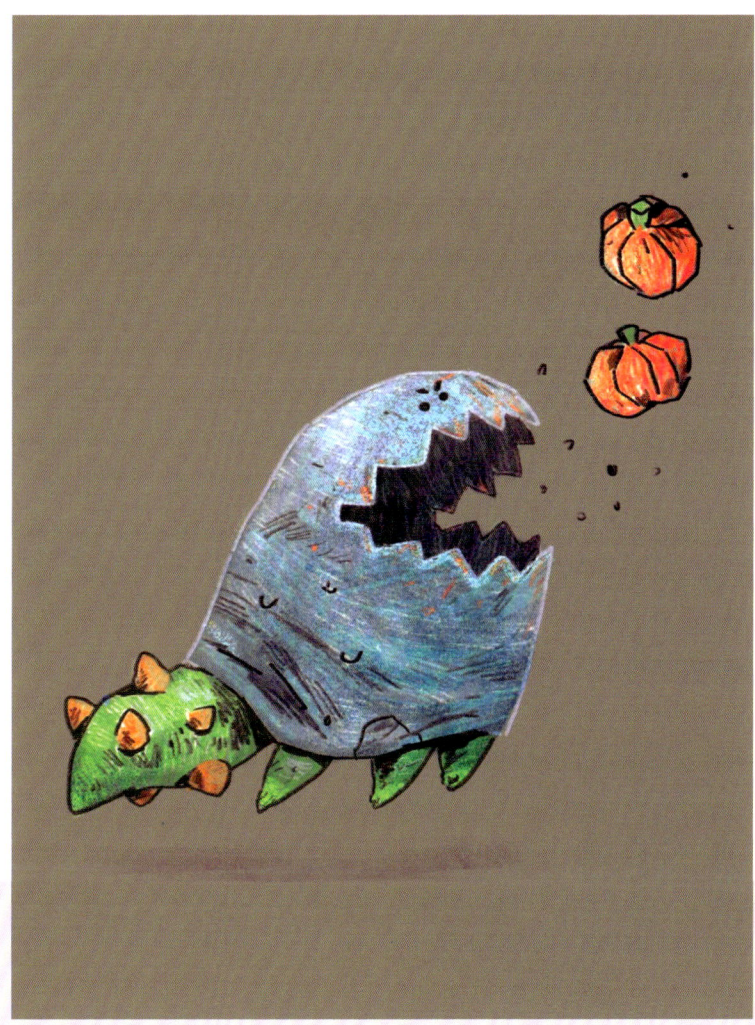

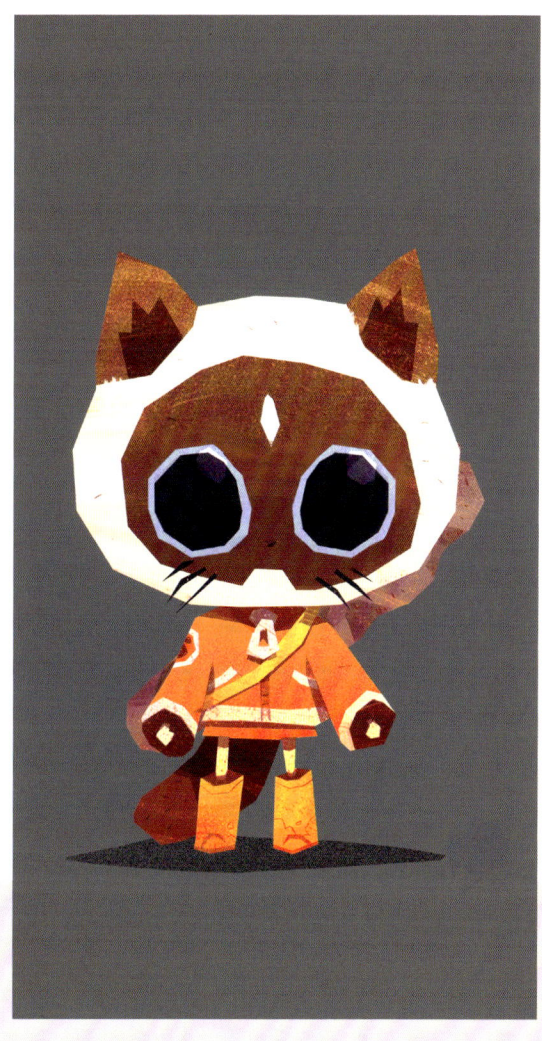

How do you impose those boundaries in your own work? Do you plan what you want to draw, or is your process more experimental?

I need to have an idea going in for what I'm going to draw. Will it be a structure? Will it be a cute character? Experimenting can be fun, for sure, and I still do it from time to time, especially when I see an inspirational art style.

Honestly, though, I do this a lot less than I used to – is this a sign of slowly getting old?

How do you find inspiration for your characters?

I would always advise to look outside of your chosen field for inspiration, be it animation, video games, or something else. What you are seeing currently available already exists and so, in a sense, is already part of an old, dated trend. I'm a huge walker, whether within the city or out in the wilderness on a hike, and without fail I always see interesting people, doing equally interesting things. I can find inspiration from people's fashion, the sports they play, even just how they move. It may sound obvious, but just get out and explore, look at people. And, of course, always be watching the latest movies, anime, and TV, just to see what designers are currently up to.

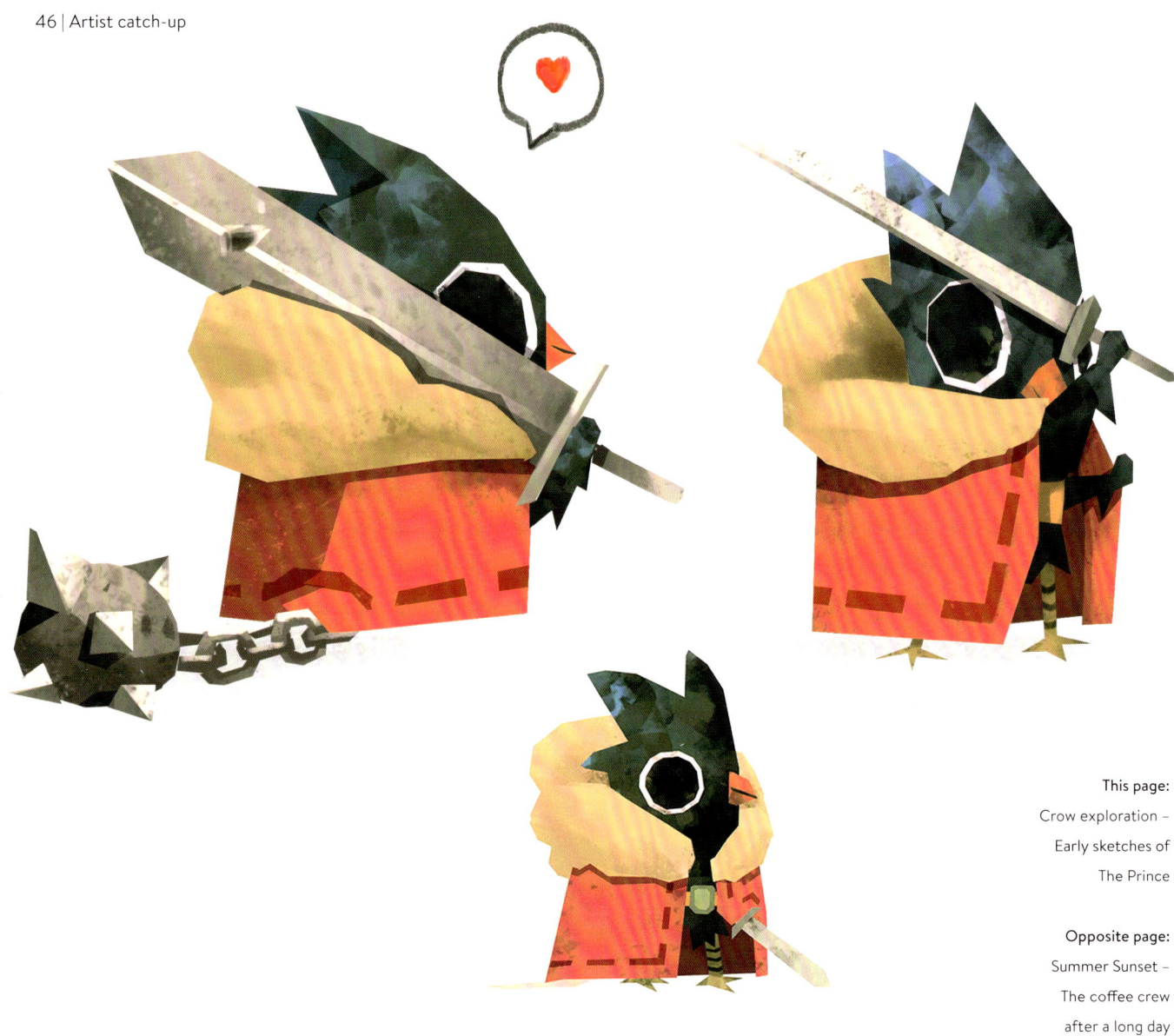

This page:
Crow exploration –
Early sketches of
The Prince

Opposite page:
Summer Sunset –
The coffee crew
after a long day

What do you think is the most important element of creating good character designs?

Fundamentally, I think a good character design is something someone can easily describe and draw from memory after having only seen it once or twice. I'm not a huge fan of over-detailed designs, I like plain, simple ideas – they seem more iconic to me. I believe Mario and Sonic have endured so long due to their extremely simple and clever designs. And of course, all the great games, too!

Who and what are the biggest influences behind your art style?

In recent years, huge influences on me have been Mike Mignola and Chris Bourassa (the main art director of Darkest Dungeon). They've given my work a slightly more angular look, even if the art I create in my free time still has a softer feel. Other huge influences would be Akira Toriyama, Katsuhiro Otomo, and Masashi Kishimoto. Recently, I've been really getting in to Hirohiko Araki's manga Jojo's Bizarre Adventure.

Thanks for chatting with us Trudi! Do you have any projects coming up we should be looking out for?

Currently I'm working on future downloadable content for Darkest Dungeon 2, and there will be console releases of the game soon, too. We plan to support the game as long as possible, with new characters, environments, and game modes!

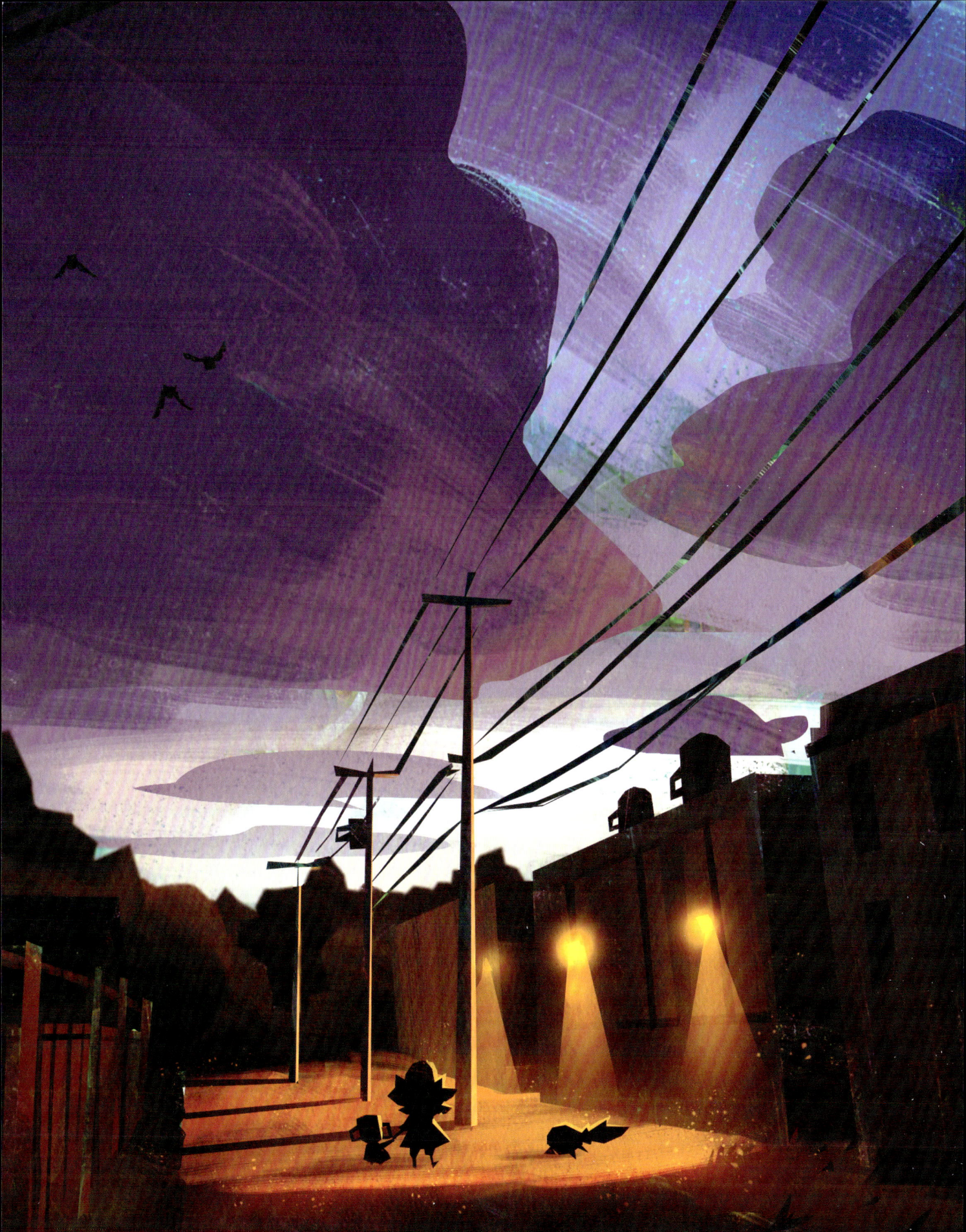

THE ECO-WARRIOR POSE

YAROSLAVA APOLLONOVA

In this mini feature I want to walk you through the process for creating a character based on a single-word prompt: ocean. I immediately had this idea of a modern girl who's upset with the whole world for throwing plastic and non-renewable things into the ocean. For this tutorial I will be using Procreate on my iPad Pro.

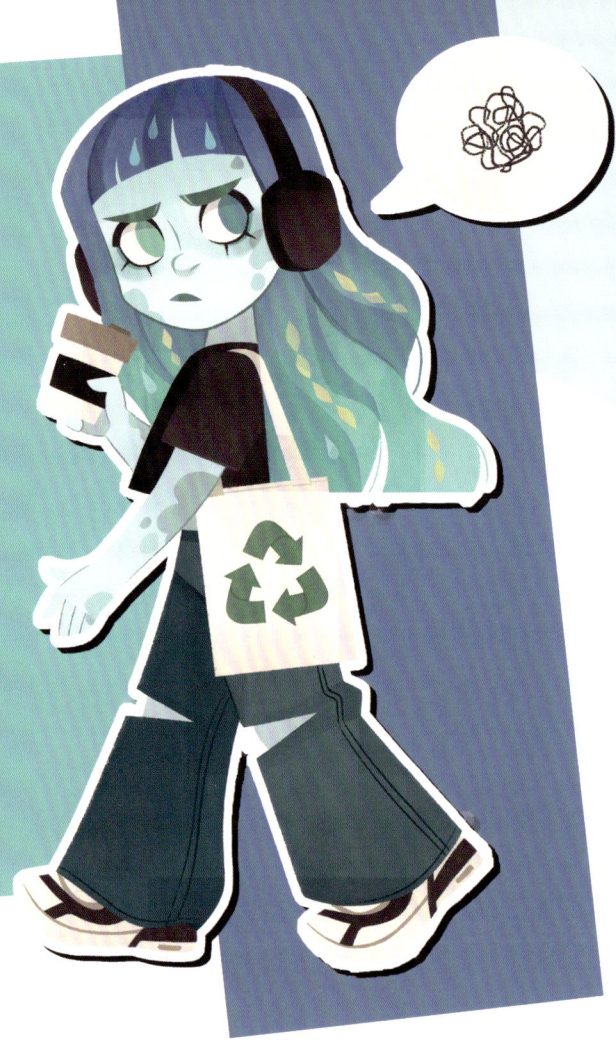

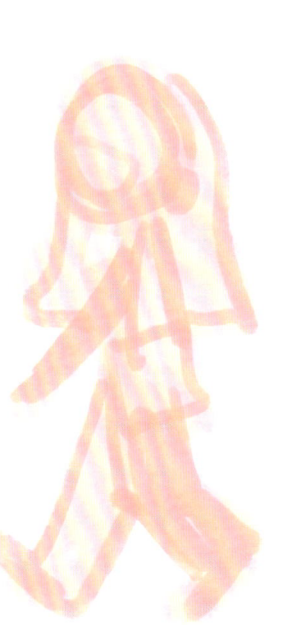

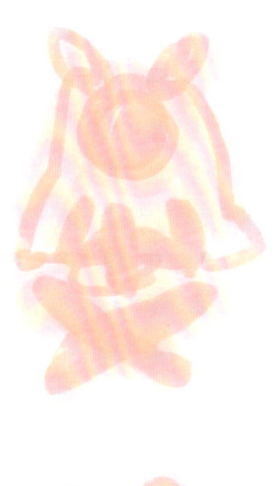

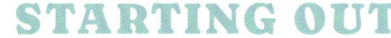

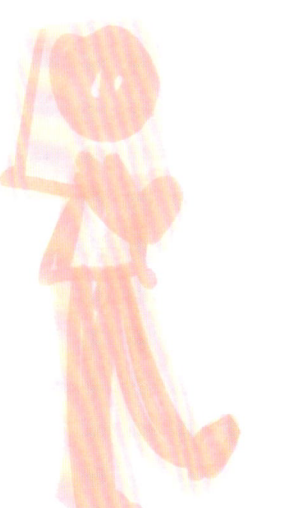

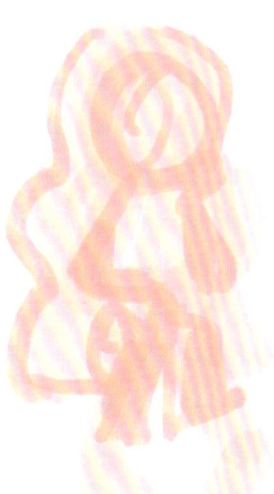

STARTING OUT

I always start with very rough thumbnails. I use a gouache brush to quickly define possible figures. Don't spend too much time here – this step should literally take you no more than a few minutes.

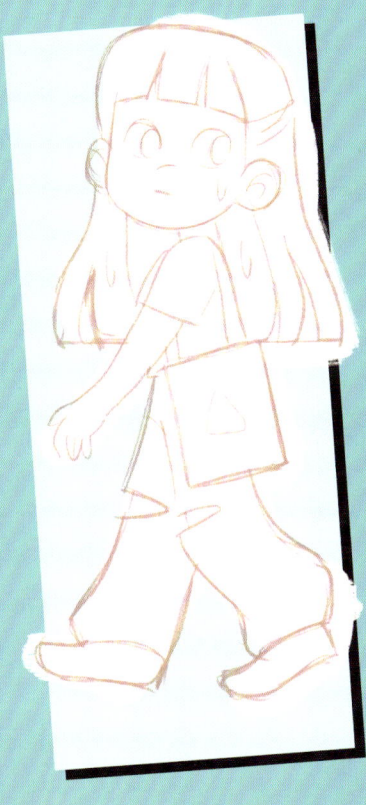

'CONCENTRATE ON THE MOOD OF THE CHARACTER'

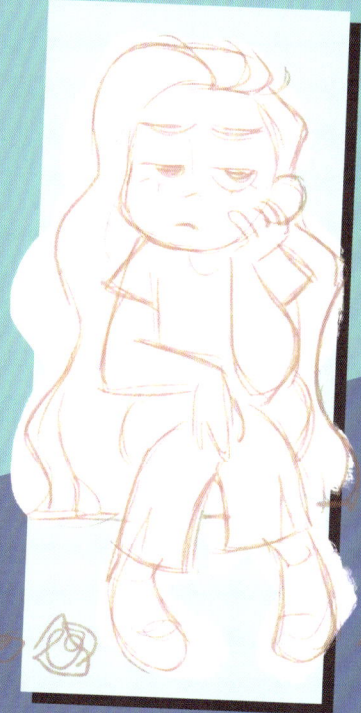

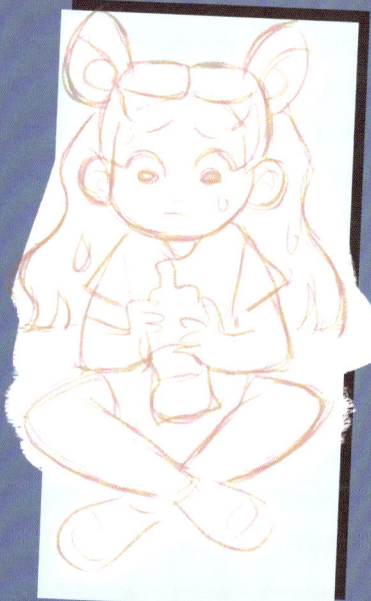

FIRST SKETCHES

Now it's time to make our first clean sketches. At this point I experiment with at least five different emotions to see how the character matches my original idea. Try to concentrate on the mood of the character – the small details are not important this early on in the process.

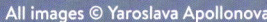

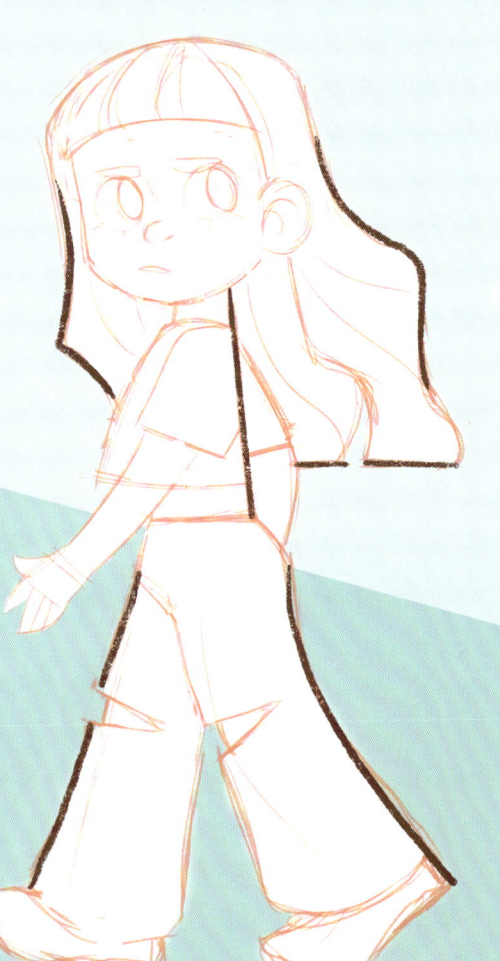

CLEANING UP

In my first sketch the girl looks too basic, so I need to give her a bit more character. What I like here is that she is almost turning her back at the viewer and walking away – I'm using the pose to amplify her emotions and attitude. I slightly tilt her head to the side in order to make her feelings even stronger.

ACCESSORIZE THIS

Once you are done with simple shapes and have a final pose, don't forget to add some extras. I feel the urge to bring back her tote with the 'Recycling' logo on it, as well as give her a reusable cup, and headphones that she uses to shut everyone out.

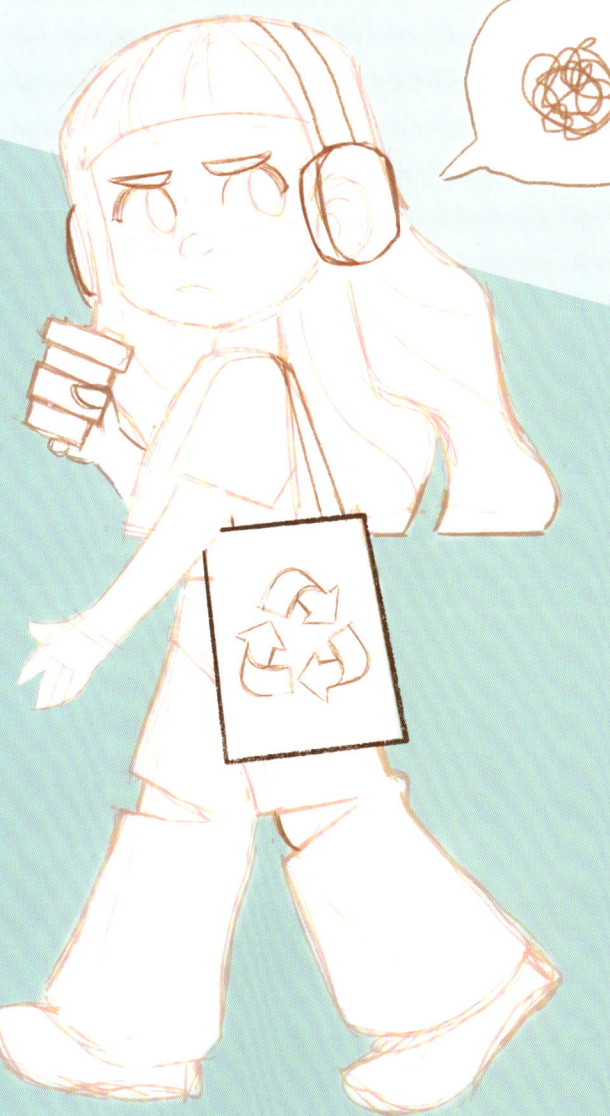

'I'M USING THE POSE TO AMPLIFY HER EMOTIONS AND ATTITUDE'

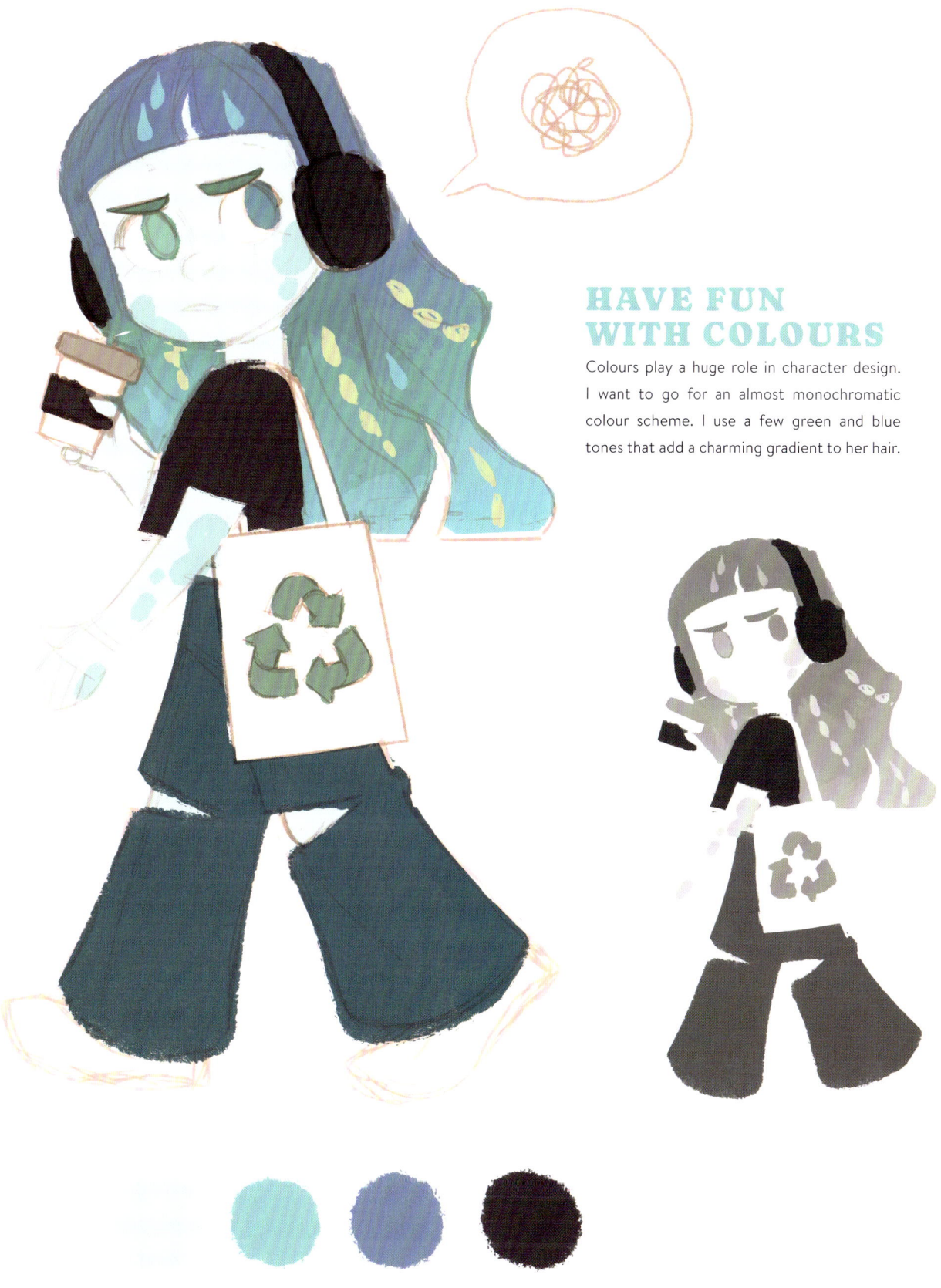

HAVE FUN WITH COLOURS

Colours play a huge role in character design. I want to go for an almost monochromatic colour scheme. I use a few green and blue tones that add a charming gradient to her hair.

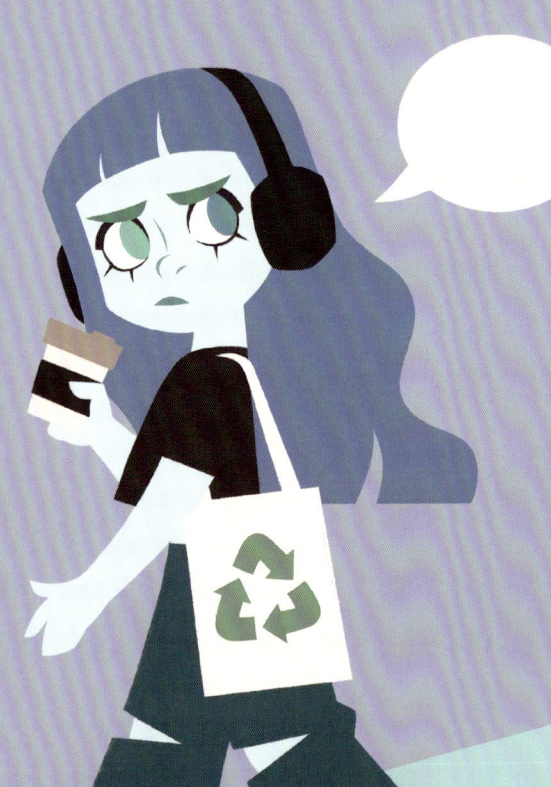

‘USING INDIVIDUAL LAYERS FOR EACH ELEMENT, I CAREFULLY FILL MY BASIC SHAPES’

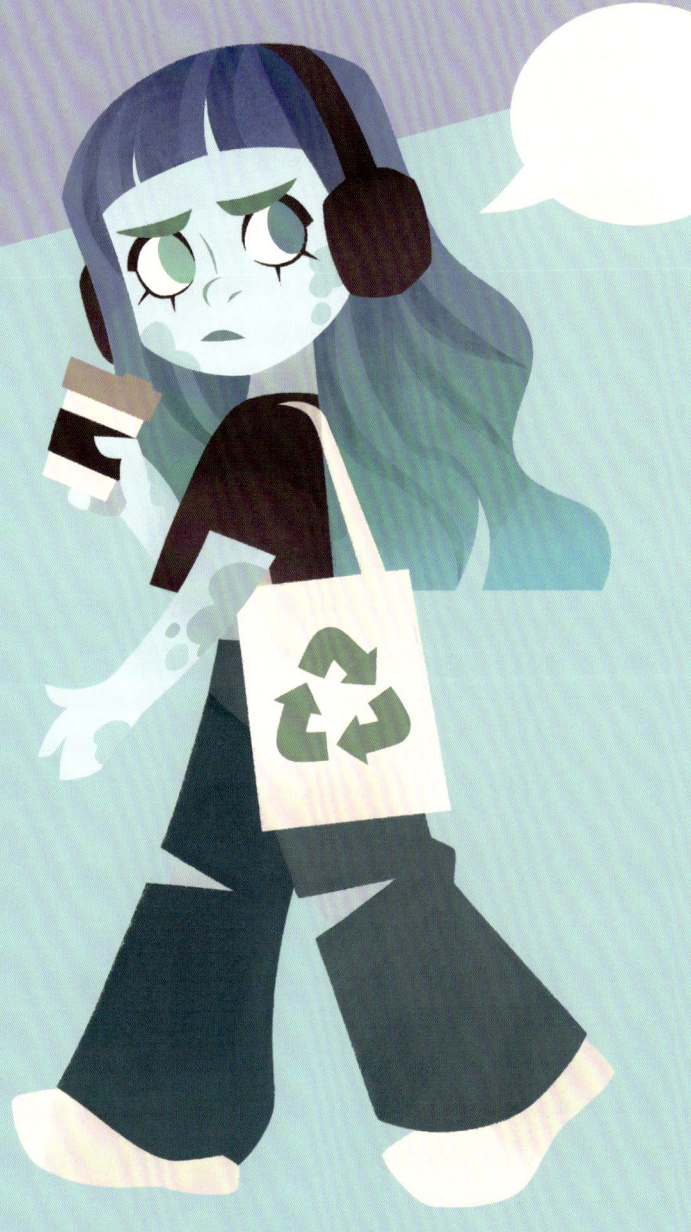

STRENGTH THROUGH SHAPES

Using individual layers for each element, I carefully fill my basic shapes. If your shapes don't look clean, hide the sketch and work with just the eraser until you feel satisfied with your forms.

ADDING TEXTURE

Adding texture is my favourite step, it immediately makes the work look 'half done'. Alpha Lock your layers and use brushes of your choice to add a bit of texture to the shapes. Add a new Clipping Mask layer above each element to add more details and shades where needed.

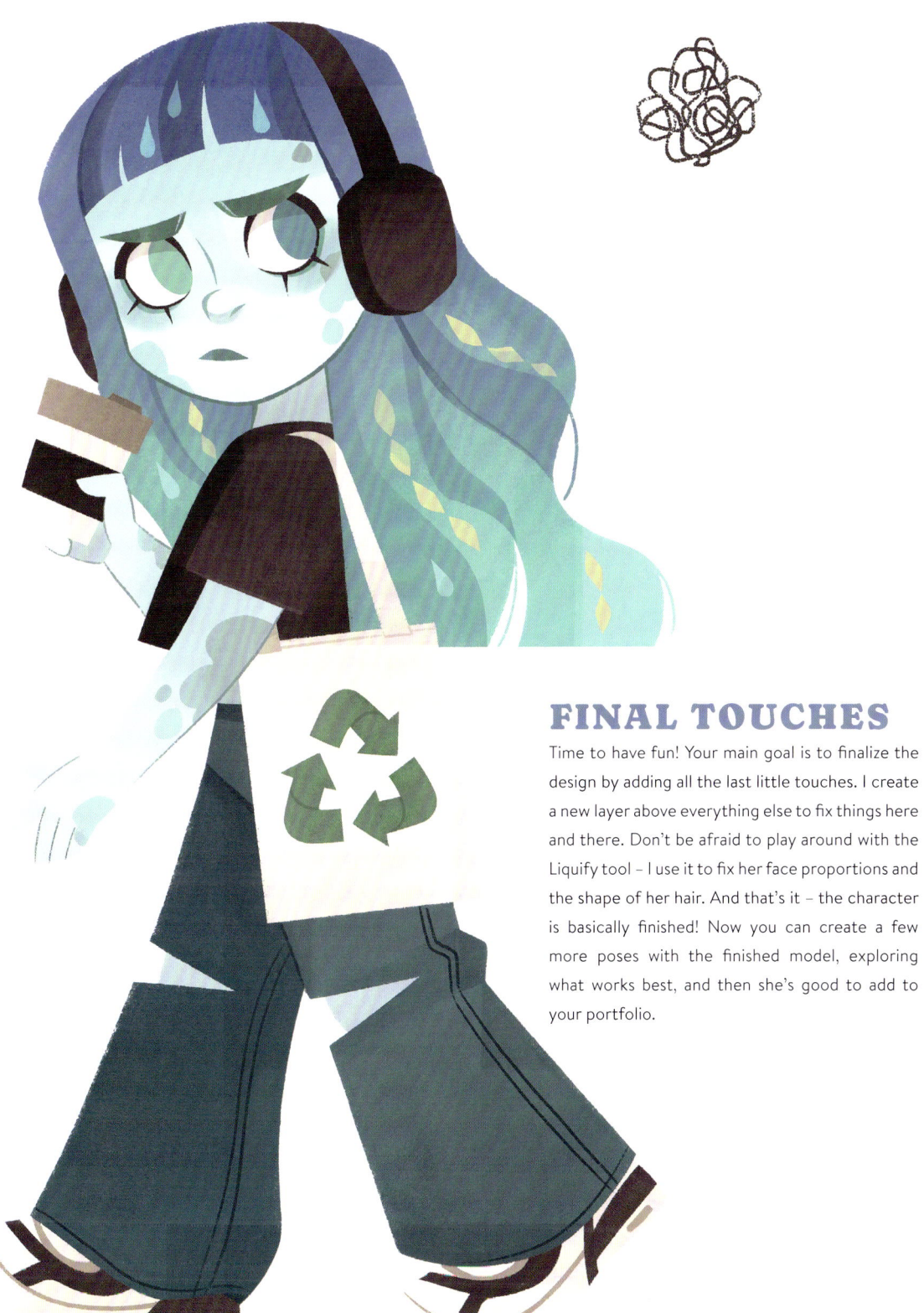

FINAL TOUCHES

Time to have fun! Your main goal is to finalize the design by adding all the last little touches. I create a new layer above everything else to fix things here and there. Don't be afraid to play around with the Liquify tool – I use it to fix her face proportions and the shape of her hair. And that's it – the character is basically finished! Now you can create a few more poses with the finished model, exploring what works best, and then she's good to add to your portfolio.

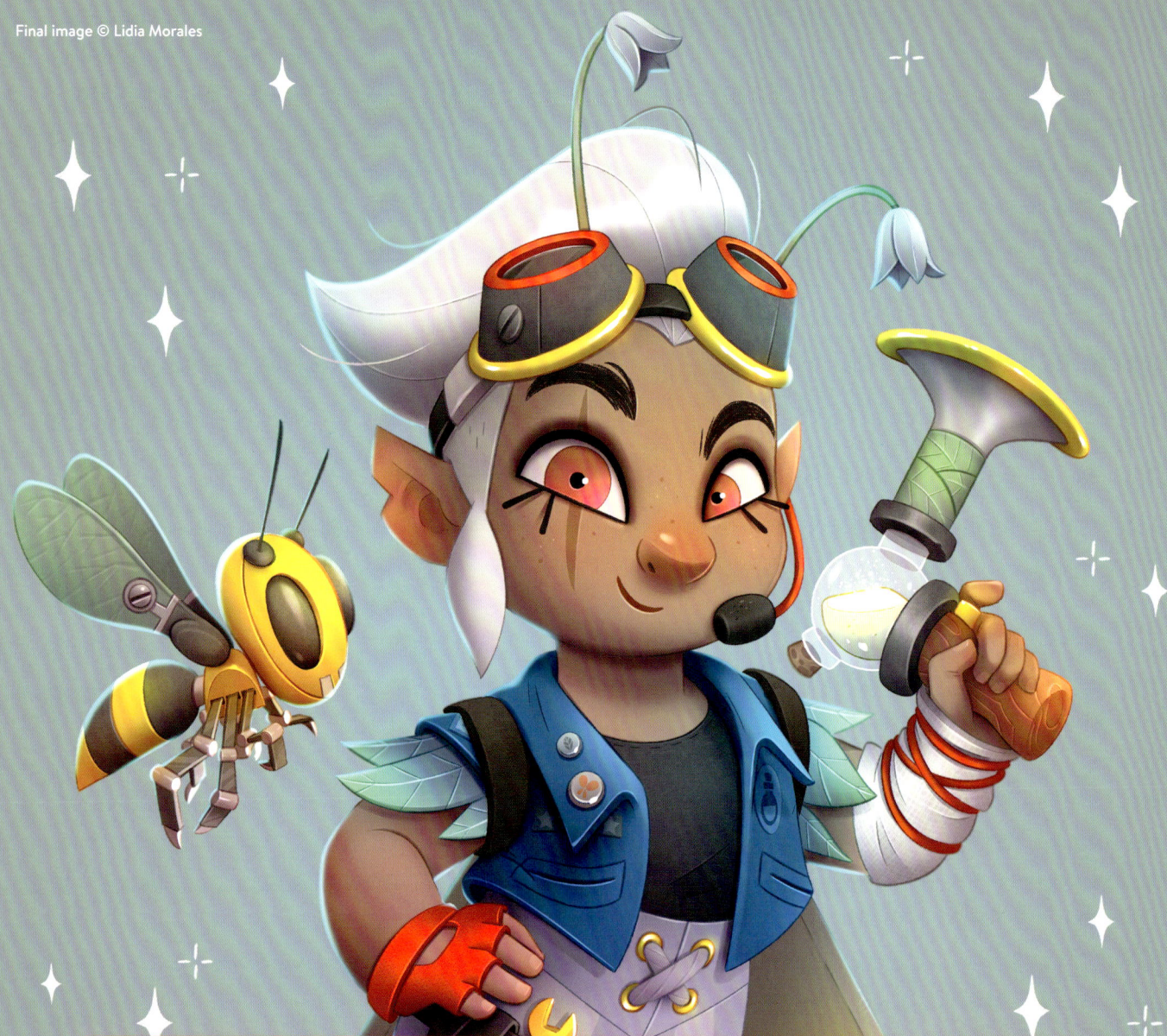

FAIRY IMPORTANT PERSON

LIDIA MORALES

The main goal of this tutorial is to share with you my character-design process, from the first ideas to the final art, using mainly Photoshop. To do this, I'm reimagining the classic character Tinker Bell, from J.M. Barrie's *Peter Pan*. Tinker Bell is a fixer-upper who can mend pots, pans, and kettles. Her voice sounds like a tinkling bell, understandable only to those familiar with fairy language. By following the tips and simple steps in this tutorial, you will have everything you need to bring a character to life!

BEFORE WE BEGIN

Creative block is commonplace for many artists, so if you're struggling to get started, don't worry! A simple way to avoid getting stuck is to train your creative mind by drawing every day and to prioritize expressing yourself by drawing things you're passionate about. Draw with a purpose, experiment, play, and have fun. Always try to develop your own vision while also visually solving a job. For this piece, I need to ask myself what version of Tinker Bell I want to create.

UNLOCKING A GOOD STORY

You're at the beginning of the design process: the conceptualization of the character. You need to start from a clear idea or a small log line (a sentence that summarizes the story). Keep in mind that the character will evolve along with the narrative – they must overcome a conflict that will change them as an individual, as this is how the audience will empathize with them. For my story, Tinker Bell has no wings, but wants to fit in with the other fairies. This narrative conflict is the spine that moves a story forward and leads the character towards action. Without it, there is no story, and without story there is no character.

This page (top): My sketchbooks and notebooks are sources of inspiration and help me avoid a creative block

This page (bottom): I start by defining the purpose behind the character

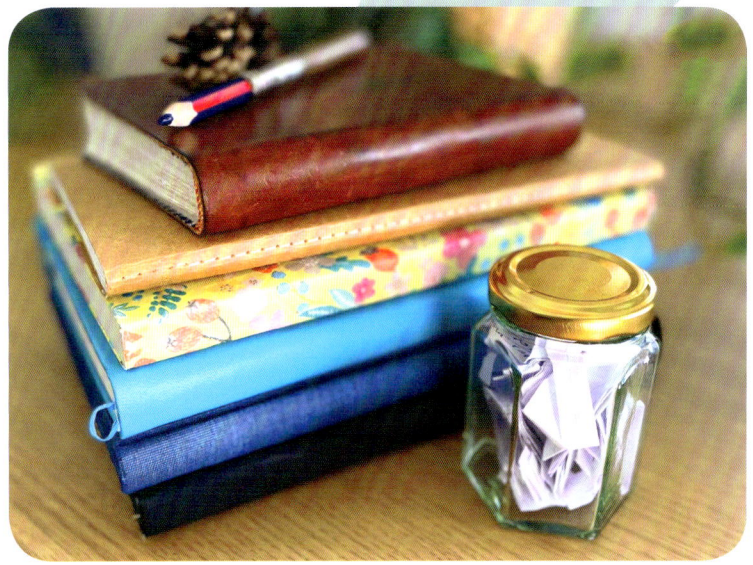

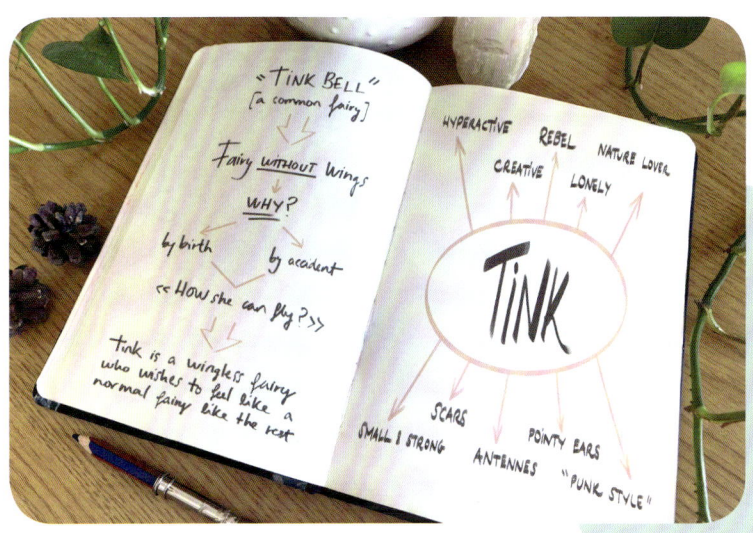

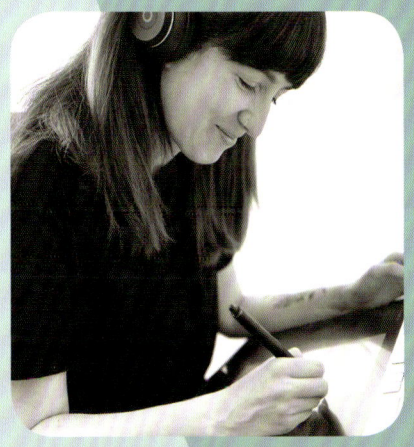

GETTING CREATIVE

Here are some practical tricks to help train your creativity.

- Always carry a small notebook with you to write down or draw any idea, so you can turn to it when you lack inspiration.

- Keep a dream journal – it will be an infinite source of creativity.

- Design characters based on fruits, vegetables, or household objects.

- Write down several nouns, adjectives, and verbs, on separate pieces of paper. Mix them in a jar and then grab a few. You'll get multiple combinations that will spark your imagination.

- Practice life drawing whenever you can.

- Walk through nature, relax, and be inspired.

WARM UP

Fill your notebook with organic shapes, then turn them into faces with different expressions, letting the random shapes inspire you. This famous exercise will free you from expectations and encourage you to have fun and play with your drawings.

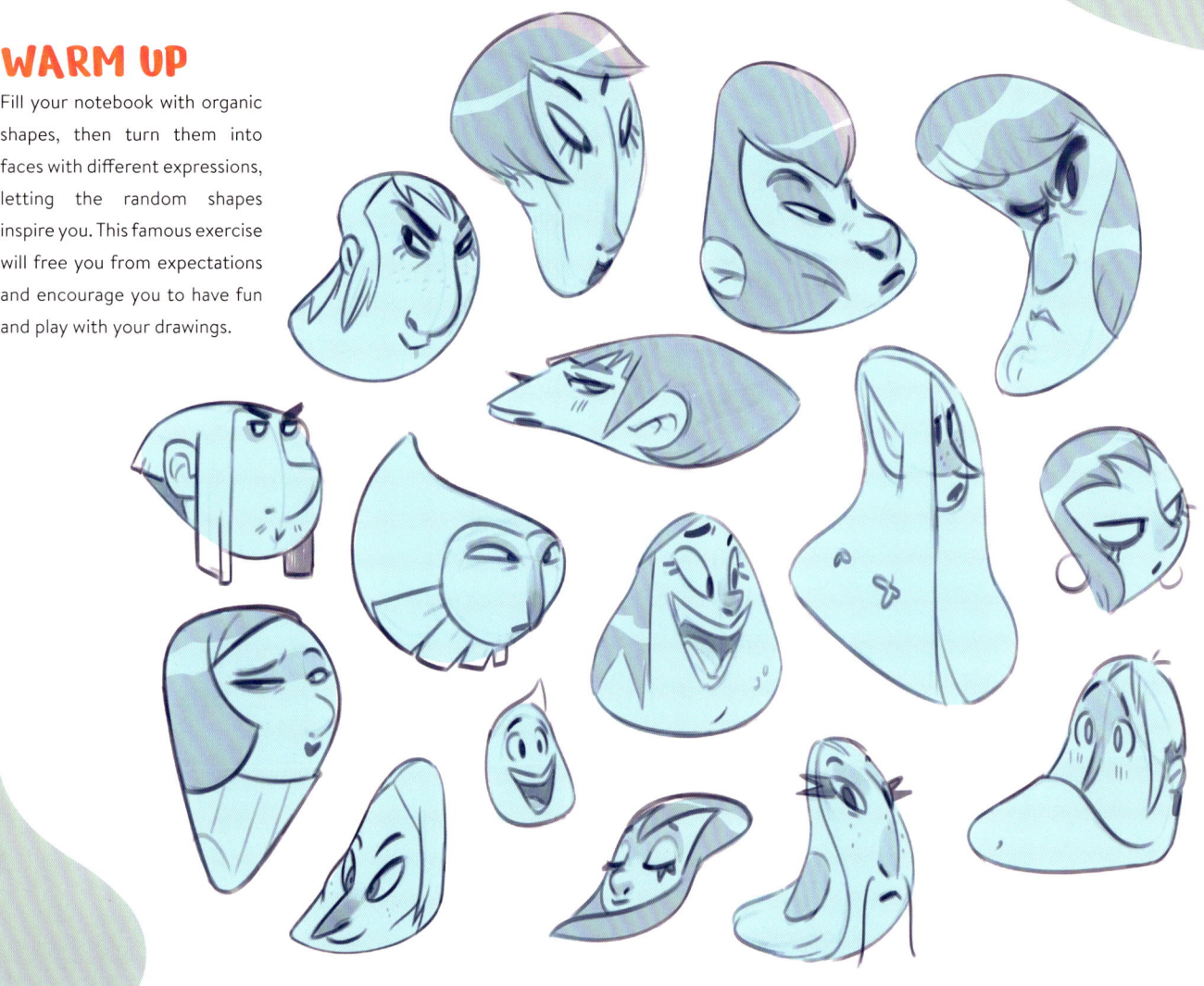

INSPIRATIONAL REFERENCING

Once you have a clear concept of your character, I suggest that you design a mood board. Collect all kinds of visual elements (photos, colours, materials, textures) that are related to your main idea. Use the references as a resource, both to understand things you've never drawn before and to delve into certain topics you like. I take pictures of nature and use them as a resource to better understand how to use flowers for Tinker Bell's antennae, and to explore possiblities for her wings. Be mindful and avoid deliberately copying or relying entirely on the ideas you find. It's more interesting to study how artists solve certain problems and then integrate their ideas into our own work.

IDEATION AND EXPLORATION

It's time to play and unleash your creativity! Without a doubt this is the most fun part of the process. I recommend you keep a sketchbook to be able to capture your ideas as soon as they arise. Don't discard any idea. Draw without filters. As you explore your ideas, you'll start to make decisions about how you want the character to look. I start with Tinker Bell's face and then move on to her general structure. This step should feel like a relaxing exercise; I don't focus on the details, but I take note of everything I find interesting, like the flower antennae and hairstyle.

Opposite page (top): I take pictures of nature to inspire me and learn about what I want to draw

Opposite page (bottom): I always draw my first ideas in my sketchbook

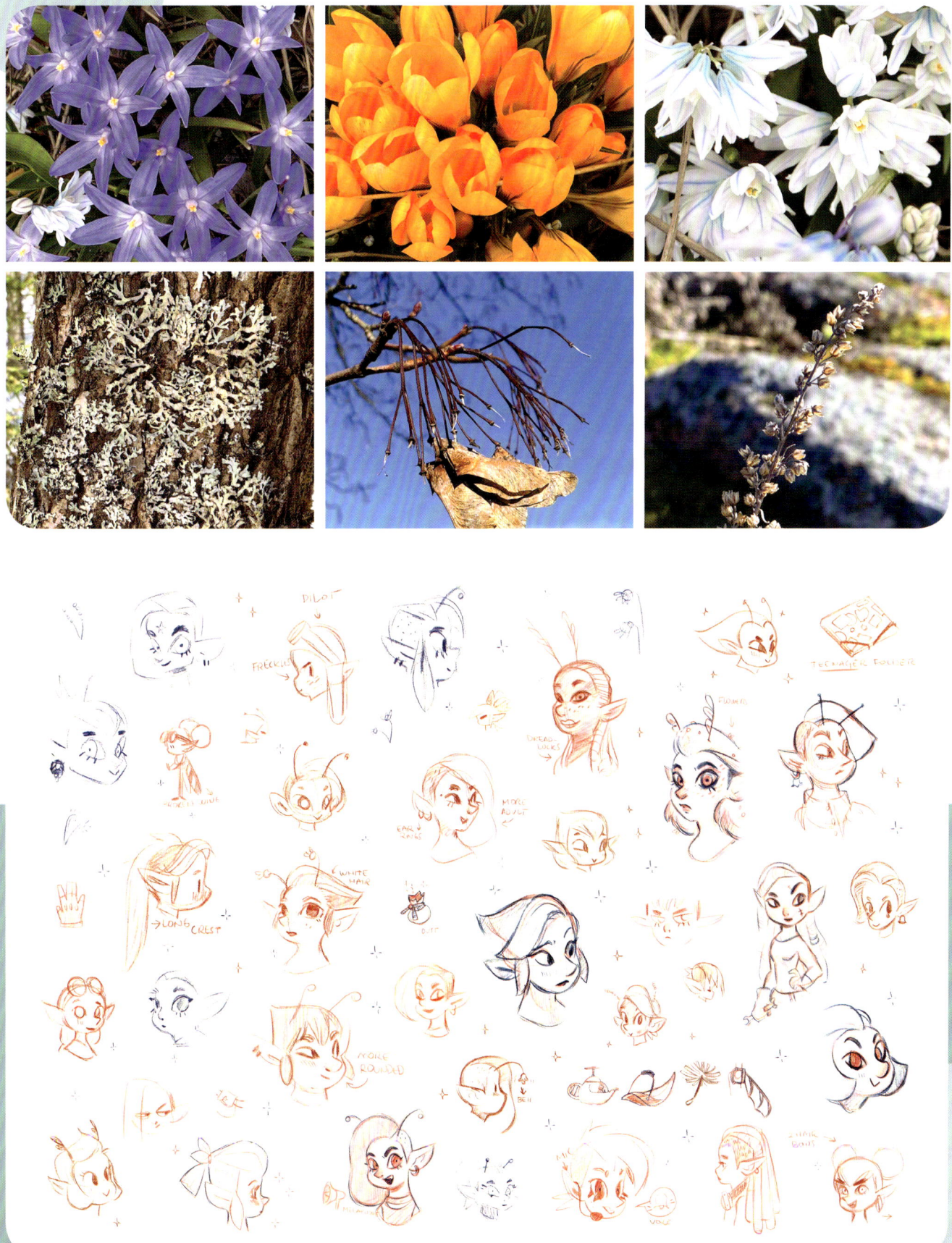

CHARACTER PSYCHOLOGY

Beyond the fact that a character must be pleasant to look at and technically competent, they also need to be charismatic and feel authentic. If you want others to empathize with your character then you first need to make that connection yourself. I explore adding depth to Tinker Bell through imperfections and contradictions, imagining how she experiences everyday situations. I try to think of her as a polyhedral being, whose personality will have aspects of both light and dark emotions.

THE SCIENCE OF SHAPES

Next, we need to consider the psychology of shapes. The form our character takes will influence how we think of the character. We perceive round designs as friendly, protective, and harmless. Square characters conjure feelings of safety and seriousness. Finally, a triangular shape suggests power and danger. I explore different proportions for Tinker Bell. I want to draw a small but chubby fairy, with strong arms – I don't want her to have a stereotypical body shape.

DUCKING THE LADDER EFFECT

To prevent your character from looking dull you should avoid the ladder effect, where every element of their body is of equal size. To achieve this, follow the small / medium / large rule by composing your character of unequal proportions – this will make them look more dynamic and iconic. The more variations they have, the more special they will seem. I apply this rule to Tinker Bell's body, giving her a medium-sized head, a small torso, and large legs. Remember to simplify the shapes, break the symmetry, and exaggerate the part of the body that you feel is most relevant to your character's personality. You can use the Liquify or Free Transform tools in Photoshop to quickly modify your drawing.

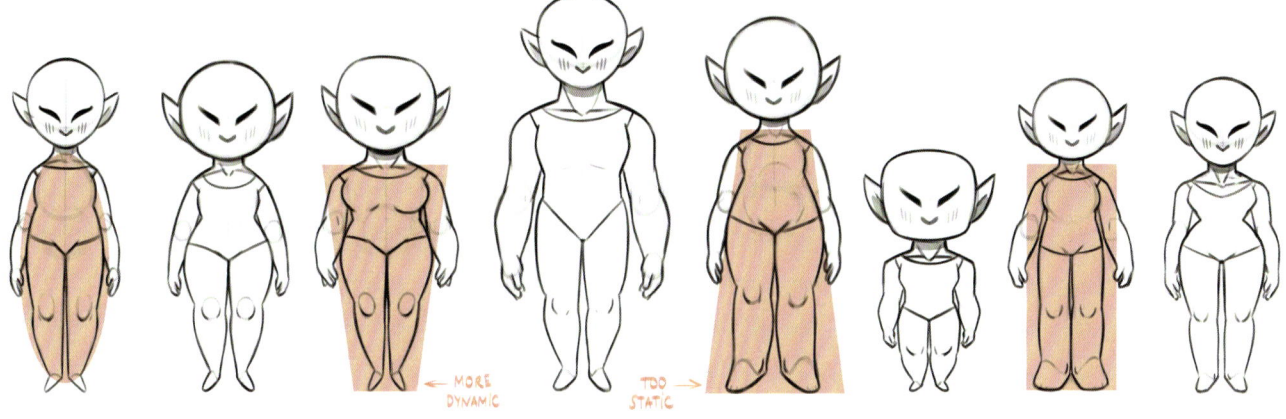

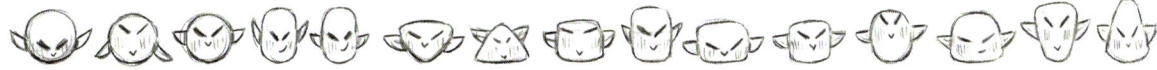

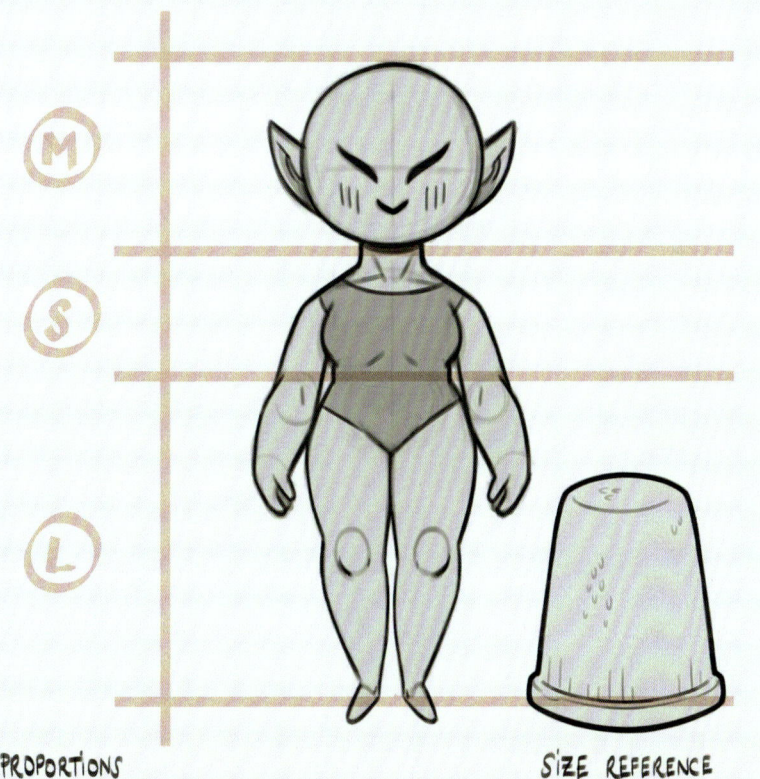

PROPORTIONS

SIZE REFERENCE

SHAPES

Opposite page:
Explorations of ideas and personalities for my Tinker Bell character

This page (top):
Playing with basic geometrical shapes looking for the perfect fit

This page (bottom):
Checking the proportions for my character's body type

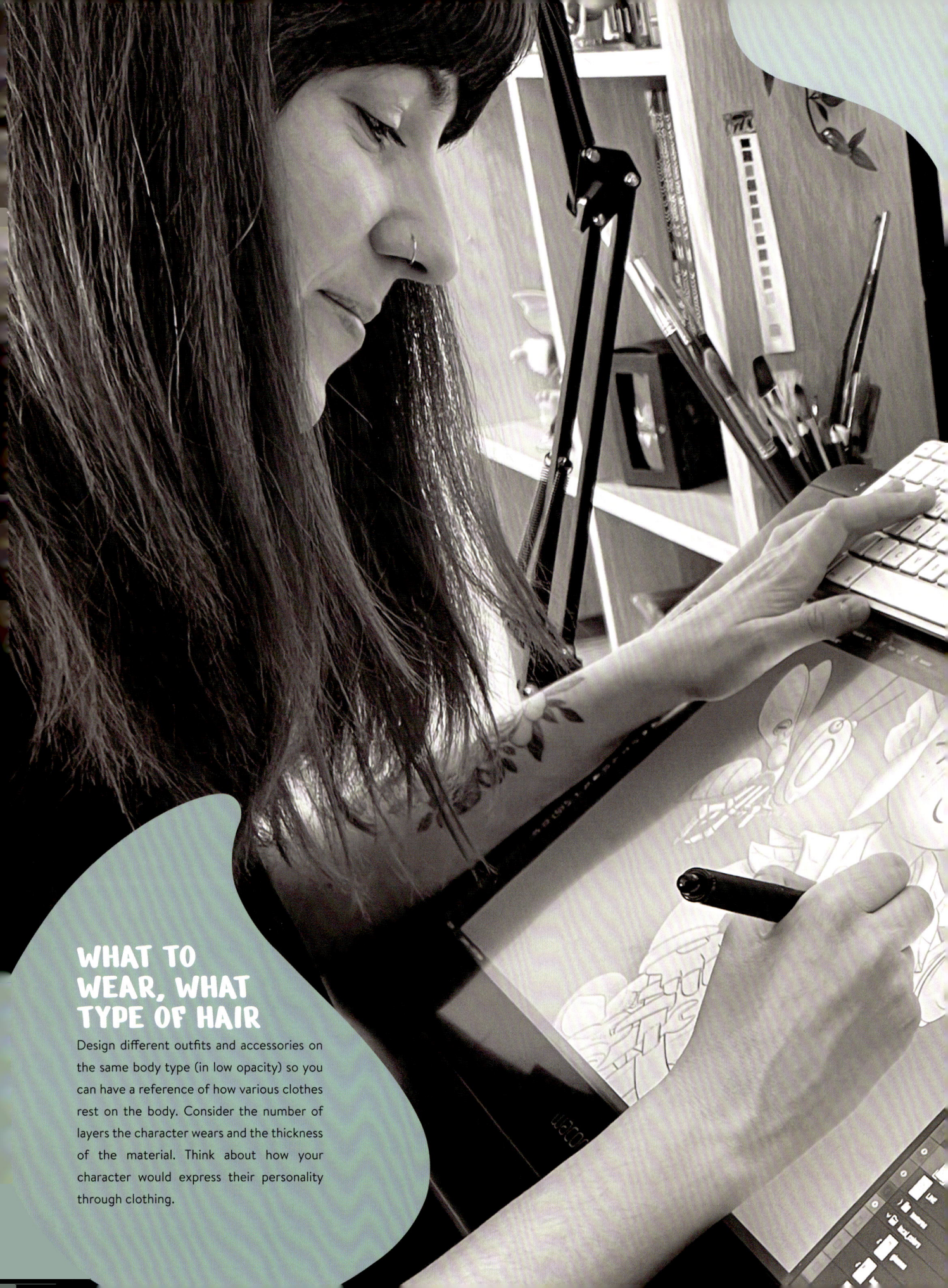

WHAT TO WEAR, WHAT TYPE OF HAIR

Design different outfits and accessories on the same body type (in low opacity) so you can have a reference of how various clothes rest on the body. Consider the number of layers the character wears and the thickness of the material. Think about how your character would express their personality through clothing.

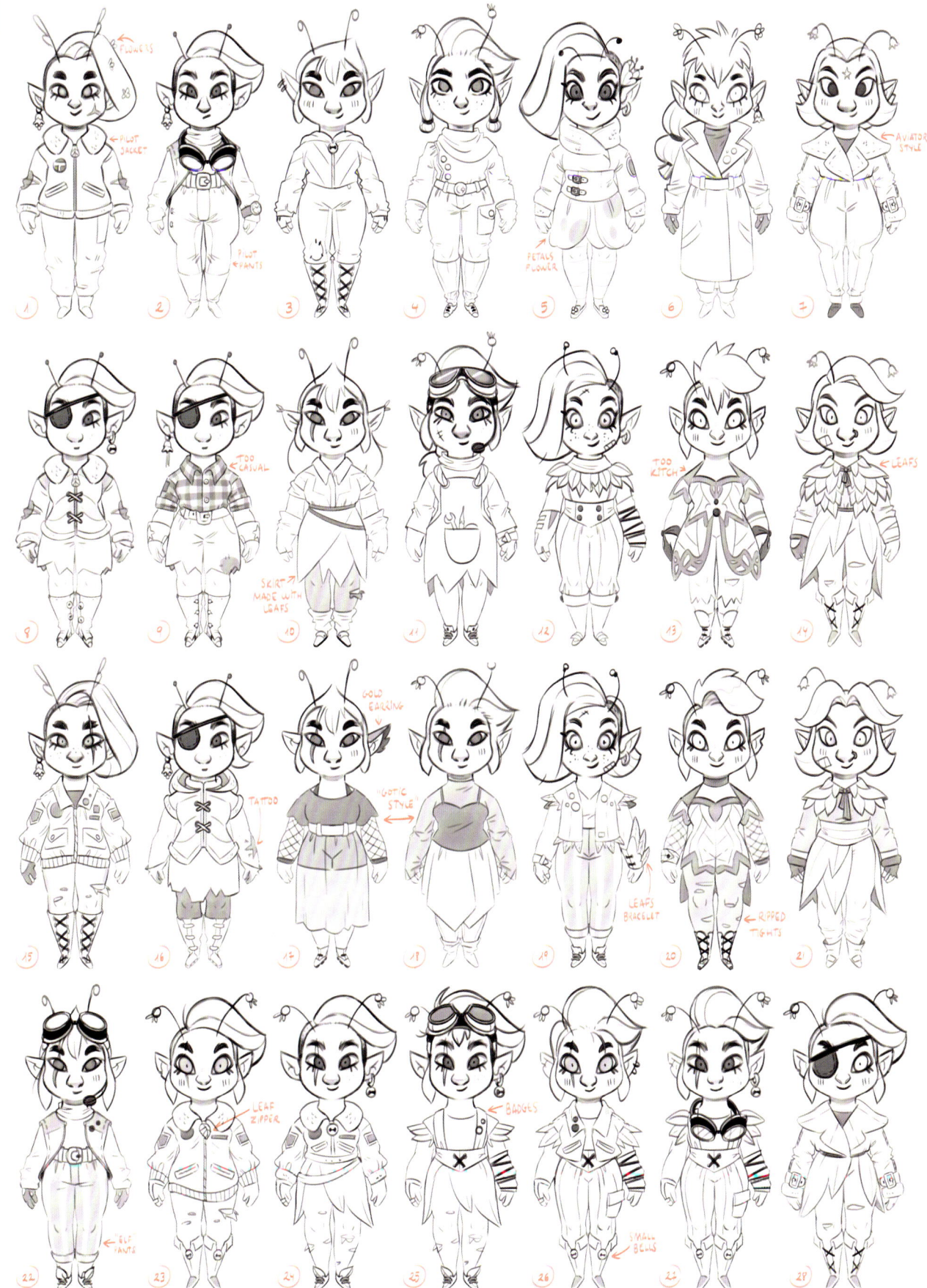

Having fun exploring outfits and hairstyles

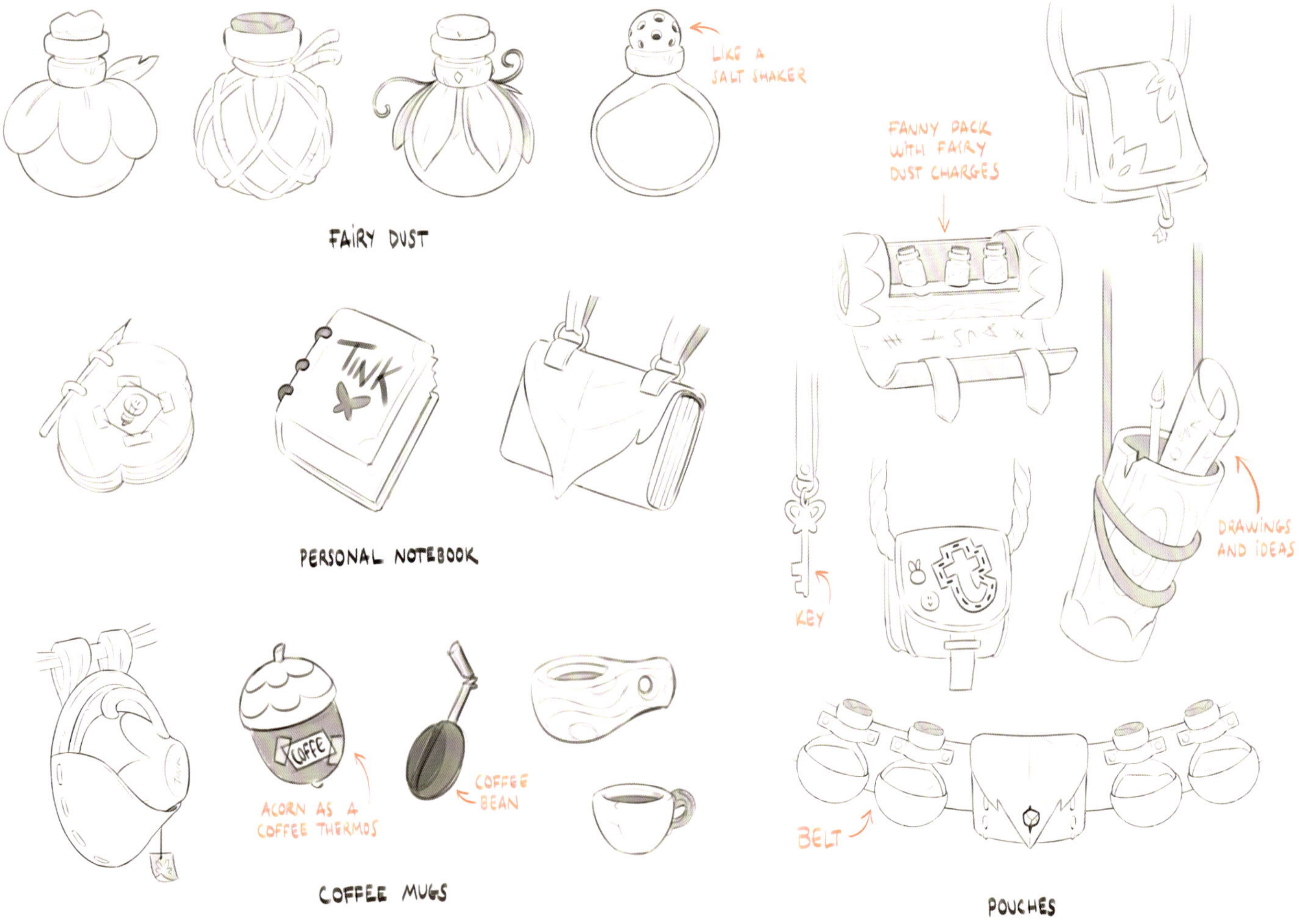

FAIRY DUST

LIKE A SALT SHAKER

FANNY PACK WITH FAIRY DUST CHARGES

PERSONAL NOTEBOOK

KEY

DRAWINGS AND IDEAS

COFFE

ACORN AS A COFFEE THERMOS

COFFEE BEAN

COFFEE MUGS

BELT

POUCHES

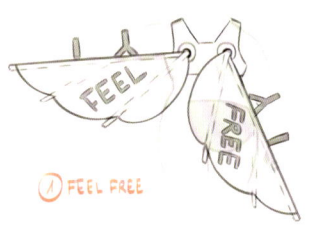

① FEEL FREE

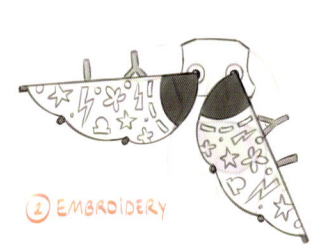

② EMBROIDERY

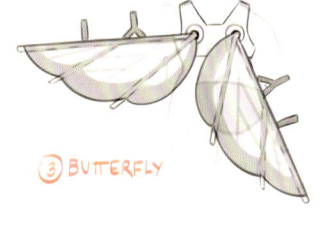

③ BUTTERFLY

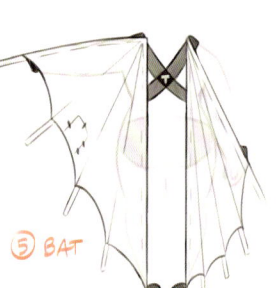

⑤ BAT

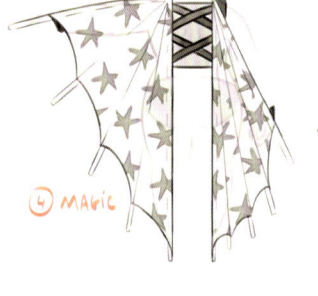

④ MAGIC

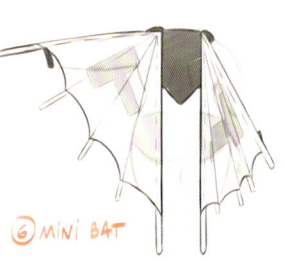

⑥ MINI BAT

THE IMPORTANCE OF PROPS

A simple way to give credibility to your character is through props. They add context to your character and reflect the world they inhabit. Take the time to think deeply about the character's world, establishing rules and creating internal logic. Ask yourself, 'What if…?'. What if, in Tinker Bell's magical fairy world, nature and analogue technology coexist? Asking myself this question leads me to design a fairy-dust pistol, among other prop ideas.

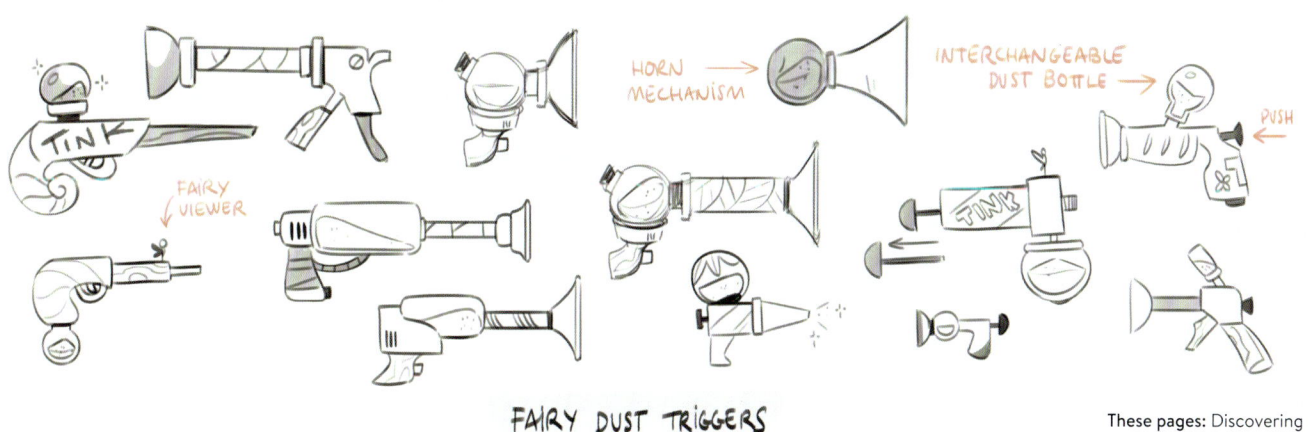

FAIRY DUST TRIGGERS

These pages: Discovering Tinker Bell's world through her props

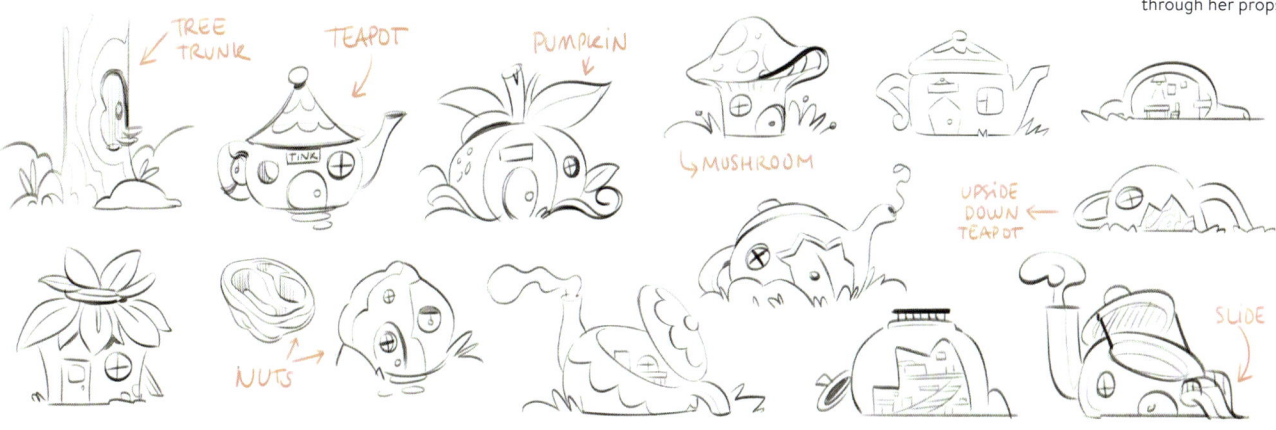

TINKER BELL'S HOME

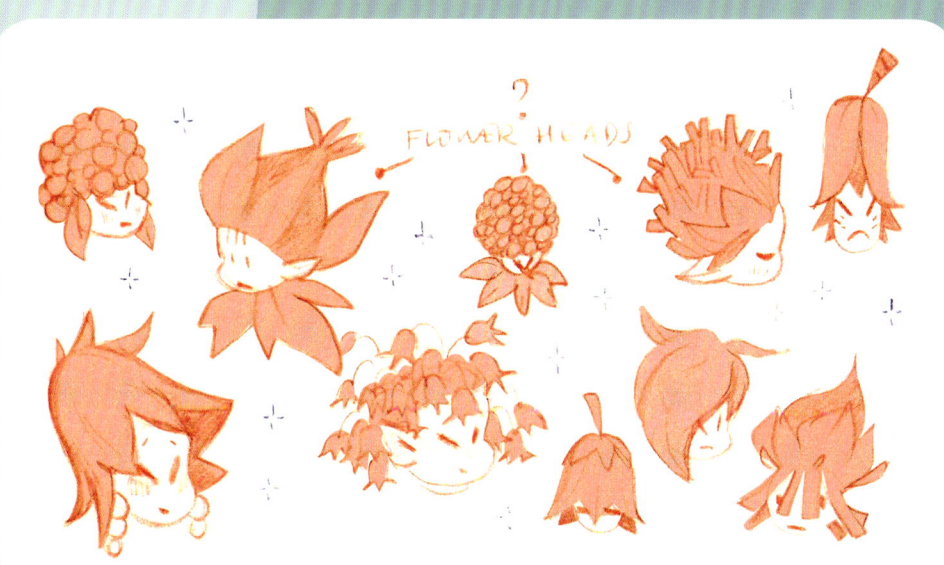

TRASH CAN

Most ideas can be good and should not be mentally dismissed without enough exploration, but it's also important to make decisions and try to be efficient. Therefore, although it would have been interesting to explore the flower heads, I didn't consider the silhouette easy to identify as a fairy.

FINALIZING THE DESIGN

The time has come to make some decisions about the final character design. Review all the work you've done so far: notes, first ideas, sketches, outfits, and props, to define and draw your final character. I suggest you draw a detailed front and back view of your character naked and clothed, along with all the props they will be wearing, to check that everything looks well balanced. I create a front and back view of Tinker Bell, thinking a lot about the position of the scar, microphone, earring, and the inclination of the belt and hair. I'm looking for harmony throughout the design.

This page: Front and back views of the final Tinker Bell design

Opposite page (top): Exploring different facial expressions

Opposite page (bottom): Working on the structure, volumes, and silhouette of the character

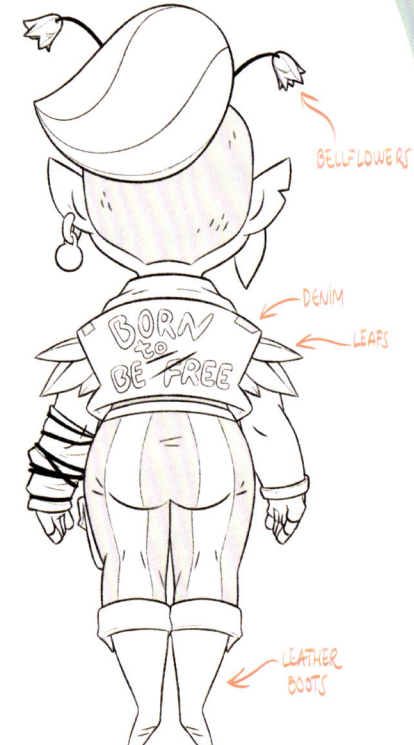

CREST
SCAR
PATCHES AND BADGES
GLOVE
BELLS
BELLFLOWERS
DENIM
LEAFS
BORN TO BE FREE
LEATHER BOOTS

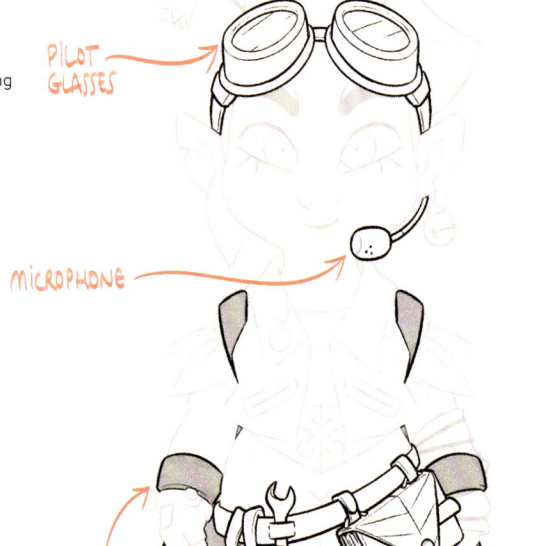
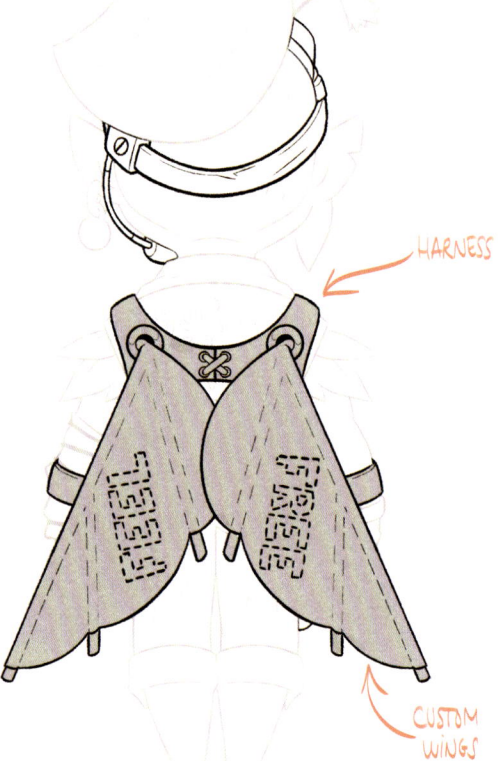

PILOT GLASSES
MICROPHONE
WRIST WRAPS
BELT WITH ACCESSORIES
HARNESS
CUSTOM WINGS

SQUASH IT STRETCH IT

When creating your character's facial expressions, it's a good idea to look at your own face in a mirror and use it as a guide. Squash and stretch your character's face to show each expression, considering the line of action. Next, take the basic emotions - joy, sadness, disgust, fear, anger - and combine two of them to create secondary expressions. I find it effective to draw characters from a high point of view to convey sadness, and from a low point of view to express joy.

STRUCTURE AND POSE

In order to create a good structure and pose for a character, begin by drawing three-dimensional volumes that follow the lines of action. Give them perspective by placing them inside a cylinder with a straight horizon line in the centre. Consider the weight of the character and how gravity affects them. Flipping the drawing horizontally will help you spot any anatomical errors. I ensure Tinker Bell's silhouette is legible, avoiding symmetry and showing off her limbs and props.

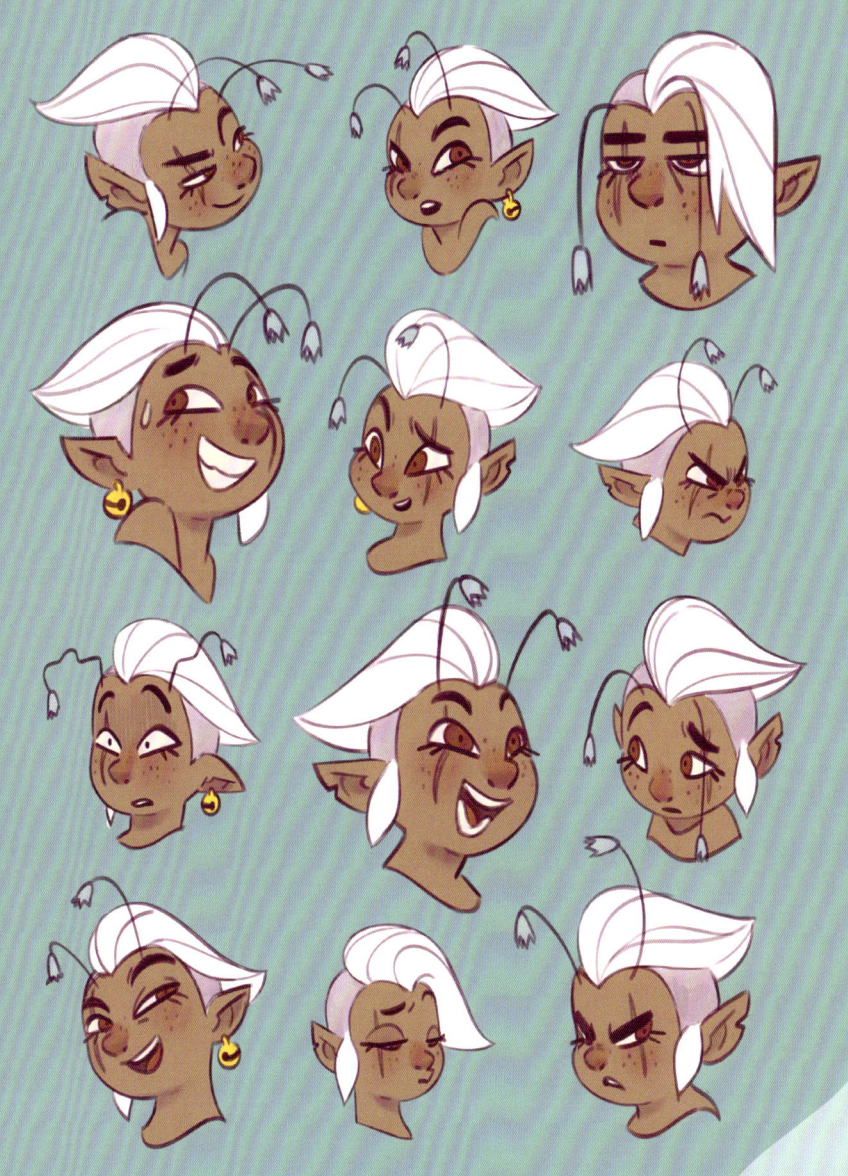

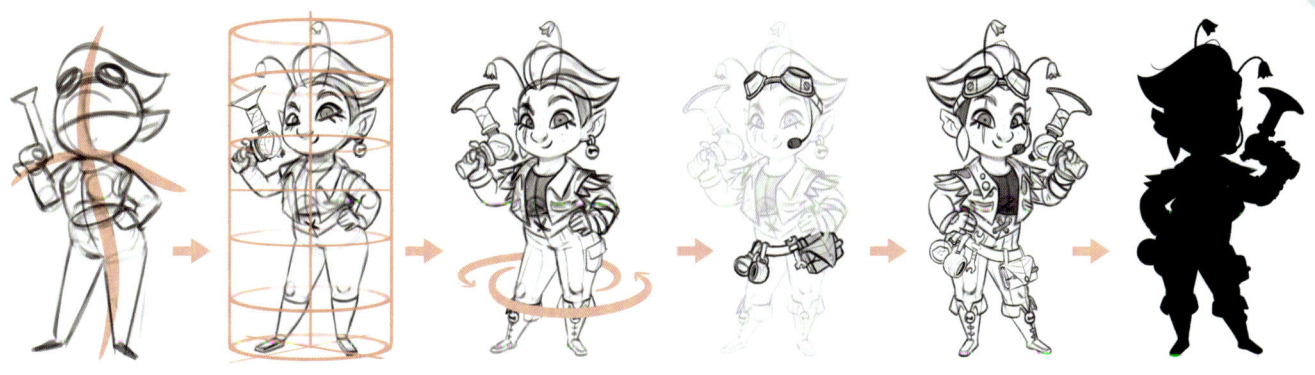

SELECT A SIDEKICK

A main character is rarely alone in their story, so I design a tiny robotic bee, built by Tinker Bell to join her on her adventures. Imagining the two of them interacting and facing different situations together will enrich the design.

THE COLOUR TEST

Colours can have a positive or negative effect on a viewer, so it's important to choose carefully. I recommend creating a few different colour tests for your character. I use my sketch as the top layer (set to Multiply mode) as a reference and paint on another layer with solid colours at 100% Opacity. Next, I create a balance between analogous colours (close on the colour wheel) and complementary colours (opposite on the colour wheel). I use desaturated tones between them as a bridge, controlling where the point of higher contrast is. Finally, I check the colours in greyscale to avoid overlapping values.

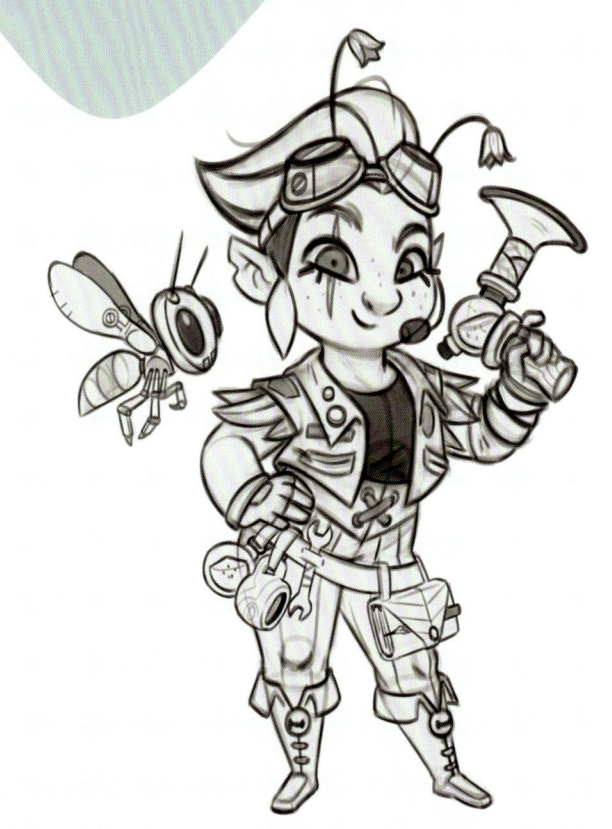

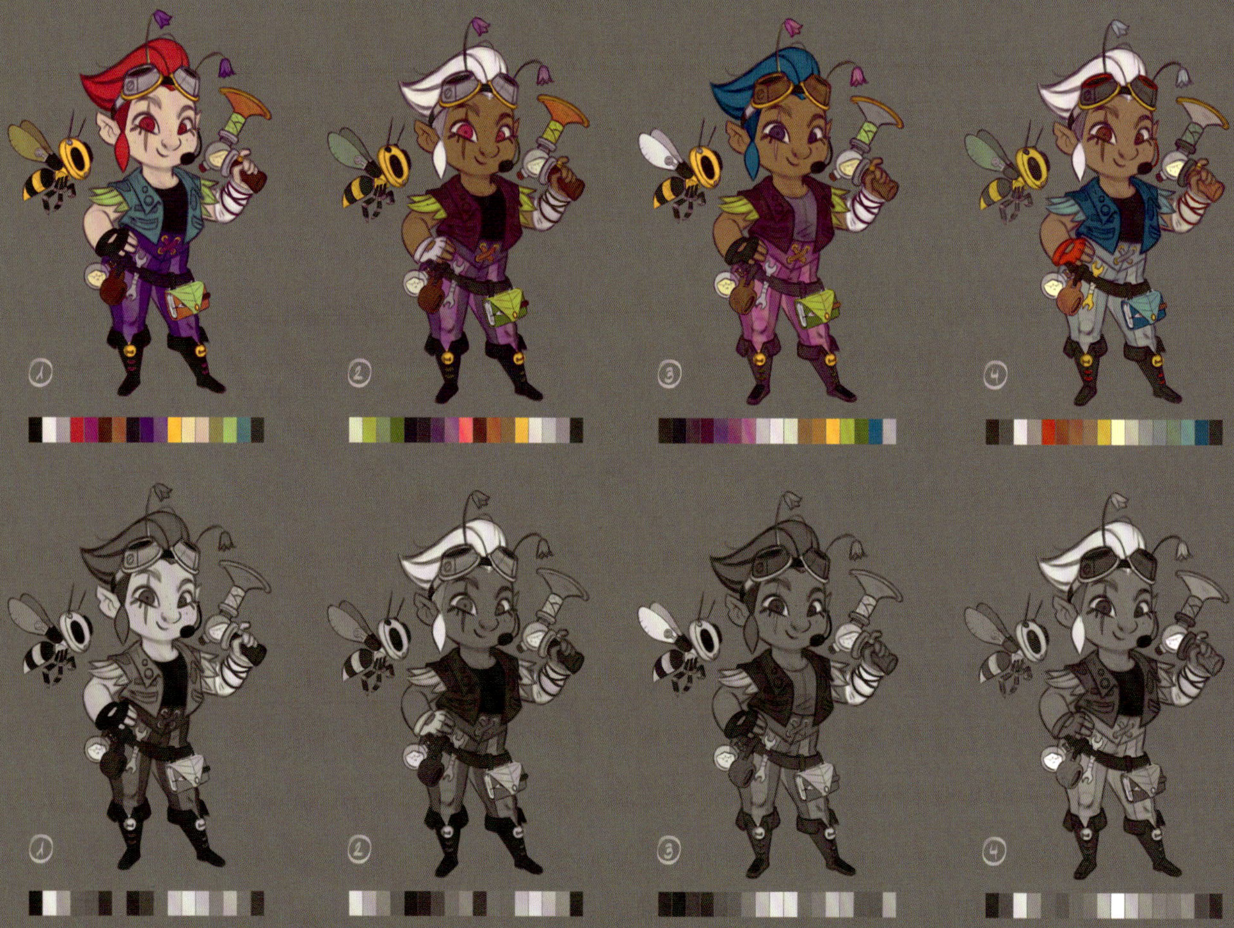

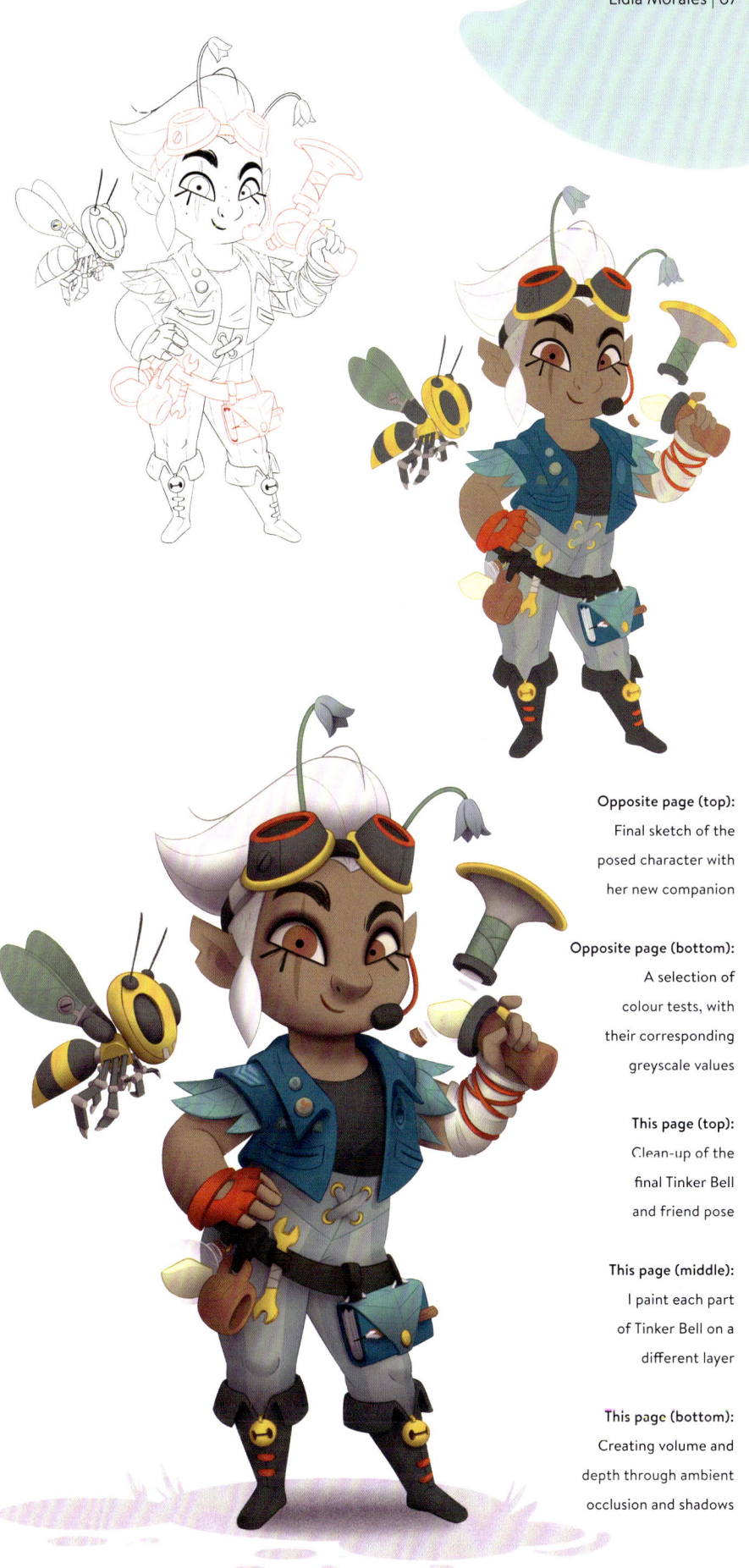

THE CLEAN UP

I place the sketch on a layer in Multiply mode (with low opacity) and then, on another layer, redraw Tinker Bell, maintaining the volumes, and rectifying them if necessary. During this step, don't just trace over the sketch – try to improve it. Refine the shapes and avoid parallel lines and tangents. Be careful with the line and be decisive with the stroke in order to maintain the intention of the sketch. Flip the character horizontally to check if they still work, since any failure of the sketch will be multiplied in the clean-up.

LOCAL COLOURS

Local colours are those that are not affected by light. Take your favourite option from the colour test and keep it in the corner of your screen as a reference. Under the clean-up drawing, I create a base layer of Tinker Bell's silhouette and paint it with local colours, with each of her parts on a different layer.

RENDERING SHADOWS

On another layer, in Multiply mode, paint the ambient occlusion with a smudge or textured brush, taking into account the direction of the light, adding the character's own volume, and highlighting the contact areas. Duplicate the layer and reserve the areas that move away from the light source. Consider adding texture to certain materials to give them richness. Finally, in a layer below, add the shadow the character casts against the ground.

Opposite page (top):
Final sketch of the posed character with her new companion

Opposite page (bottom):
A selection of colour tests, with their corresponding greyscale values

This page (top):
Clean-up of the final Tinker Bell and friend pose

This page (middle):
I paint each part of Tinker Bell on a different layer

This page (bottom):
Creating volume and depth through ambient occlusion and shadows

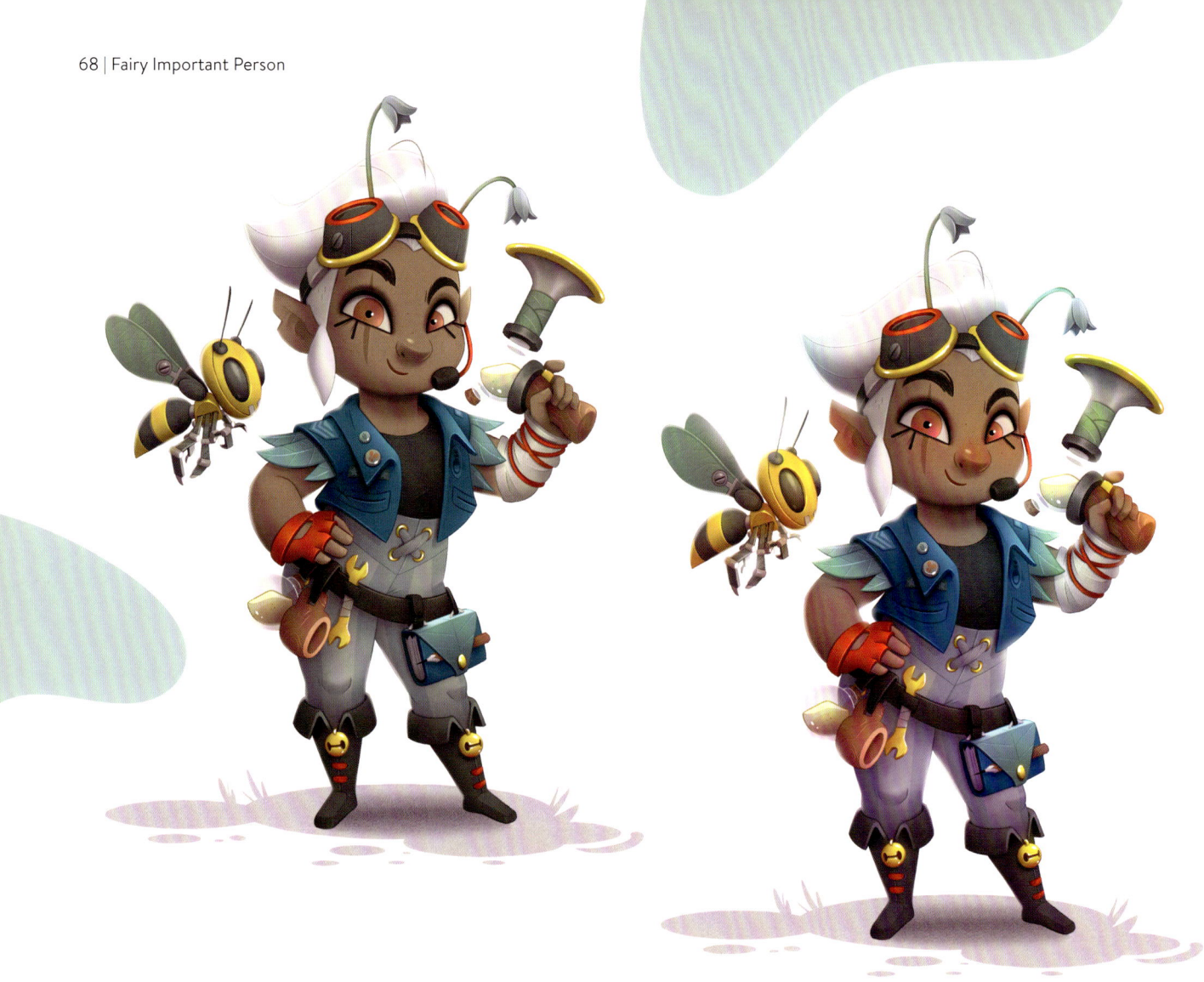

LIGHTING THE SCENE

The character must reflect the light of the colour that exists in the environment – its intensity will depend on the material of the surface and the proximity to the light source. To illuminate Tinker Bell in a simple way, I create a layer for the diffused light in Overlay mode, above the shadows, and then paint (with the same colour as the environment) the areas most exposed to light to better define the volumes. To bring the character to life I add specular light to objects that have a higher refractive index, and rim light to create an outline effect.

POST-PRODUCTION EFFECTS

On a new layer, in Overlay mode, I add a scattering effect to the ears and nose to show light passing through them. You can also apply this effect to the cheeks and fingertips. In another layer (with the same properties) I add different colour points with the Gradient tool to create variations in the tonality of the light. Make sure to turn down the opacity to avoid messing it up. Finally, on another layer (set to Colour Dodge) I accentuate the light from the most reflective materials, adding halos of the same colour as the object. Adding halos of white light at specific points of the contour will help integrate it with a white background.

PLAYING UNTIL THE END

I want to see the character with and without her customized wings, so I make two final versions with a different colour background. It's never too late to change your drawing, so play around with whatever you feel isn't working. You can even create a Smart object (right click on your character's layer group and select Convert to Smart Object) and adjust the Levels and Brightness in the Layer settings. My final reimagining shows a Tinker Bell born without wings – which has only made her stronger. She uses her tinkering skills to create tools to fit in with her fairy friends and be helpful to them. She is determined, independent, and an asset to the fairy kingdom.

Opposite page (left):
Working on basic lighting
to push the character

Opposite page (right):
The final version without wings

This page: The final design
featuring the customized wings
and a coloured background

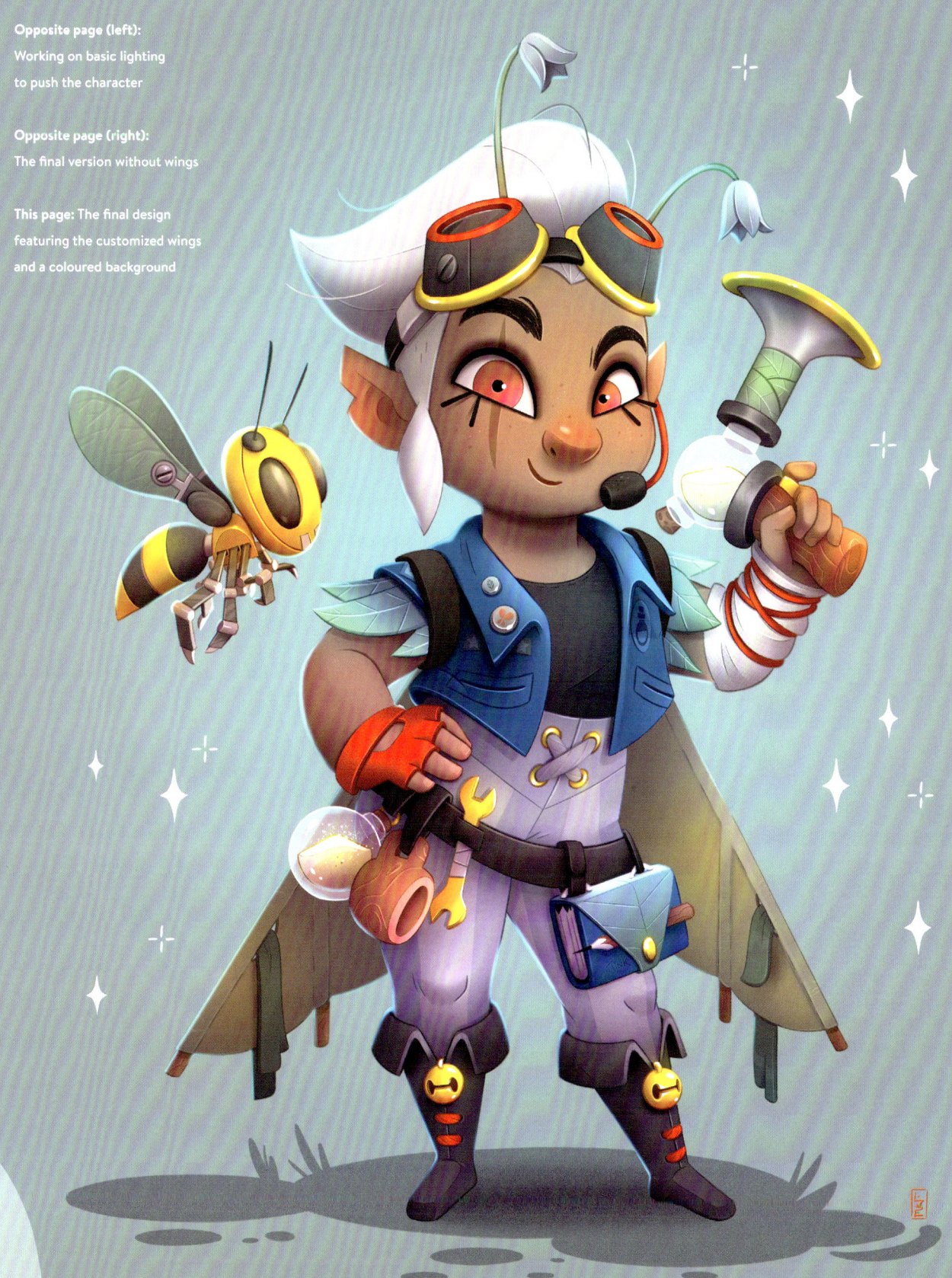

Final image © Lidia Morales

A CURIOUS CREATION

ISABELLA AGOSTI

I'm going to walk you through the ideation process of creating a character based on the prompt 'curious explorer' focusing on the main design choices I make along the way. You can use these steps as a starting point to create your own captivating and appealing characters. The most interesting thing about character design for me is that you can actually create lots of different designs starting from the same keywords – the possibilities are endless. Don't be afraid to give voice to your creativity!

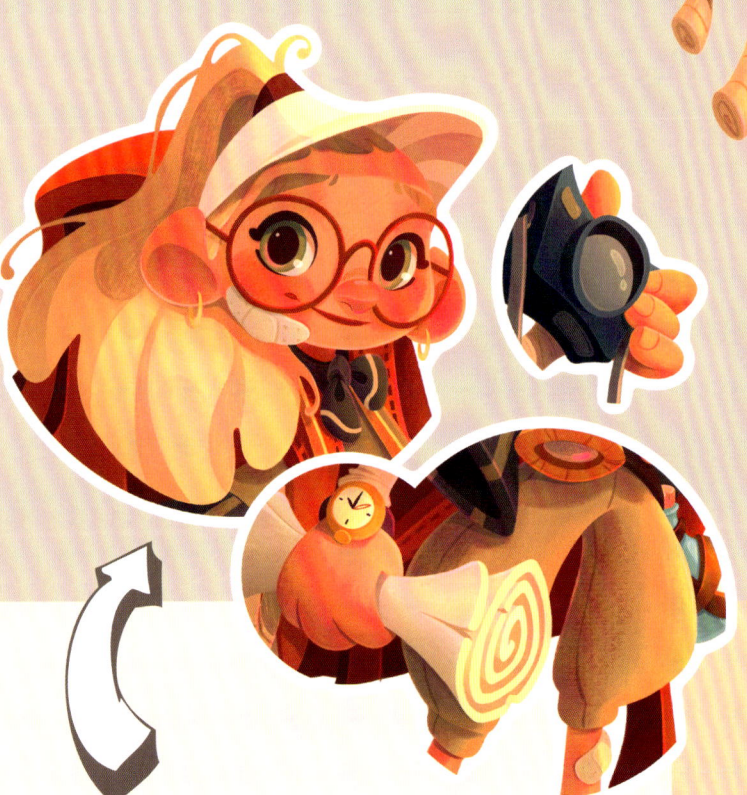

FIRST STEPS

After analysing the prompts, the idea of a friendly and cheerful character immediately pops into my mind. Since circles are the best shapes to convey these traits, I make sure to repeat them across the whole design.

make a map

Creating a character from only a two-word prompt might be a bit overwhelming. Creating a map before even beginning to sketch can help organize your ideas. Starting with the prompts, connect a few key concepts – props, clothes, character traits, and so on – and write down a few ideas for each, always keeping the initial brief in mind.

FASHION CHOICES

Clothing items play an important role in identifying a character's profession or hobby. Since my character is an explorer, I opt for comfy clothes that are also appropriate for expeditions.

PREPPING THE PROPS

When considering the 'curious' keyword, I give my character big eyes and glasses to see better, a camera to capture her favourite subjects, and binoculars to spy on even the shyest of animals.

'FOCUSING ON SHAPE LANGUAGE IS ESSENTIAL'

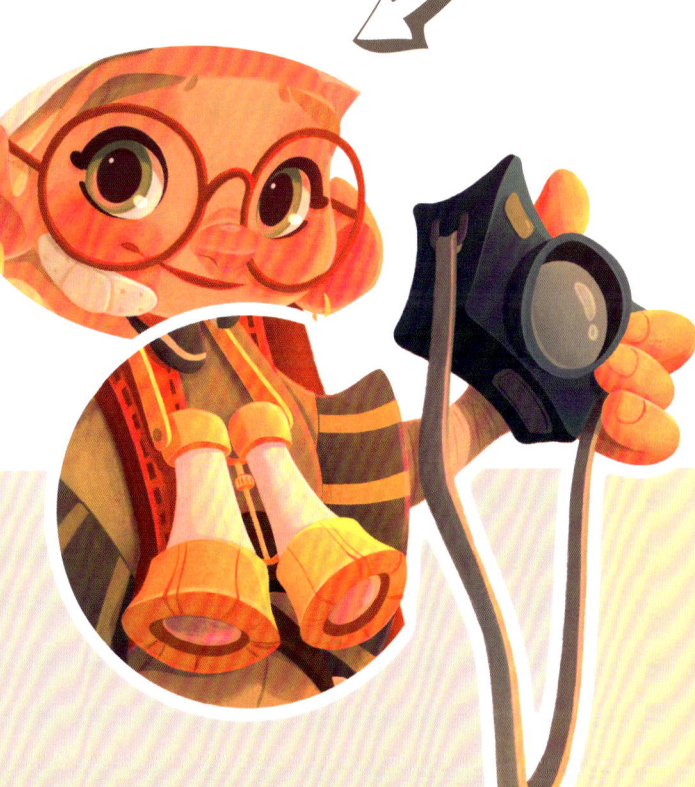

THE LANGUAGE OF SHAPES

When trying to convey specific personality traits, focusing on shape language is essential, as different shapes communicate different emotions. Circles and round shapes evoke kindness and cuteness, squares bring to mind solidity and strength, while triangles suggest evil and danger.

EXPLORING IDEAS

My character is an explorer too, so I give her a massive backpack to carry as many supplies as possible, a map to check the right direction, a compass for orientation, and a rope to brave the most difficult of routes.

LESS IS MORE

Adding too many props to a design might make it confusing. Make sure to only focus on those that make sense in relation to the other elements and that aid your character's story. I initially planned to add a torch to my design – for nocturnal explorations – but quickly realized it would have clashed with the cap my character is wearing to protect against the sun.

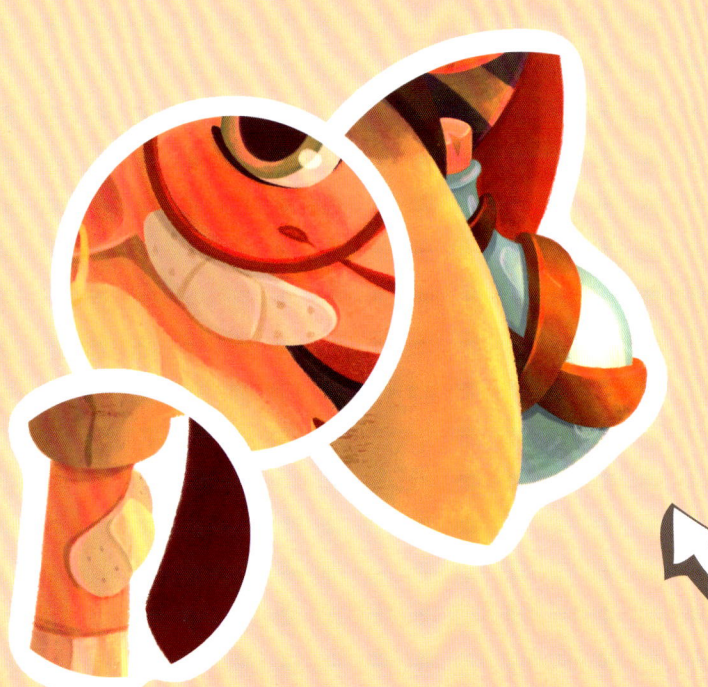

'ADDING TOO MANY PROPS TO A DESIGN MIGHT MAKE IT CONFUSING'

EXTRA ELEMENTS

After creating props related to the two keywords, have fun thinking of other elements that could add to the design, while still cohering with who your character is and what they are doing.

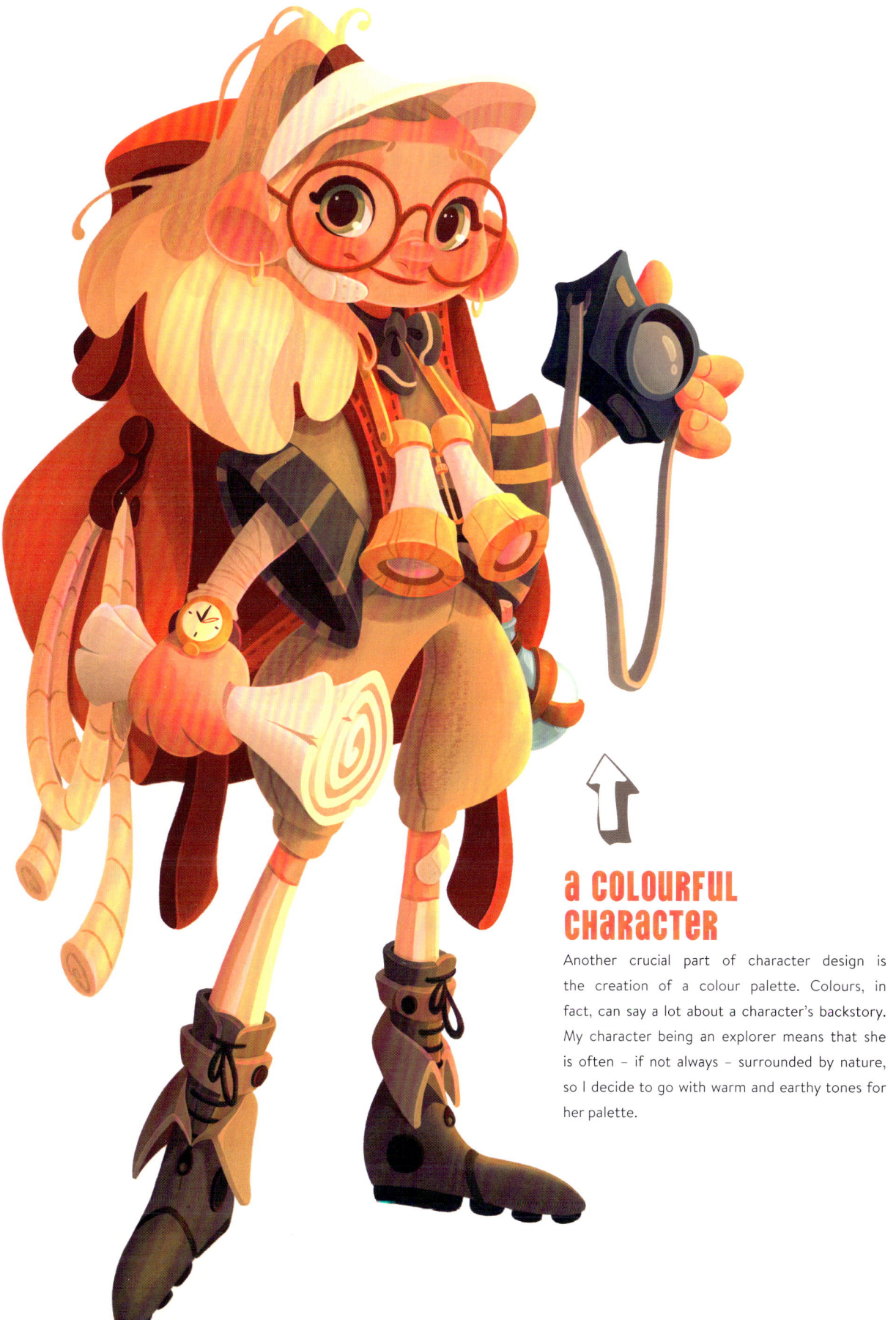

a COLOURFUL CHaRaCTER

Another crucial part of character design is the creation of a colour palette. Colours, in fact, can say a lot about a character's backstory. My character being an explorer means that she is often – if not always – surrounded by nature, so I decide to go with warm and earthy tones for her palette.

THE GALLERY

In the gallery we're proud to showcase artists producing high-quality character design and character-based artwork throughout the industry. In this issue we have inspiring designs from Ilinca Mitchell, Benjamin Denkert, and tono.

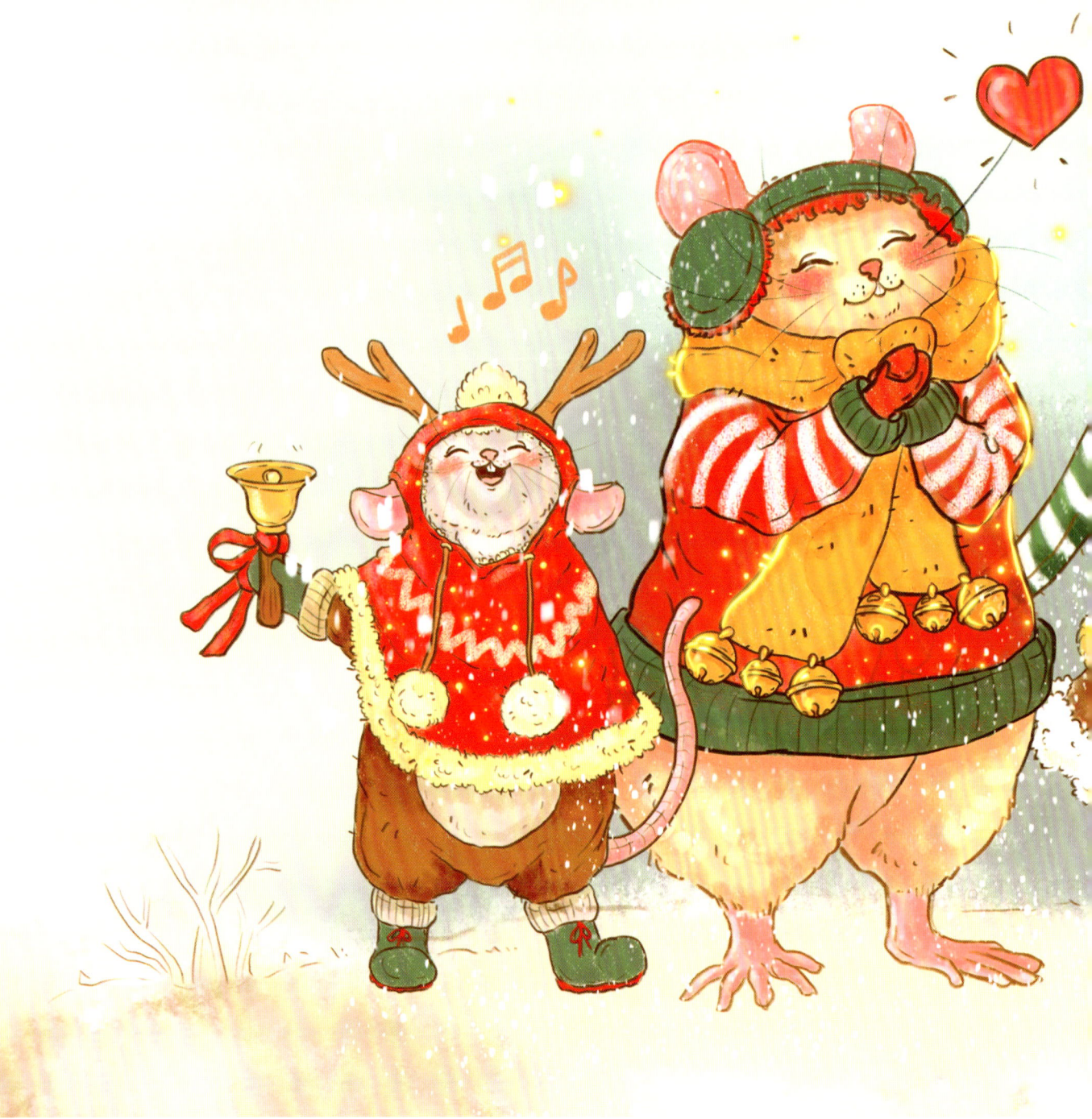

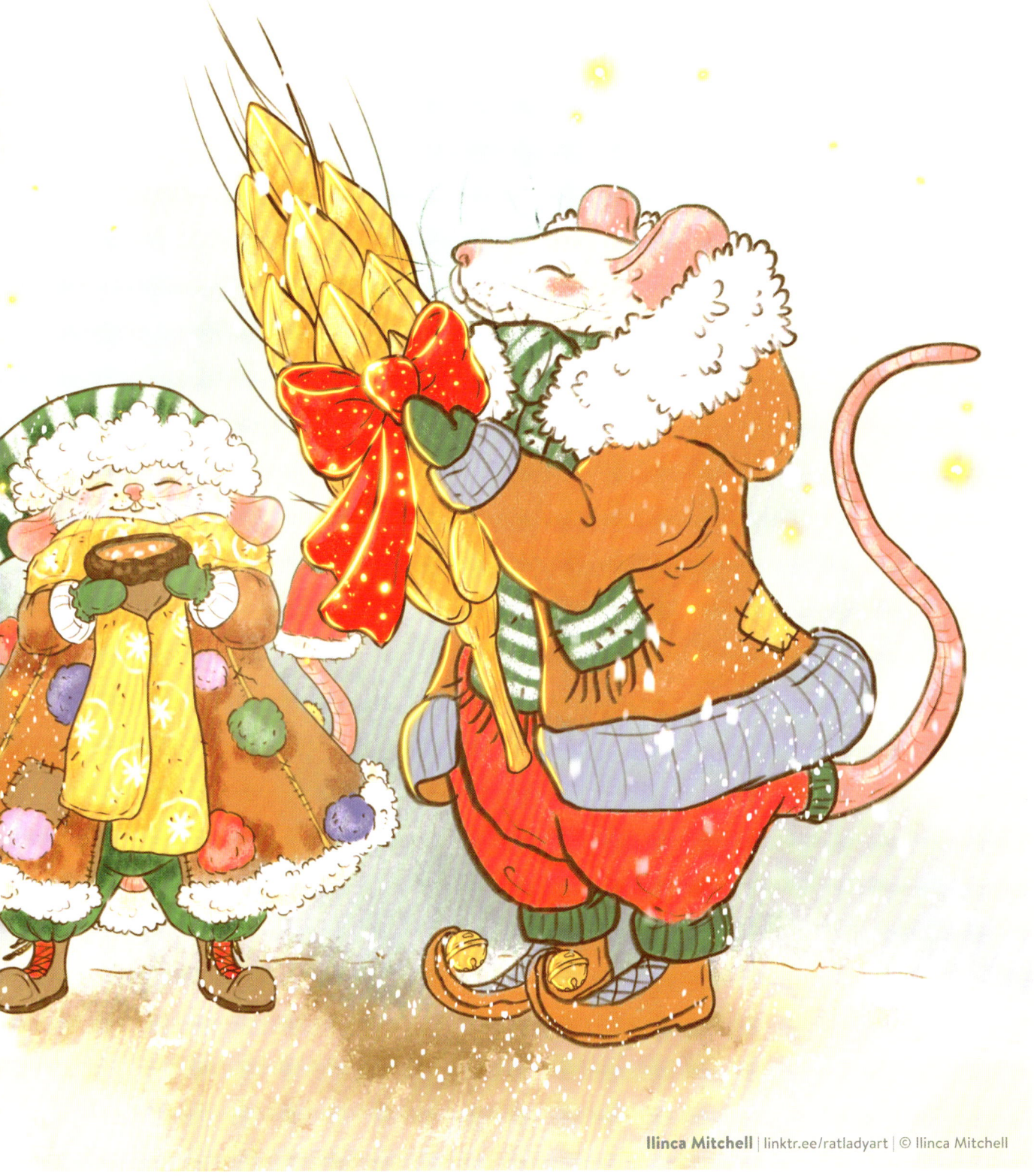

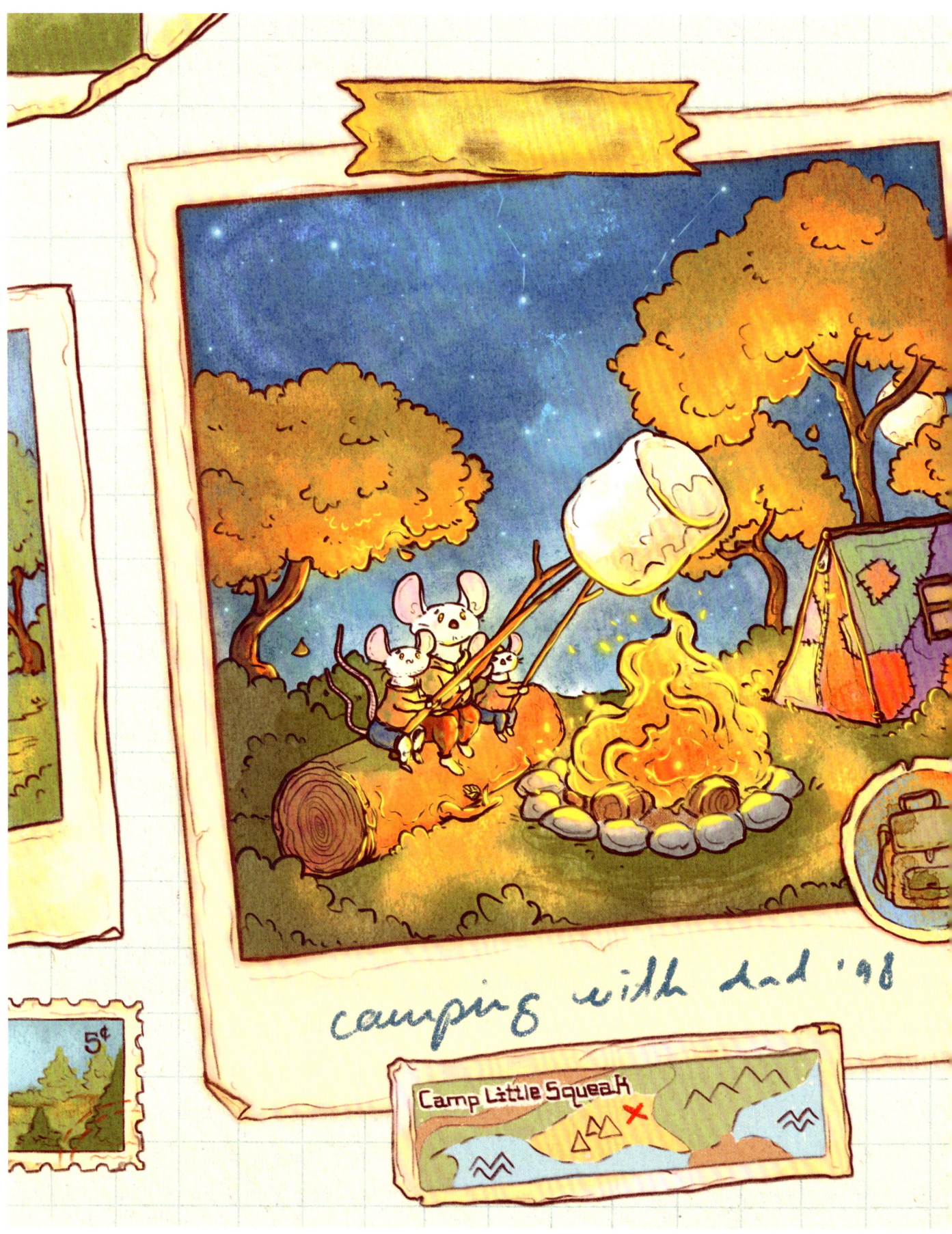

Ilinca Mitchell | linktr.ee/ratladyart | © Ilinca Mitchell

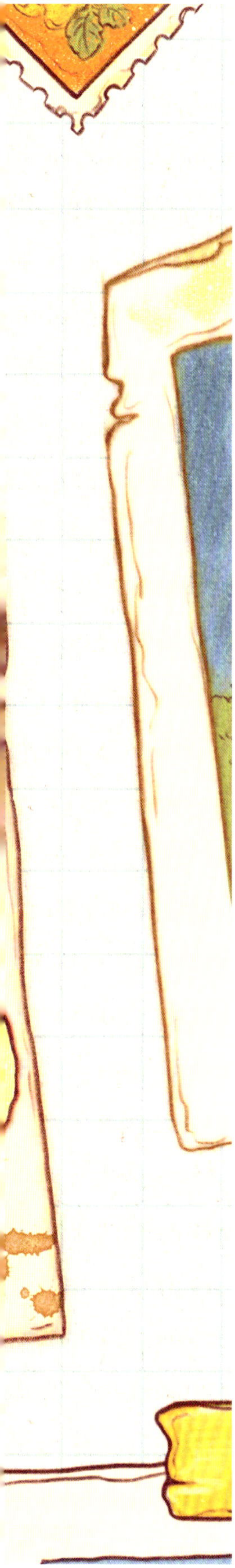

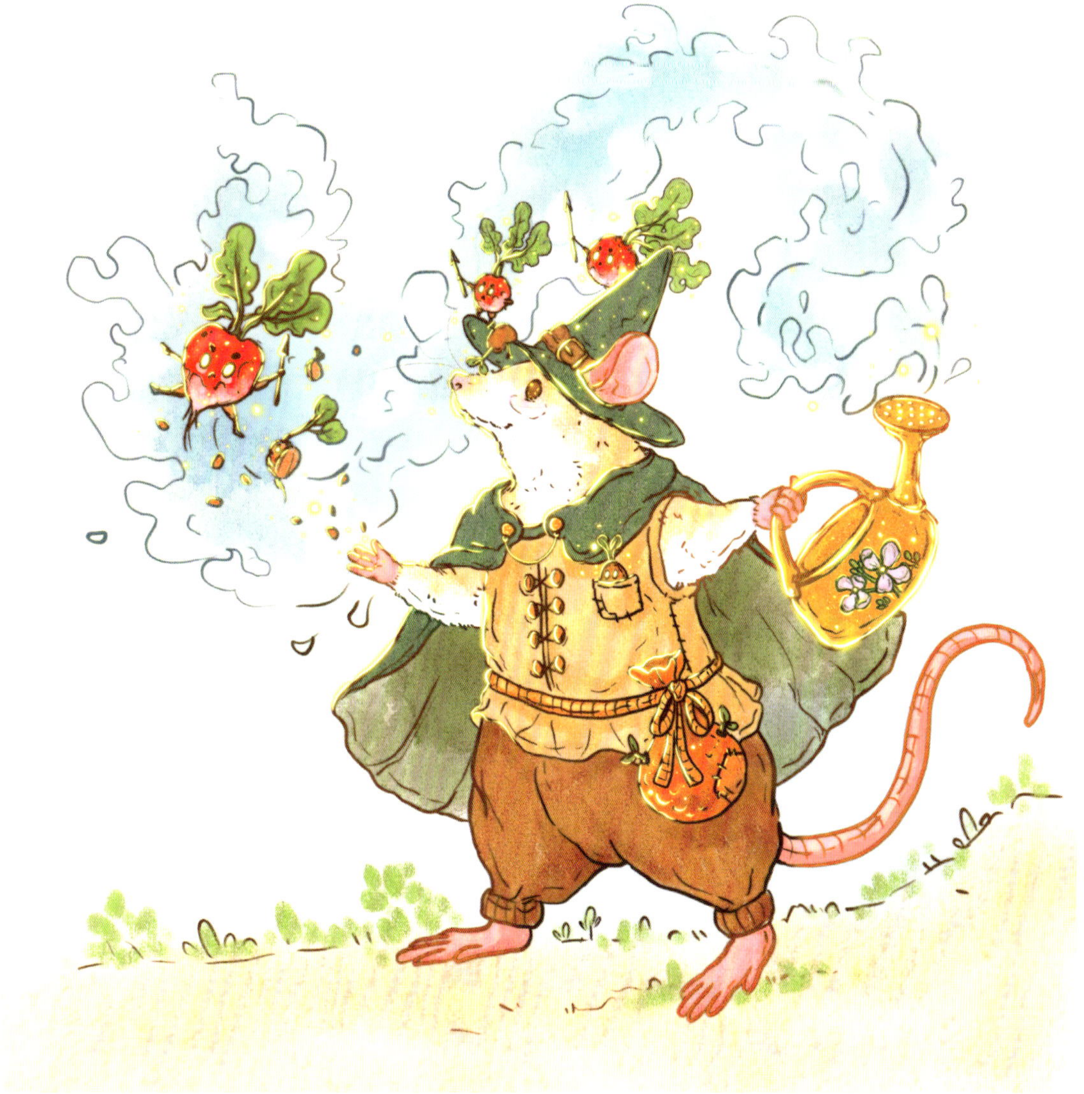

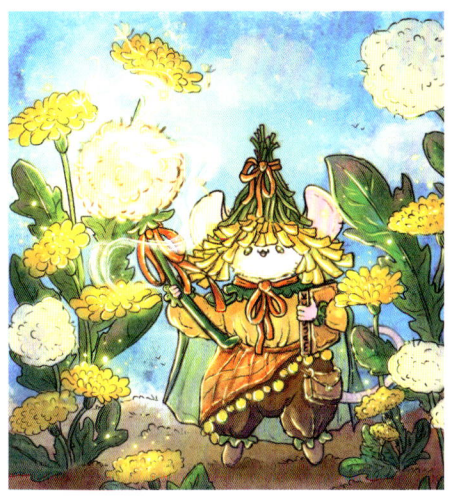

ILINCA LOVES TO DRAW WHOLESOME ANIMAL CHARACTERS GOING ABOUT THEIR DAY IN MAGICAL ENVIRONMENTS. SHE PRIMARILY WORKS IN WATERCOLOUR AND INK, BUT SOMETIMES SHE WORKS DIGITALLY IN PROCREATE. SHE HOPES HER ART WILL BRING A SMILE TO SOMEONE'S FACE!

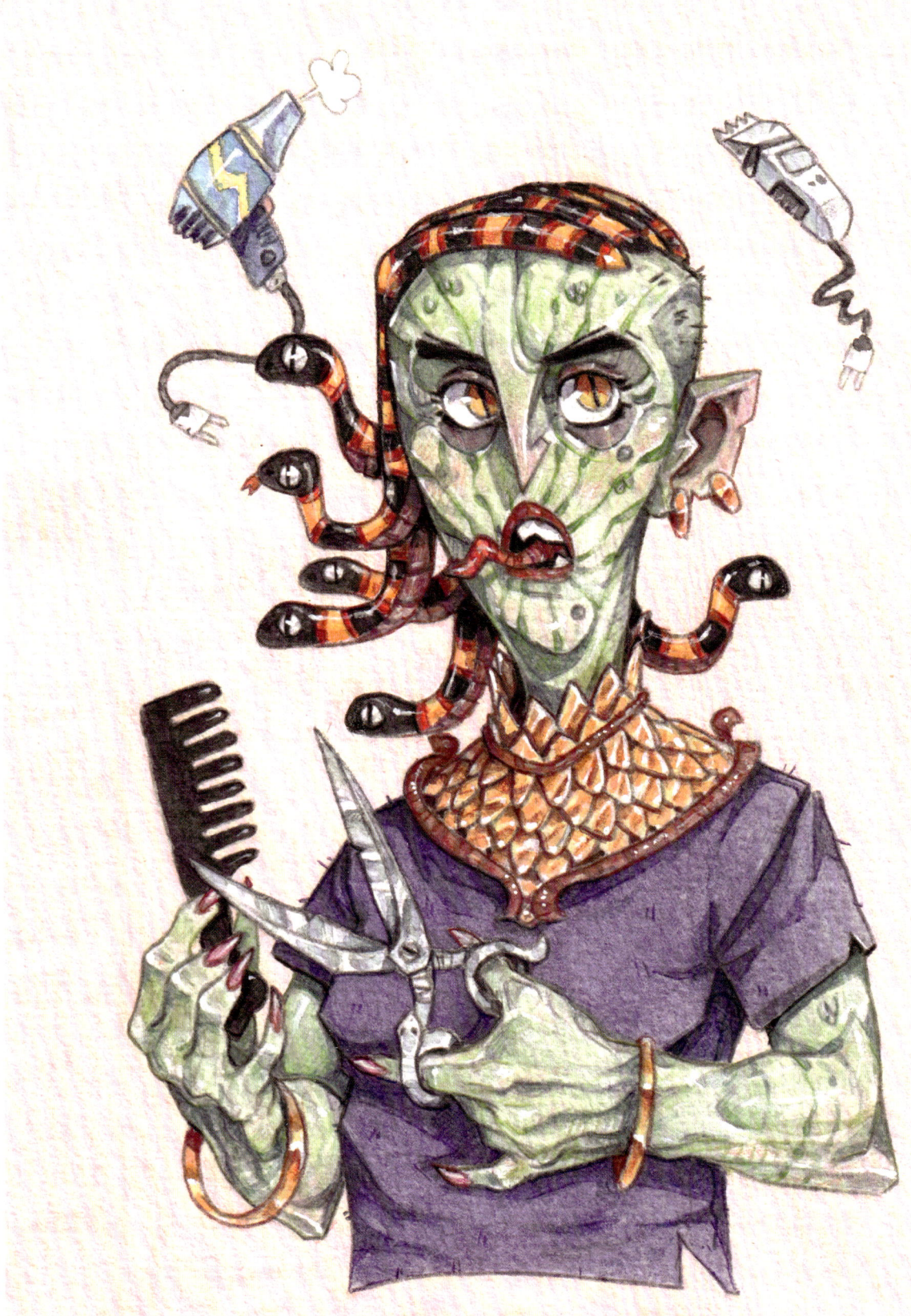

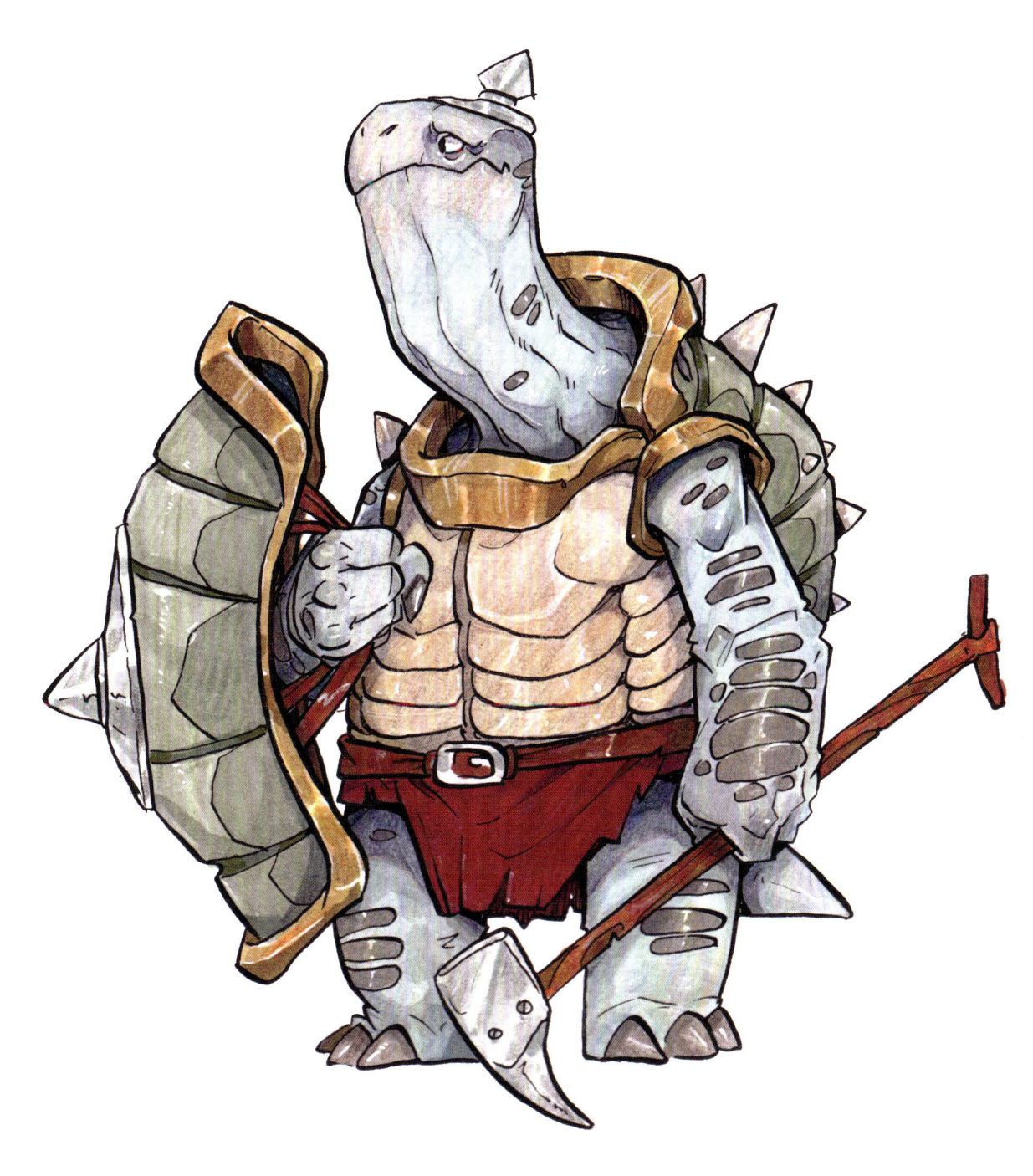

BENJAMIN IS A CHARACTER DESIGNER AND ILLUSTRATOR FROM BERLIN, GERMANY, WHO WORKS IN THE GAMES AND ENTERTAINMENT INDUSTRY. HE LOVES TRADITIONAL MEDIA AND THE FEELING OF A PEN OR BRUSH GLIDING OVER PAPER. WATERCOLOURS, MARKERS, AND DIPS ARE HIS PREFERRED MEDIUM.

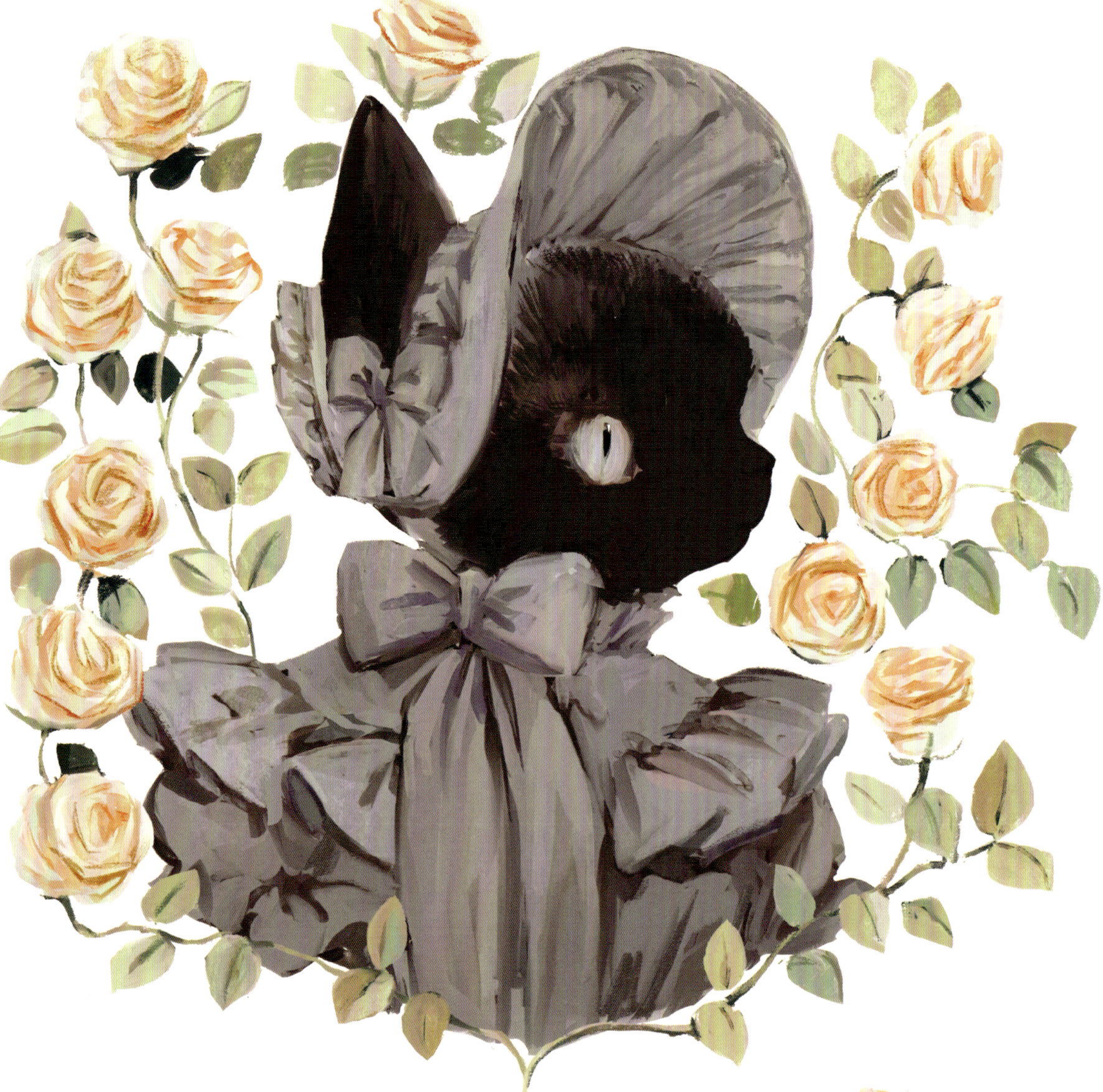

TONO IS AN ILLUSTRATOR
BASED IN JAPAN WHO
SPECIALIZES IN DRAWING
ANIMALS AND CHARACTERS
THAT INHABIT FAIRY-
TALE WORLDS. IN 2020,
SHE PUBLISHED THE ART
COLLECTION *HALF MOON*.

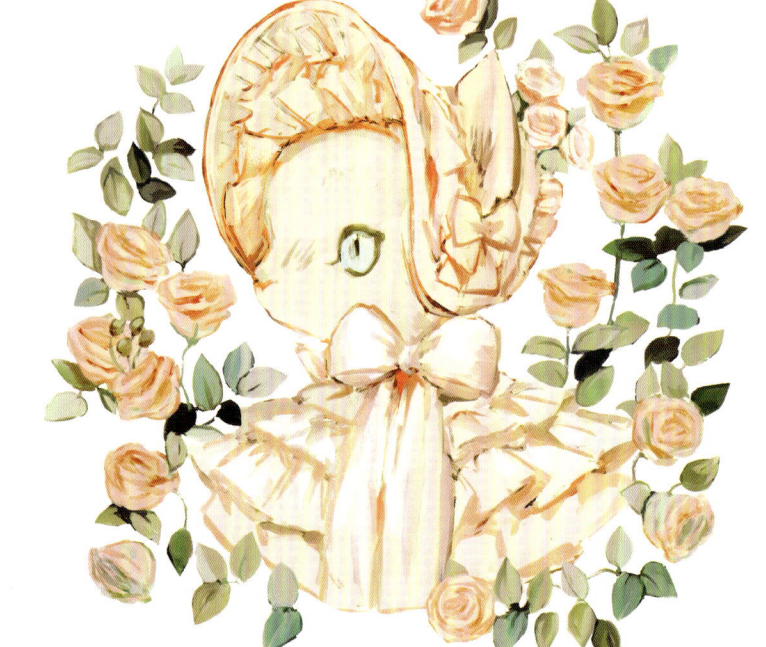

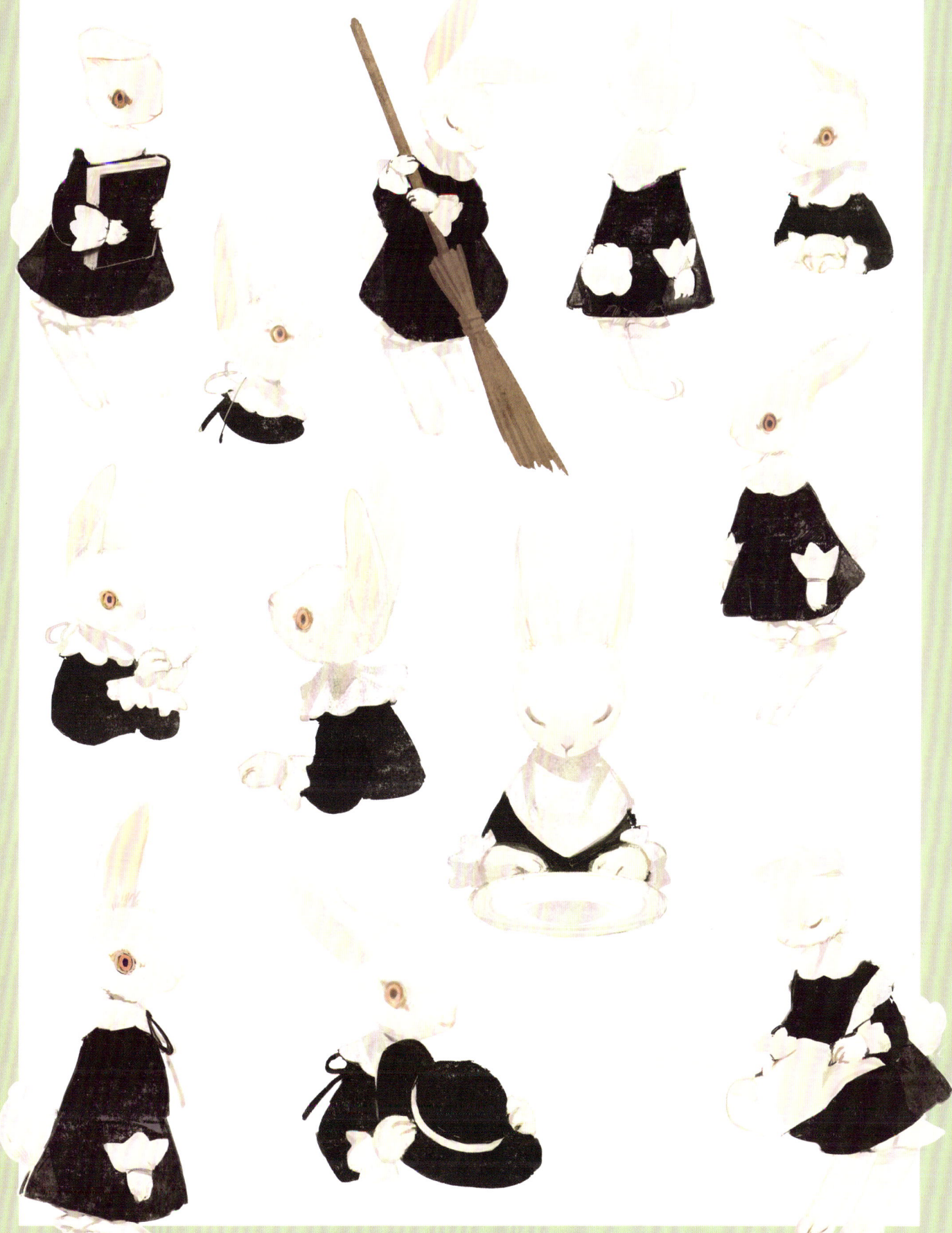

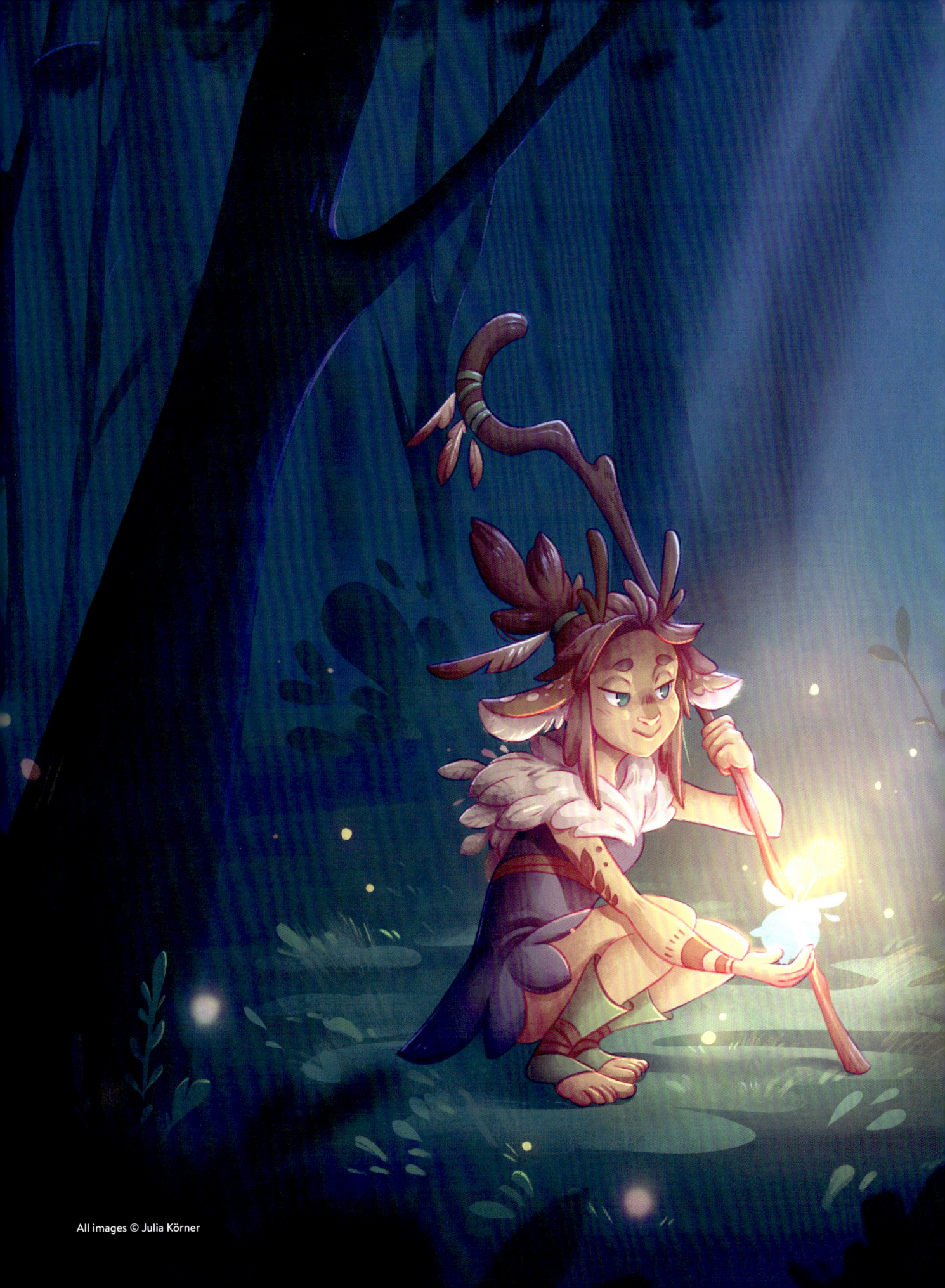

DYRU

Julia Körner, also known as Dyru, is a freelance illustrator, character designer, and visual-development artist who has worked on many projects in video games and animation, as well as children's books and magazines, including *CDQ*! We spoke to Julia about her love of watercolours, the benefits of keeping a sketchbook, and the inspirations behind her magical and warm art style.

DYRU

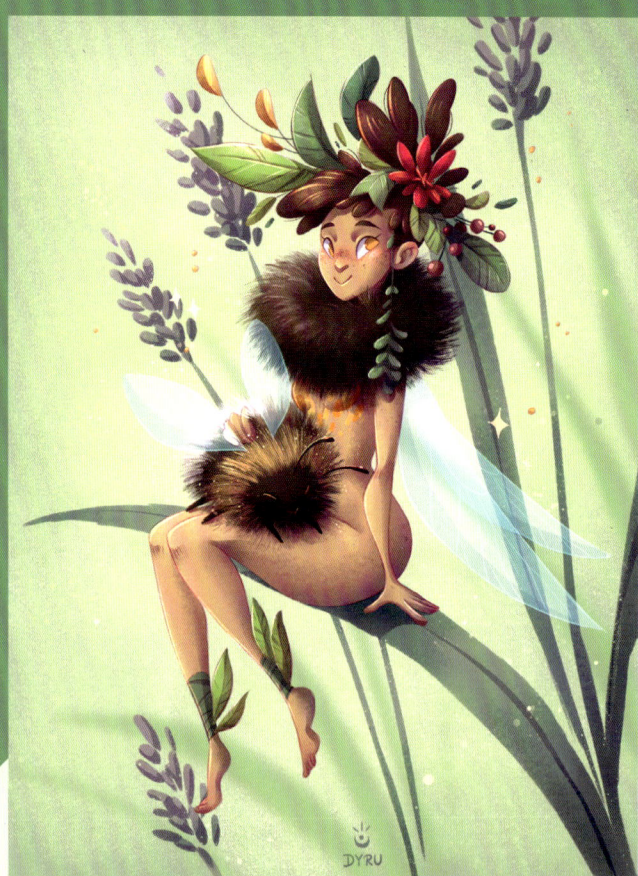

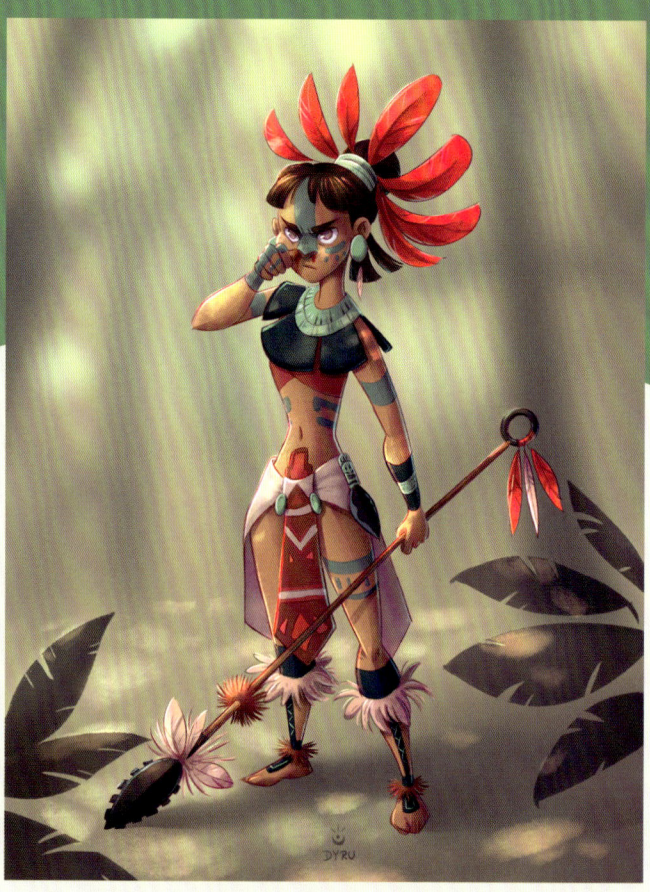

Hi Julia, welcome back to CDQ! Can you tell our readers a little about your art journey so far?

Like most artists, I've drawn since I can remember. My professional career grew step by step after I finished my Master of Arts in Communication and Graphic Design. I didn't go to a specific art or illustration university, so I sometimes think of myself as 'self-taught', but I'm not sure if that's right!

The most important moment on my journey was when I decided to see art as more than a hobby I dabbled in from time to time, and instead take it more seriously and pursue a career as an illustrator. I worked on my portfolio and attended workshops by some of my favourite illustrators, learning from their skills and career paths. Gradually, as I visited other art events and reviewed and updated my portfolio, I began to receive more and more

job requests, until I was working as a full-time illustrator. Nowadays, the biggest challenge I face is finding a good balance between client work and personal projects.

You work a lot with watercolours. What is it about this medium that you find works well for character design?

What I like about watercolour is the tactile feel and textured look that comes from using traditional media, as well as the happy little accidents that add details to each illustration. However, I wouldn't say watercolours are any better or worse for character design than other tools – they are just a medium. Characters are found through the design process, through creating new ideas, exploring fresh ways to interpret telling a character's story.

If you are looking to create characters with a specific softness or playfulness, then watercolours can definitely help bring that aspect of your designs to the fore. For this reason, I especially like to use watercolours for working on art for children's books.

This page (left): My take on one of the Character Design Challenge topics: fairy kingdom

This page (right): Another for the Character Design challenge: an angry Aztec warrior after a fight

Opposite page: A little faun girl enjoying her peaceful life in the forest. This was created for Our Planet Week

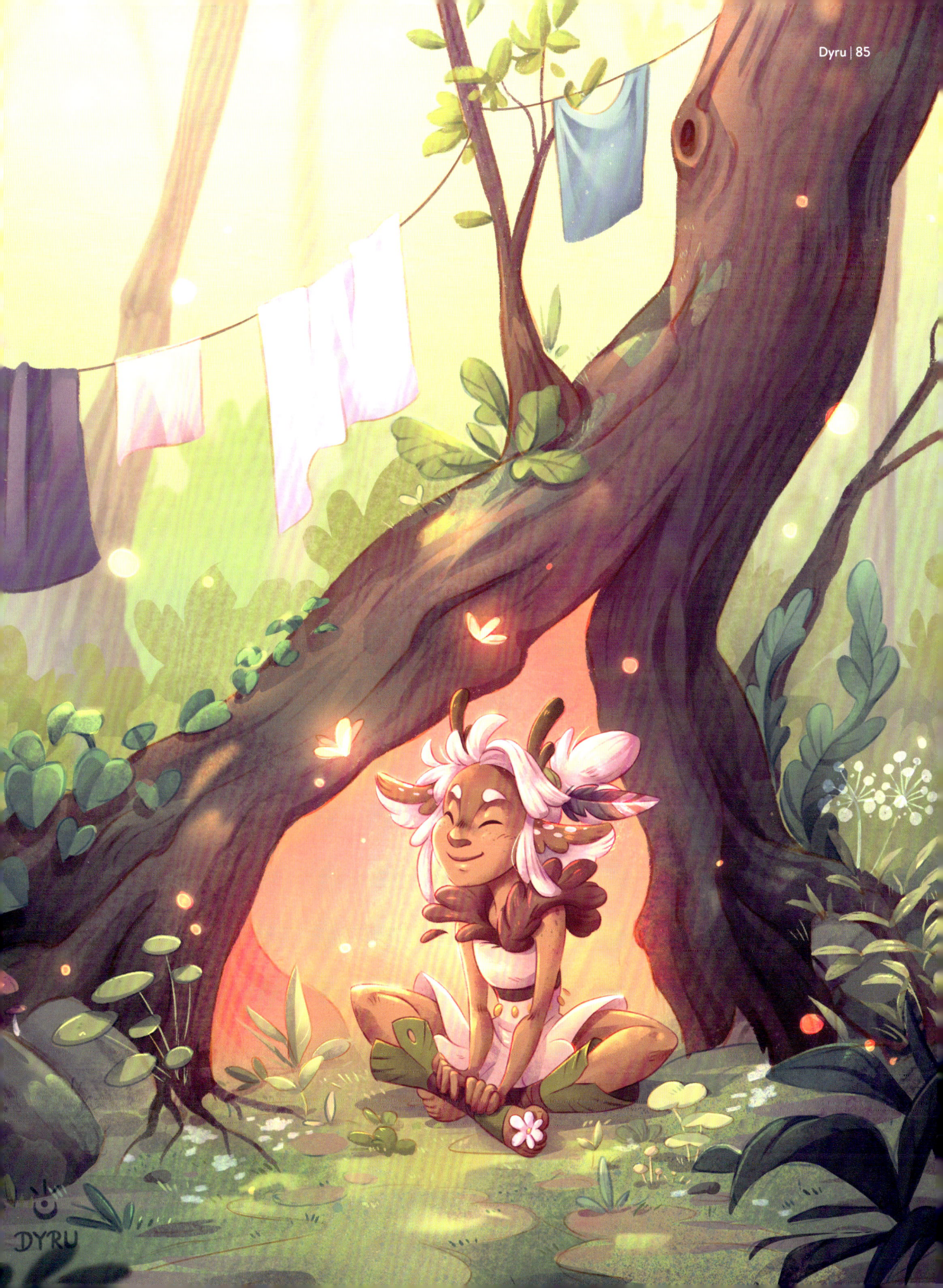

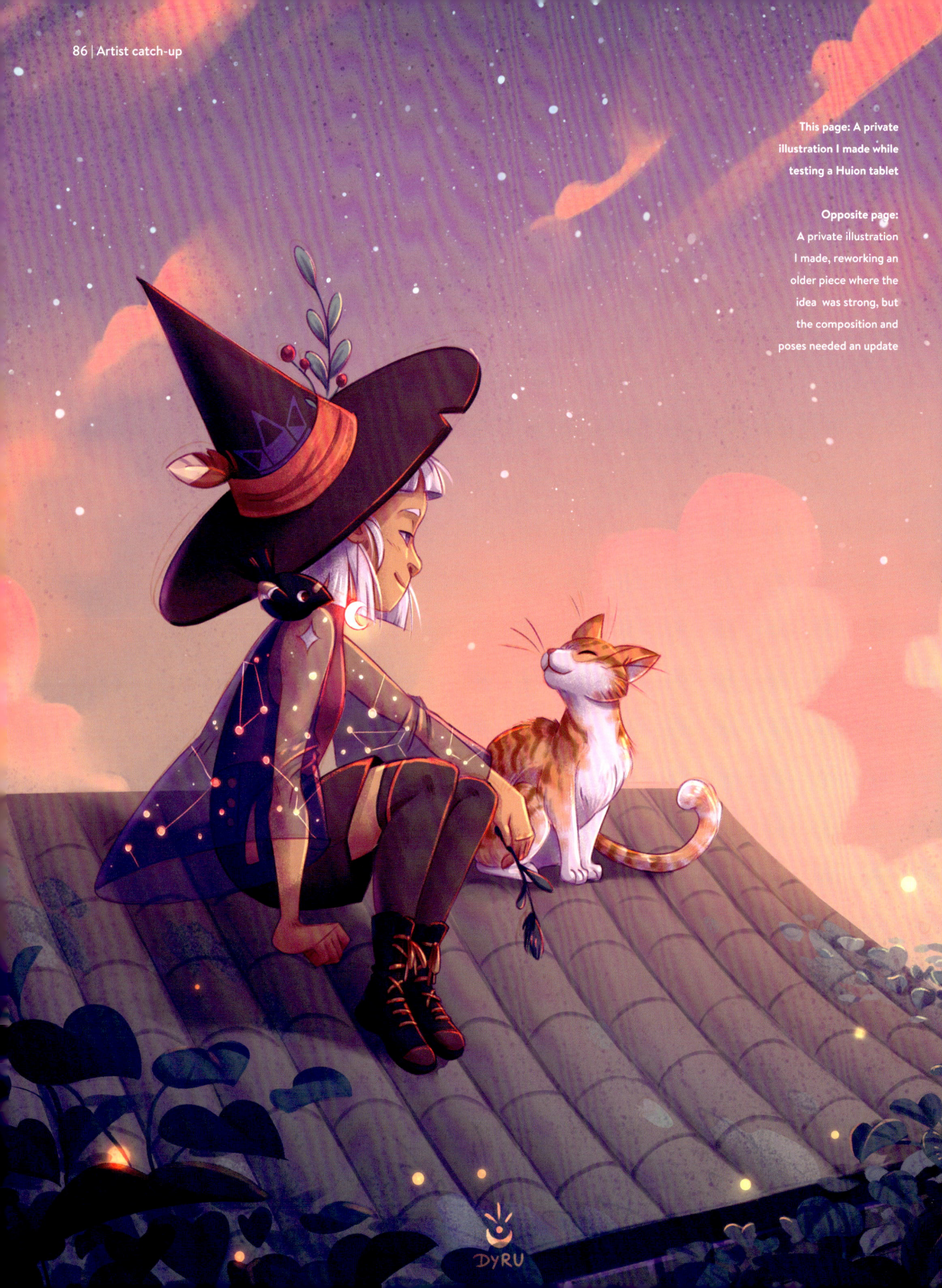

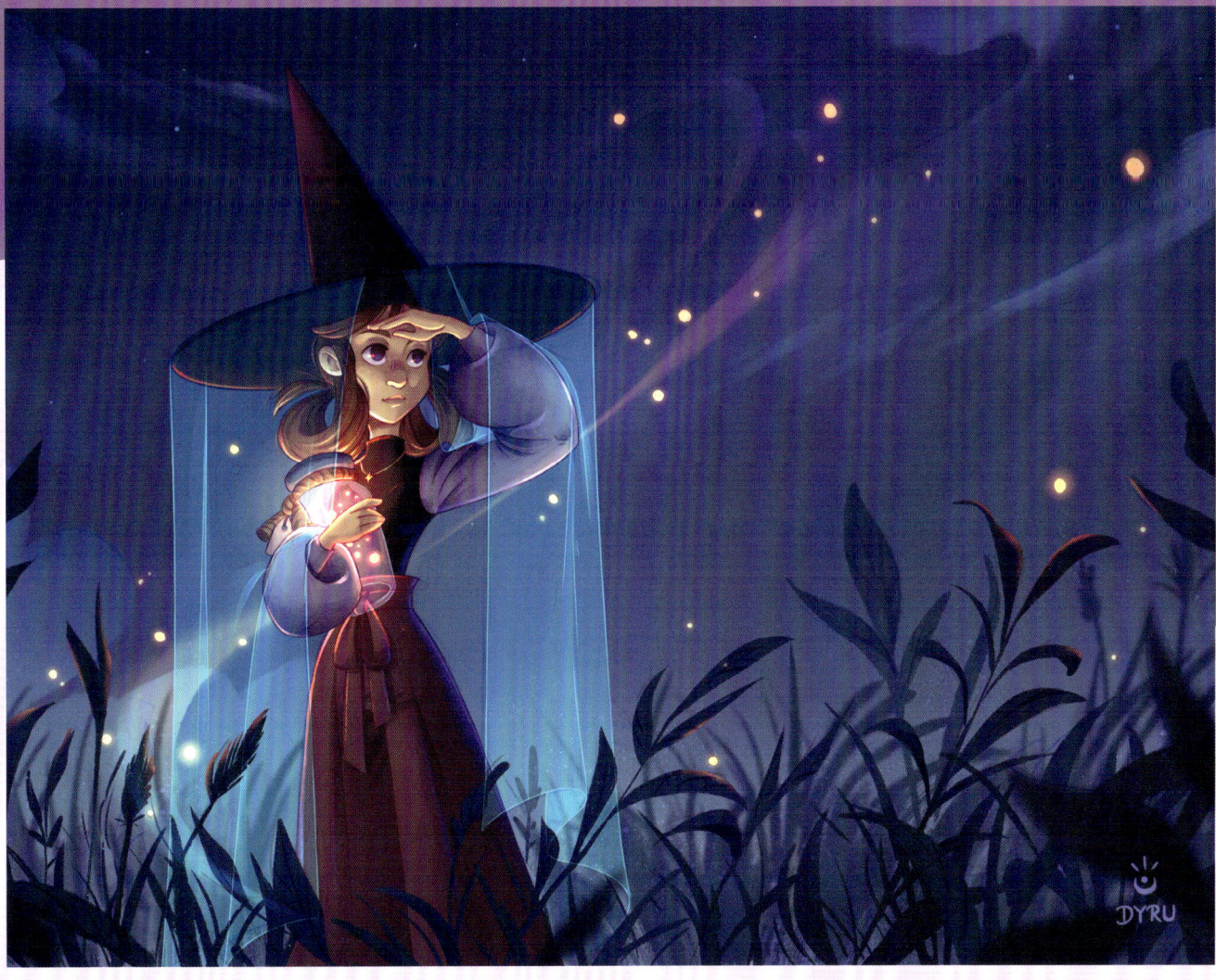

What does the start of your character-design process look like? Where do you find your ideas?

The start of my character design process is a bit different depending on whether the project is client work or private work. With client work or commissions, there is often a brief that includes the important characteristics, sometimes even fixed details about age, hairstyle, hair colour, and so on. But even for my own character designs, I like to choose a certain topic I want to explore, such as witch, forest spirit, animal adventurer, or something like that. After settling on a brief, I will often then research and find references for inspiration. I keep several Pinterest boards and saved illustrations on social media to help get started. From these explorations, I'll create a mood board to get an idea of the direction I want to take the piece. This visual collage might contain photos, crafting, costumes, studies, illustrations, and more. Next, I start sketching some of the ideas that have popped into my head so far. I like to explore different designs or variations before moving on to creating colour tests.

I love seeing pages from your sketchbook on Instagram! Why do you think keeping a sketchbook is important for an artist?

A sketchbook is like an artist's playground. Here you can explore, experiment, and fail, all without fear of judgment. I love trying different sketches for the same idea, drawing rough and ugly compositional sketches or mini thumbnails, just to catch an idea before it gets away.

As well as a place for exploring new styles, trying new tools and mediums, your sketchbook is also the perfect place for practising the basics of illustration, or particular things you struggle with. I recommend having an 'ugly' sketchbook, one that's just meant for yourself that you don't have to show anyone. In this safe space there'll be no expectations or pressure to create something awesome or beautiful. I think it's important to remember that a sketchbook doesn't have to look pretty or perfect as it's a place for preparing for final artwork or to explore and have fun.

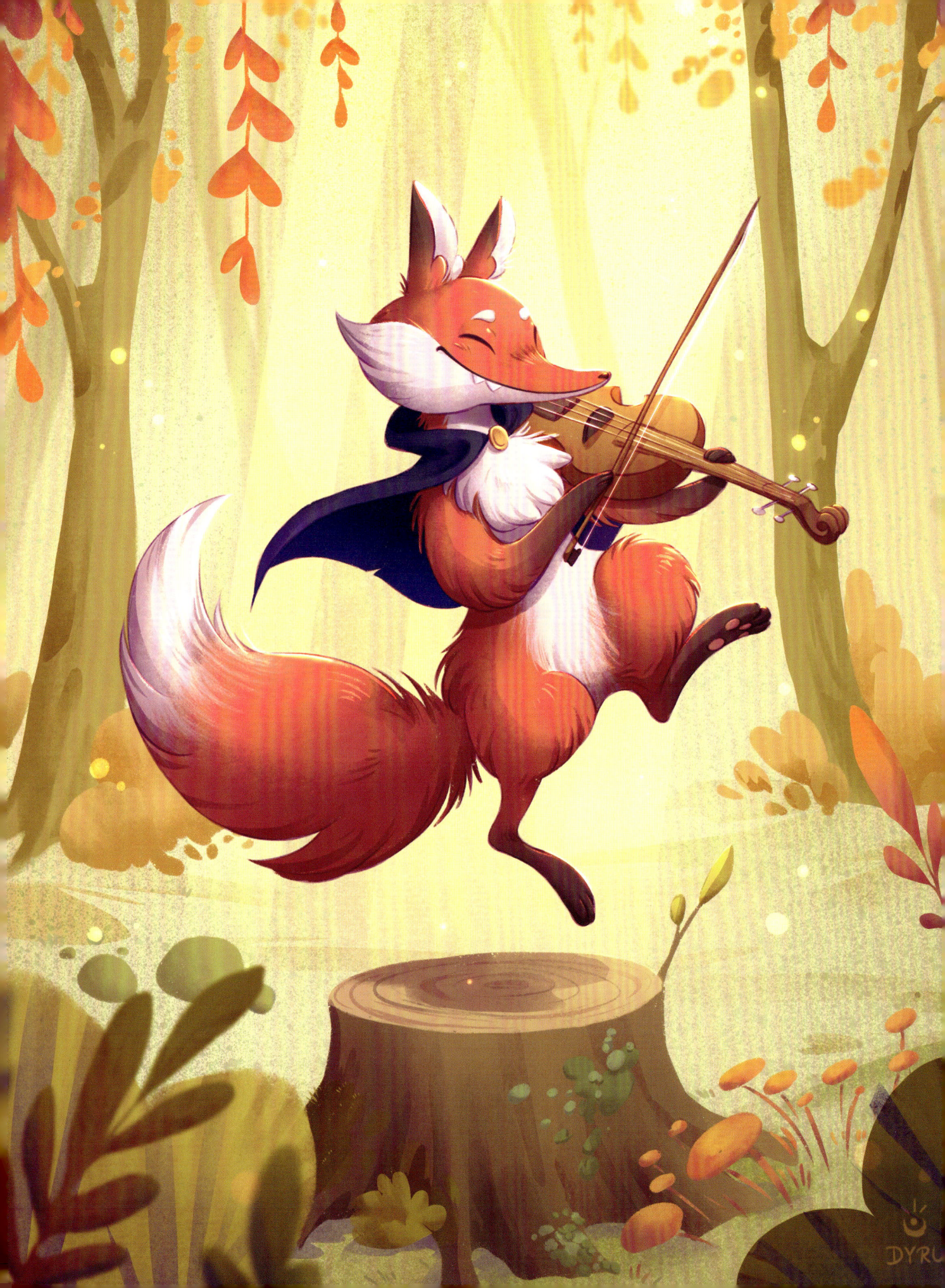

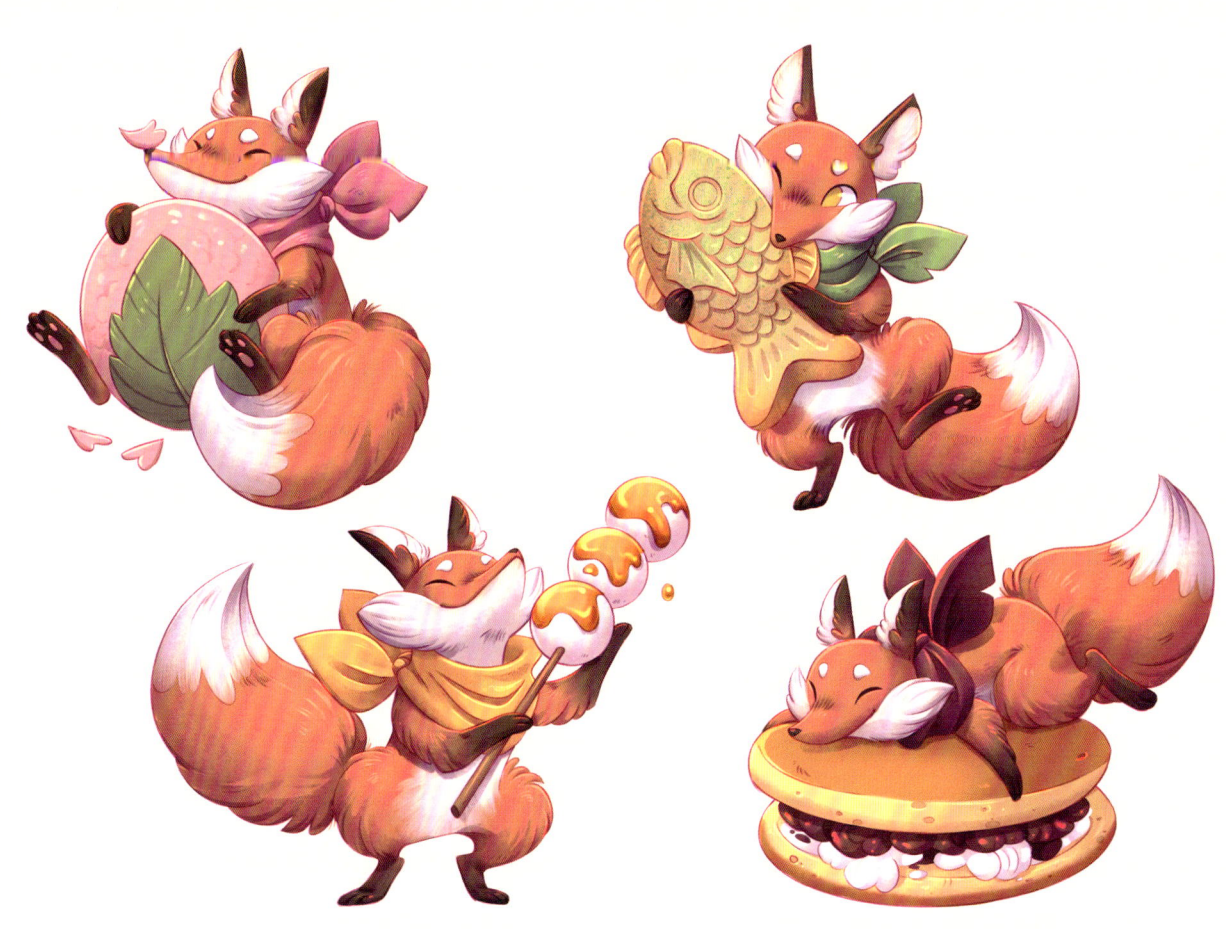

Who are the biggest inspirations behind your colourful and magical art style?

I would say for the colour part, one of my biggest inspirations is Beatrice Blue, with her beautiful way of telling a story and the emotions her colours convey. There's a lot of thought behind each colour, its brightness and saturation, something I think even non artists can pick up on, for sure. The works of Nathan Fowkes are also a great source of inspiration for how to use colours. He can smash some rough colour dots with little details onto a canvas, and you can really see a whole scenery and mood – that's so awesome. I also like a lot of the intense, special colours Natalie Andrewson uses in her Riso print artworks.

As for the magical and dreamy style I often feature in my personal works, my inspirations are artists like Djamila Knopf, with her calm, nostalgic, Ghibli-esque worlds and scenarios she creates. I also love the whimsical and other-wordly work of Heikala.

Your use of light and shadow also really stands out in your character work. Do you have any quick tips for how to use light effectively?

To achieve an impressive light and shadow effect in your illustrations, I think contrast is the key. I also try to lean into natural lighting, so I often use cold colours for shadows, like blue and purple, instead of grey tones. It's the same for light – I use yellow or orange tones to create a warm light effect. This combination creates a nice double contrast in colour value and warmth in the designs. For painting light, I like to use the Colour Dodge effect and for shadows I mostly use Multiply. Sometimes I also draw directly with the colours, depending on the mood or feeling I want to create.

Opposite page: This happy fox fiddler was created for the Character Design Challenge topic Animal Orchestra

This page: Illustrations that channel my love for Japanese sweets and foxes

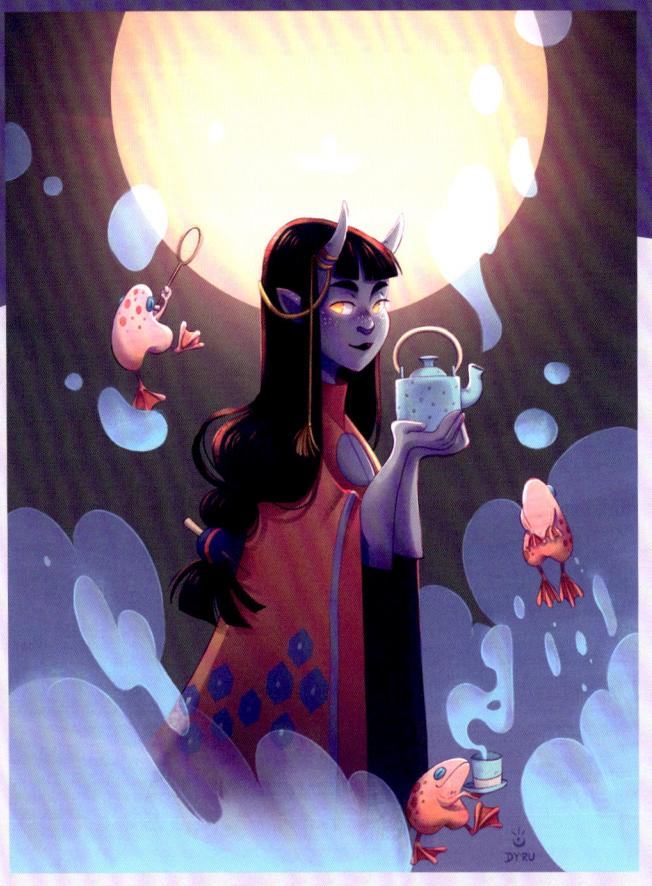

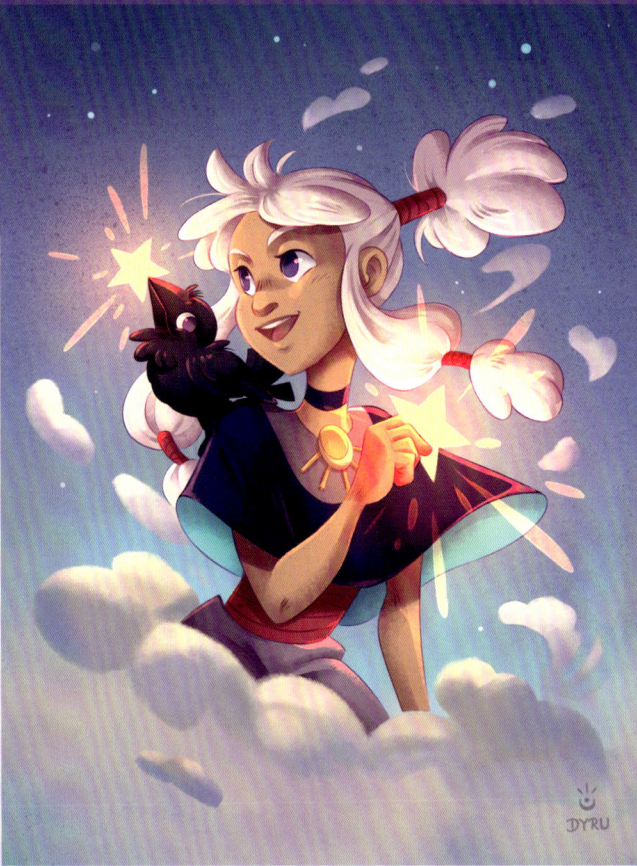

How has your art style developed over time?

In my opinion, my art style has developed from scribbly and unsure lines to a flowing, dynamic, but also clean style. These days I also feel more comfortable creating whole scenes and backgrounds, which gives me the chance to convey more through my illustrations. I used to make a sketch and directly colour it, without redrawing the outlines, correcting proportions, or anything much else. I think this gave my illustrations a bit of a wobbly, undefined feeling when I look back at them now. When I make characters now, I will redraw the design, pose, or scene anywhere from three to ten times to make sure everything is working as I hoped before I start colouring.

What tips do you have for artists just starting out that are looking to follow a similar career path?

Don't just chase the dream to work at a 'big' studio or you'll miss out on a lot of other opportunities along the way. As prestigious and awesome as it may sound to say you have worked with X or Y studio, there are a lot of smaller, really cool publishers, studios, or even private people with exciting projects out there. Especially at the beginning of your career, when you're still building up your portfolio or just starting out as a freelance illustrator, it's a lot easier to get in contact with a smaller operation than be one of a hundred artists applying for the same job at a studio. So, be open to opportunities that come along and you'll find you learn a lot from each job you take on. And as annoying as it may be these days, I think social media and your own website will still help you to be visible, so people looking for what you can offer have a chance to find you and your artwork.

Thanks for talking to us, Julia! Do you have any upcoming projects we should look out for?

For the last two years I've worked on several different games as an artist, which should start coming out in late 2023 and 2024. I worked for almost two and a half years as a visual development artist and character designer on the game *Spells & Secrets*. I also worked on a cool jigsaw from Kosmos, where I illustrated everything – I'm looking forward to holding the physical copy in my hands. I'm also planning to create my own art book which will hopefully be finished early in 2024.

Opposite page: These images were made for my own DTIYS challenges

This page: Another illustration created for a Character Dseign Challenge

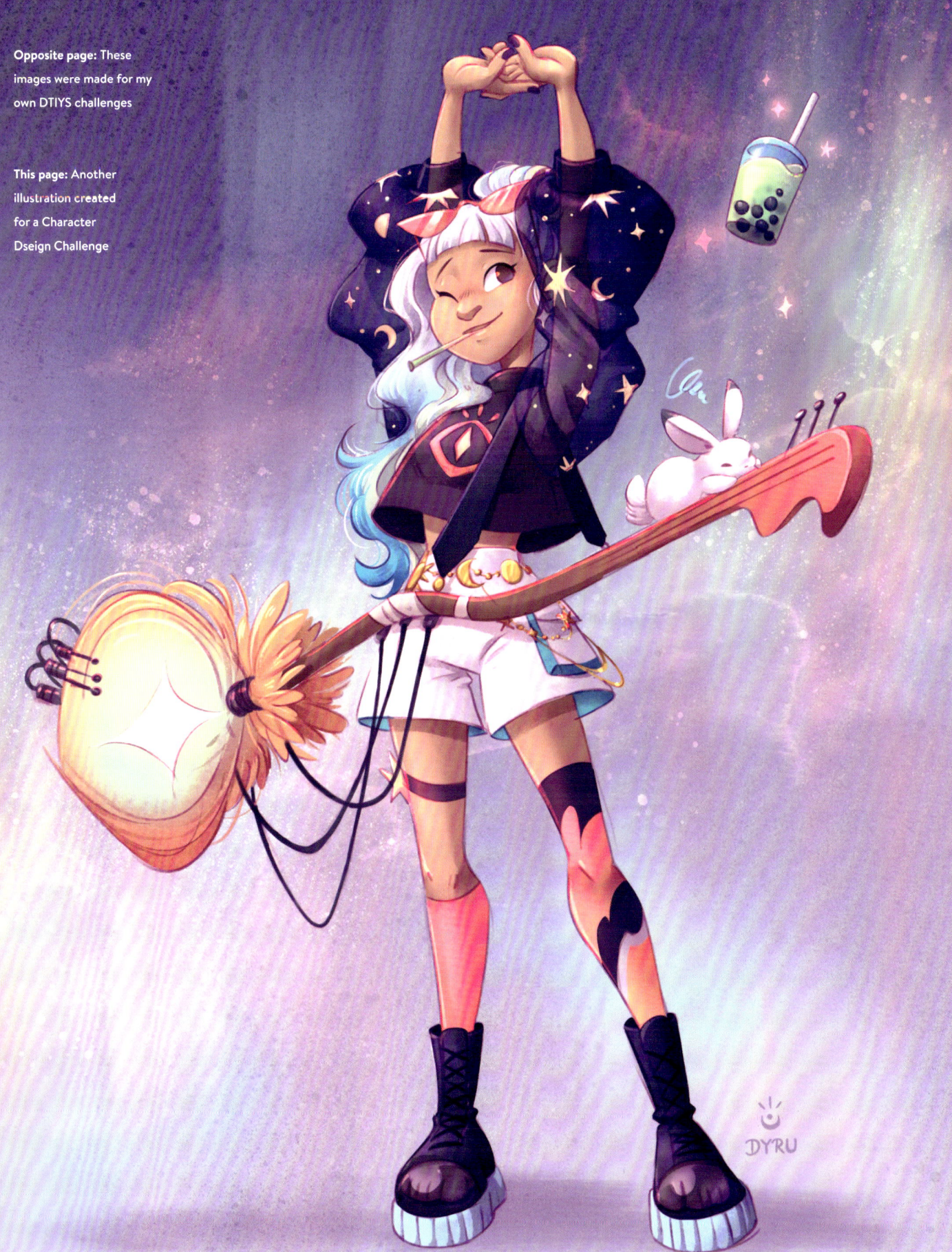

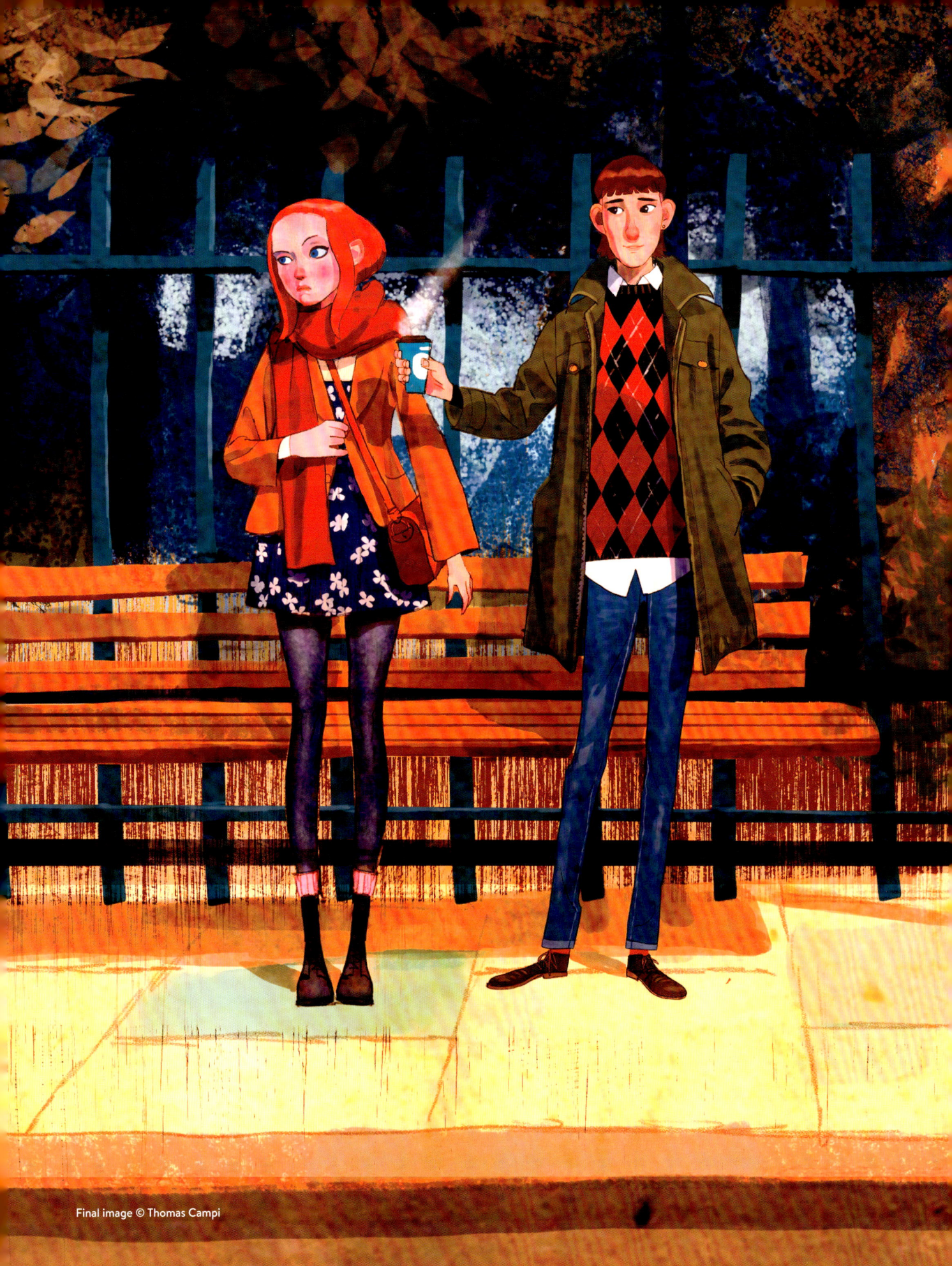

Final image © Thomas Campi

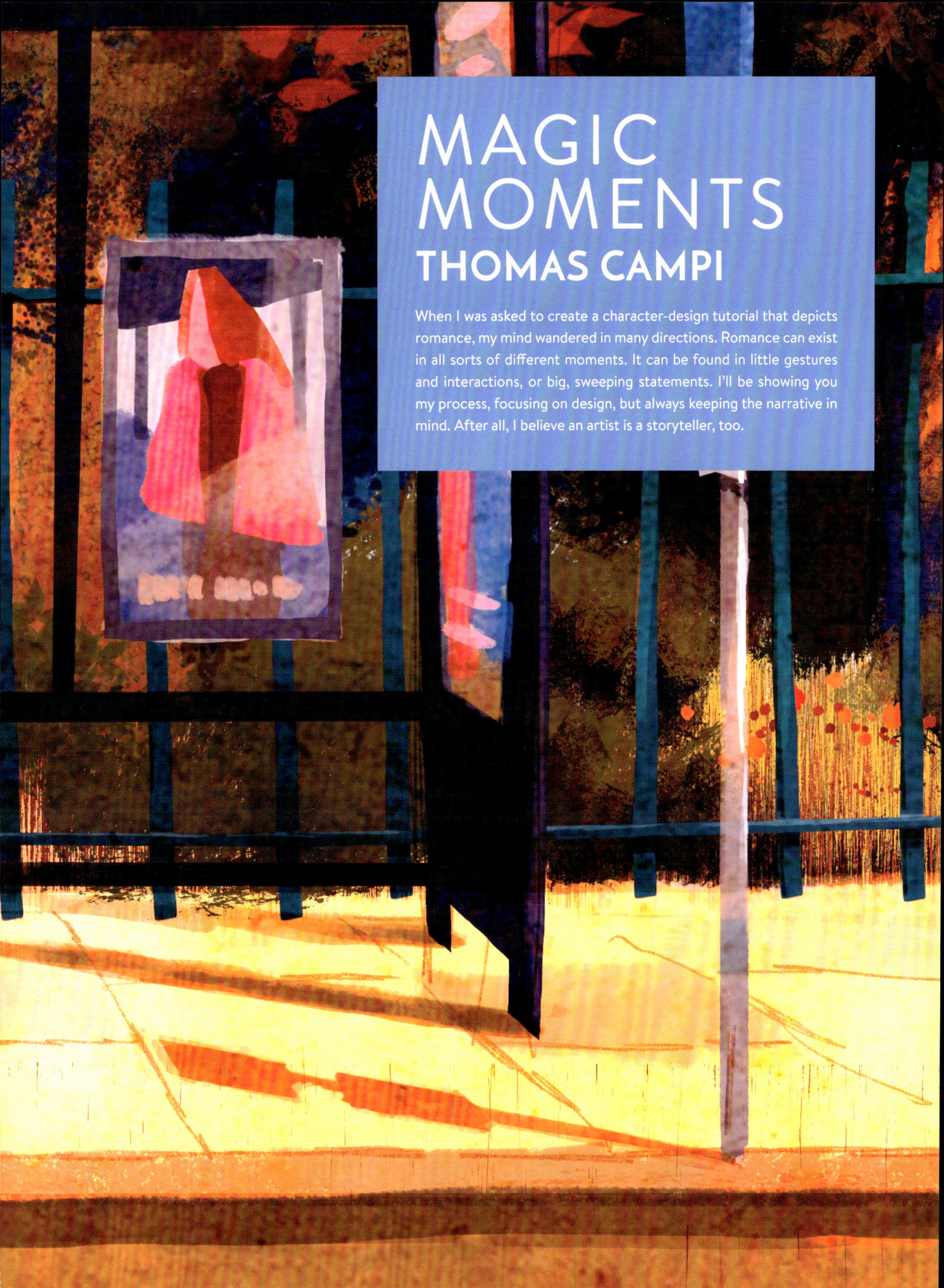

MAGIC MOMENTS

THOMAS CAMPI

When I was asked to create a character-design tutorial that depicts romance, my mind wandered in many directions. Romance can exist in all sorts of different moments. It can be found in little gestures and interactions, or big, sweeping statements. I'll be showing you my process, focusing on design, but always keeping the narrative in mind. After all, I believe an artist is a storyteller, too.

Starting out

When you first explore an idea, you will often see images flash through your mind. The theme for this tutorial is 'romance', so anything you pluck from your imagination and sketch needs to communicate that. Before you start, it's important to decide what romance means to you and how you want to represent it. You might be surprised by your own ideas and discover different possibilities for how to depict this theme, even if you've never thought about it seriously before.

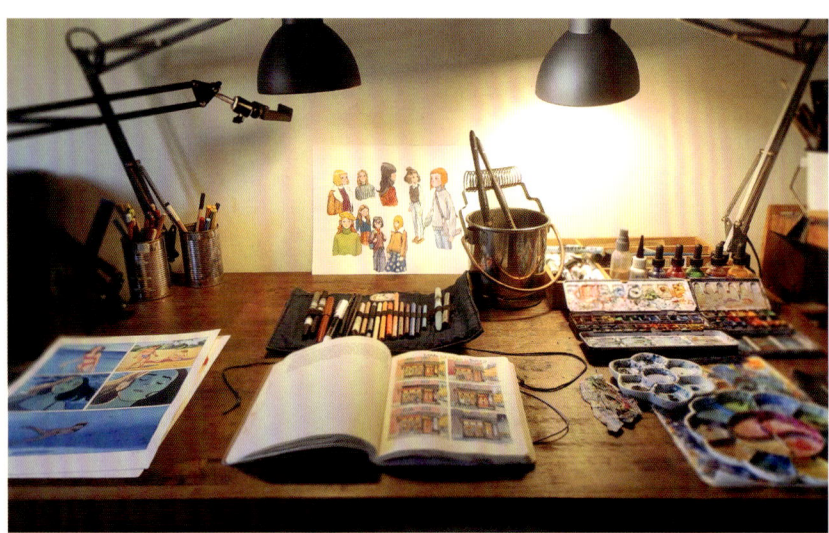

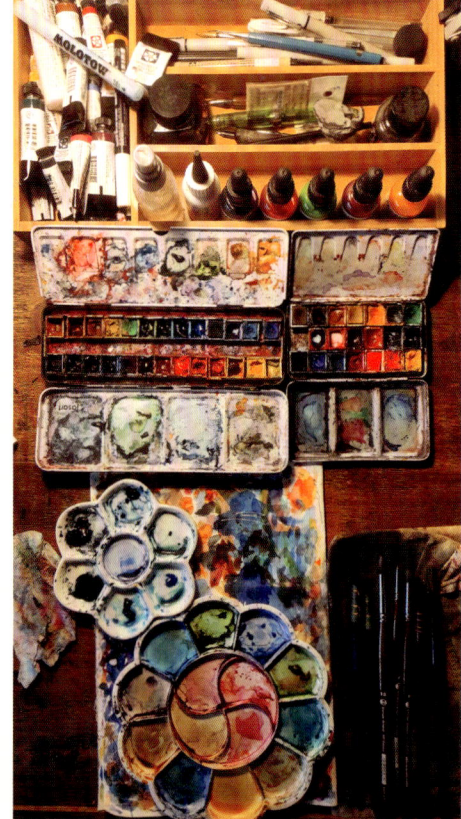

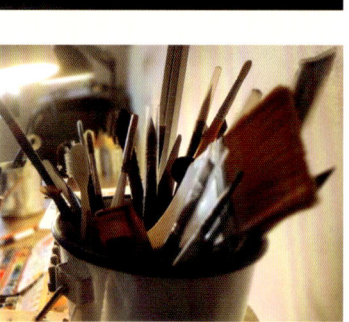

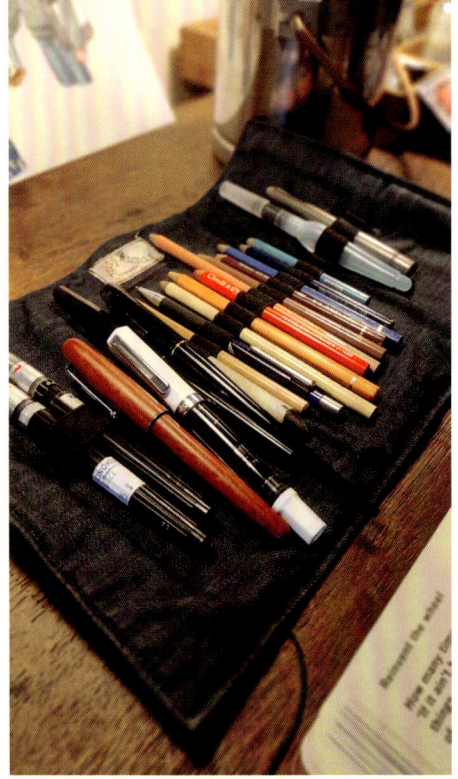

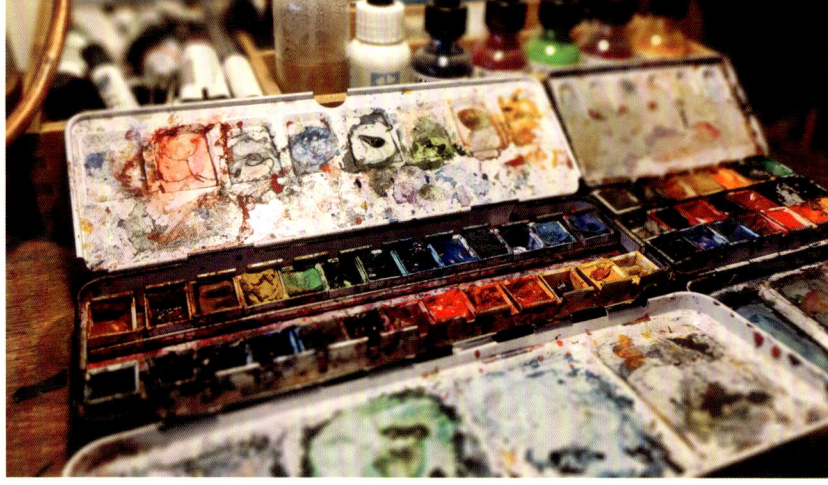

Opposite page:

Get your tools
together and
start sketching

This page:

Quick ideas for the
romantic moment
I want to show

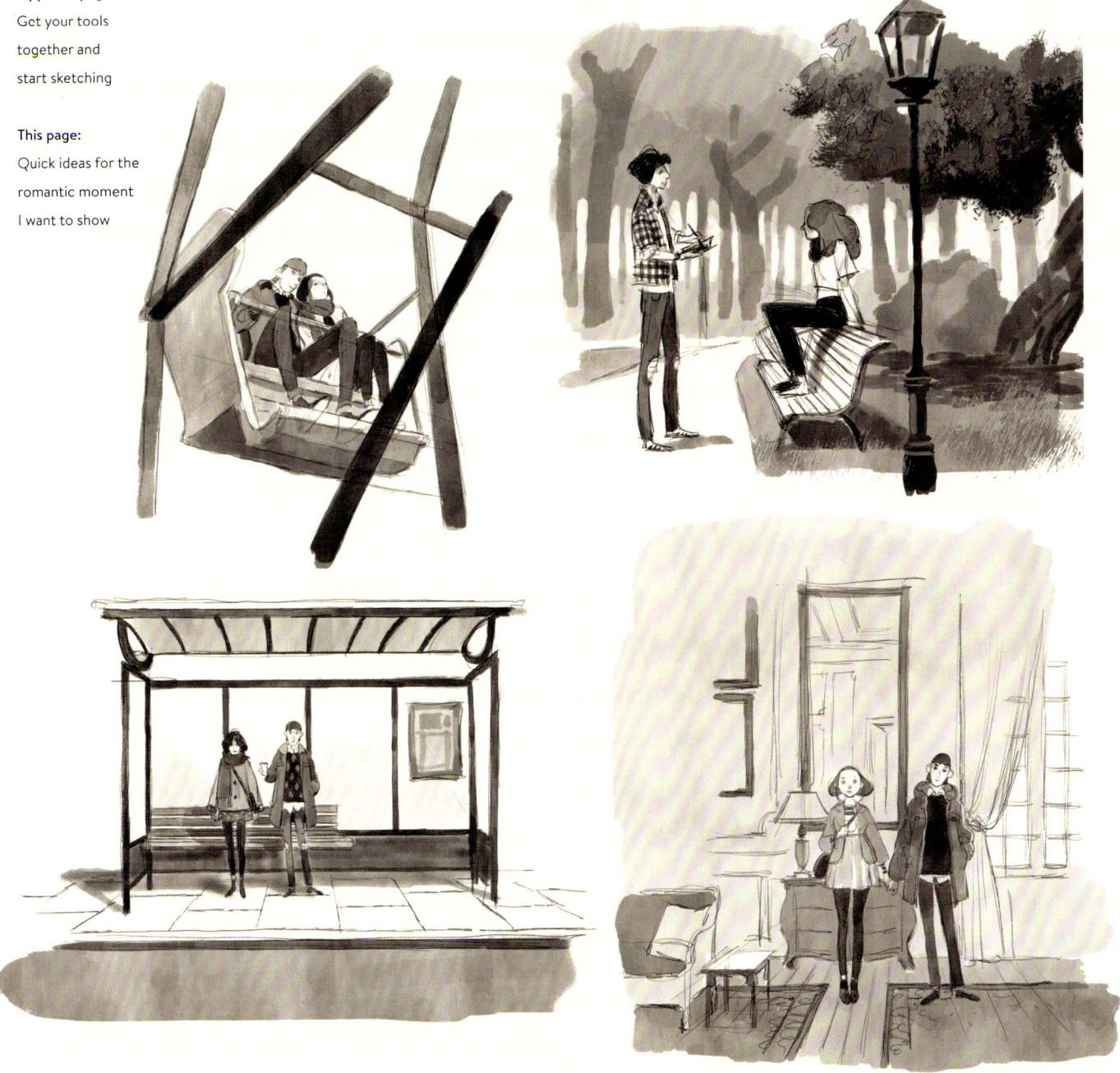

A magic spark

Sometimes, finding that initial spark of an idea can be tough. A good starting point to find inspiration is to sketch and write down ideas, associations, even memories of people you know or you might have seen around. Some of the first ideas might be very basic, unoriginal, or simply not good enough. Don't worry – this is actually very helpful.

Even if you've already sketched some of those basic ideas, you can then discard these concepts and start focusing on other directions, more confident in what works and what doesn't. That's the beauty of drawing, it's always a surprise!

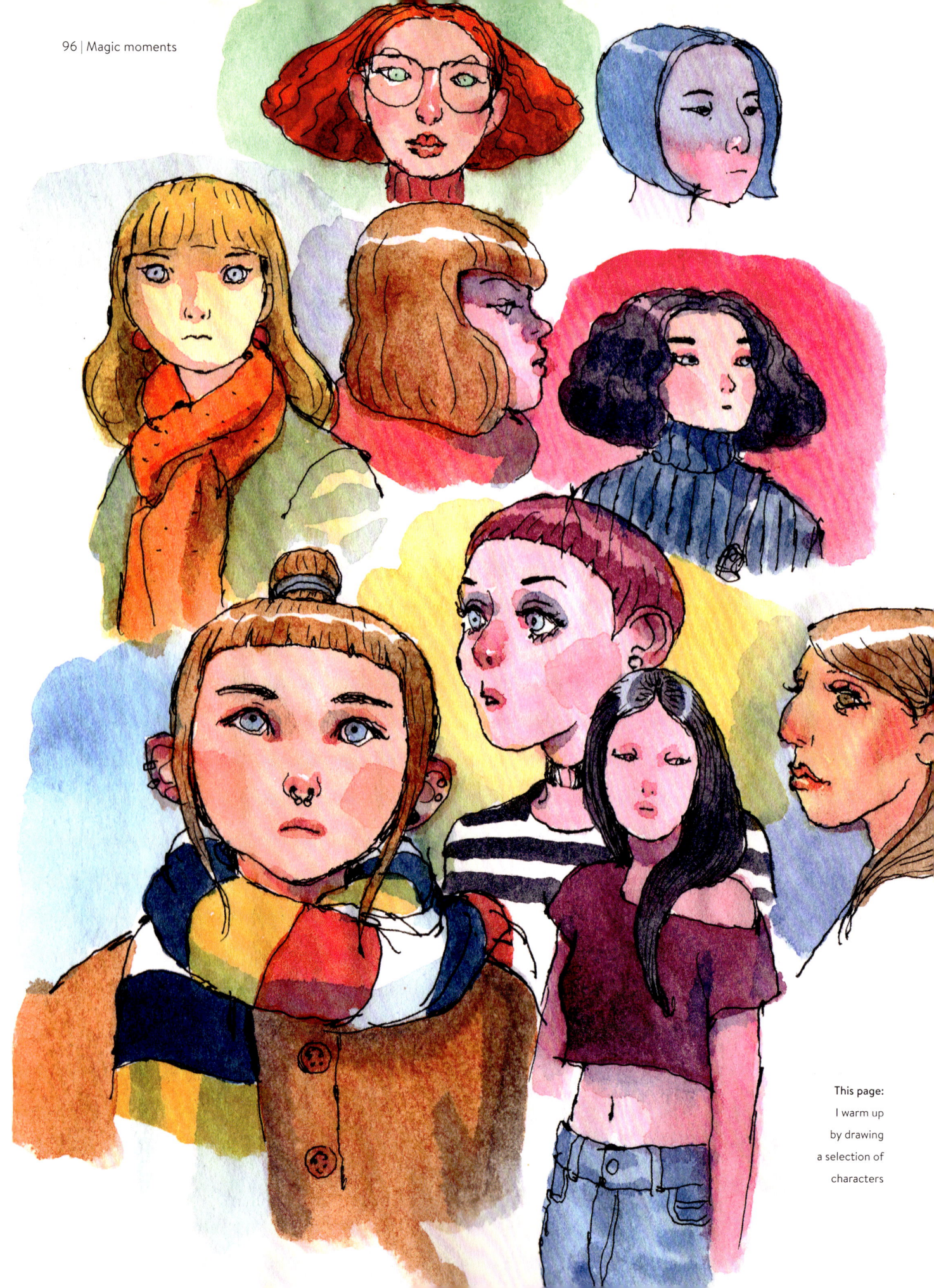

This page:
I warm up
by drawing
a selection of
characters

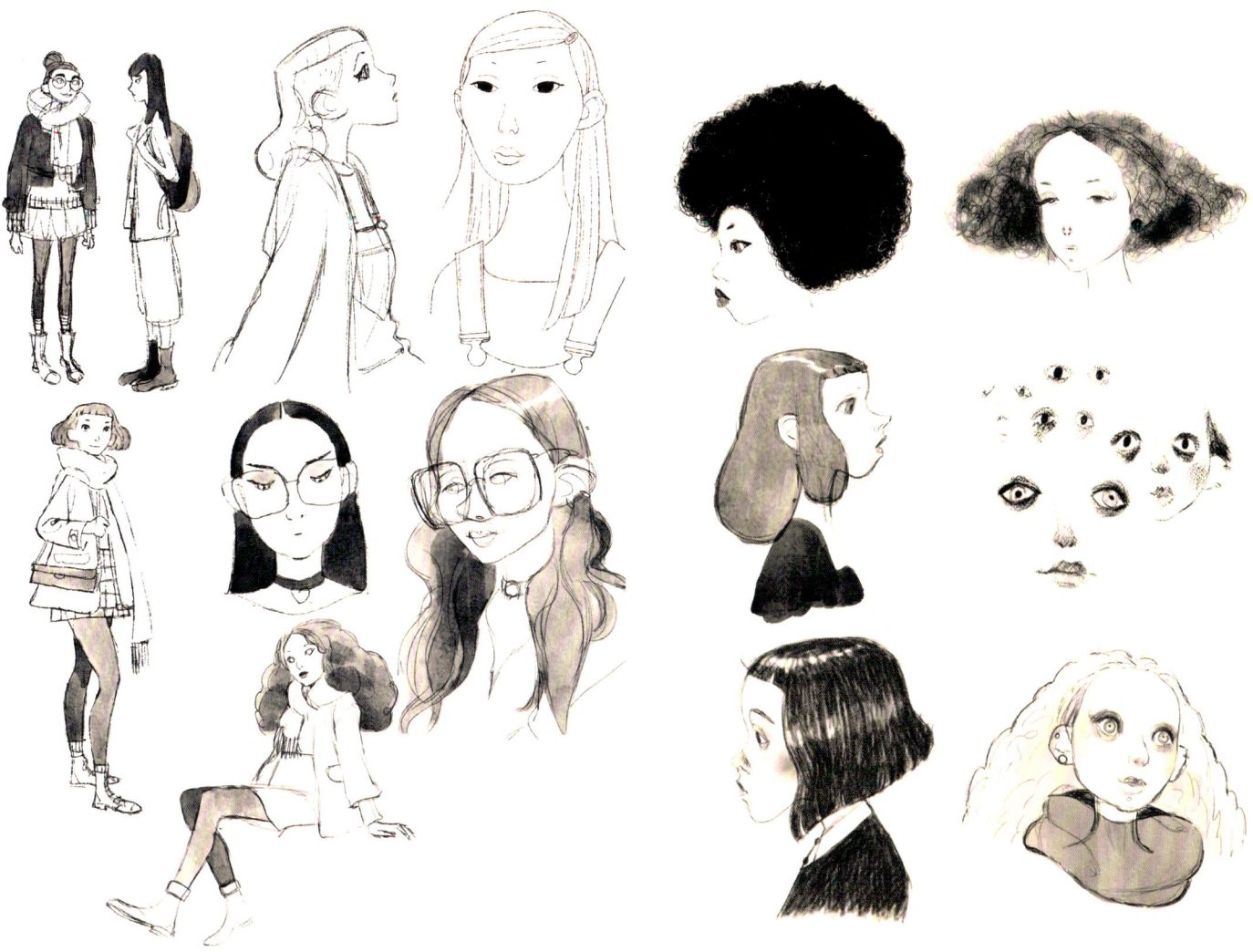

Warming up

Most of the time, your first ideas will throw up challenges – a peculiar design idea, shape, or hairstyle, for instance. When this happens, take a break and come back later. A fresh perspective can unblock your creativity. I wanted to draw a young couple, one boy and one girl, probably in love for the first time, with a specific kind of look and fashion style, but I didn't know their faces and backstory yet.

Question your characters

What do you want to communicate? Every element of your design, like shape, silhouette, outfits, props, and even poses work in service of the story you are telling. Every element needs to be clear and readable. Imagine you could talk to the characters and ask them questions: who are you? Are you in love? Is it the beginning or the end of your love story? Try to have fun with the prompt by going in unexpected directions. Keep exploring!

Two forks in the road

After some sketching and thinking, I come up with two very different ideas. One is about romance in its most pure form: a love that stands the test of time. I push this idea further by thinking of this couple as ghosts, together and happy forever. The second idea is about a more grounded manifestation of romance, exploring smaller expressions of love. I'm thinking about those actions that, no matter how small, can make you smile. For example, on a cold winter's day, a girl stands at a bus stop after an argument. Her partner approaches with a hot drink and a smile, handing her the drink, silently saying 'sorry'. I'll come back to this idea later – for now, it's time to sketch.

This page (left): Early sketches of one of my romantic characters

This page (right): Initially, my idea for a ghostly romance seems strongest

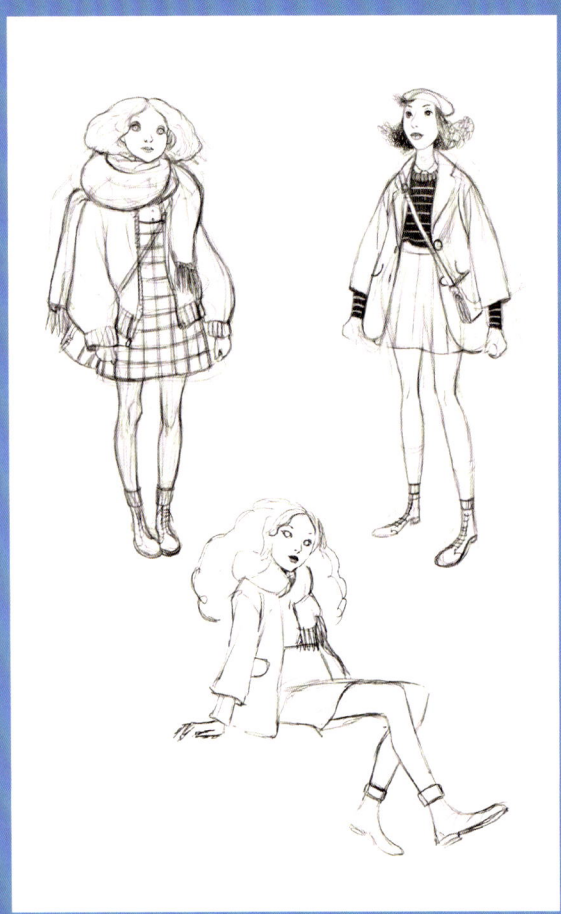

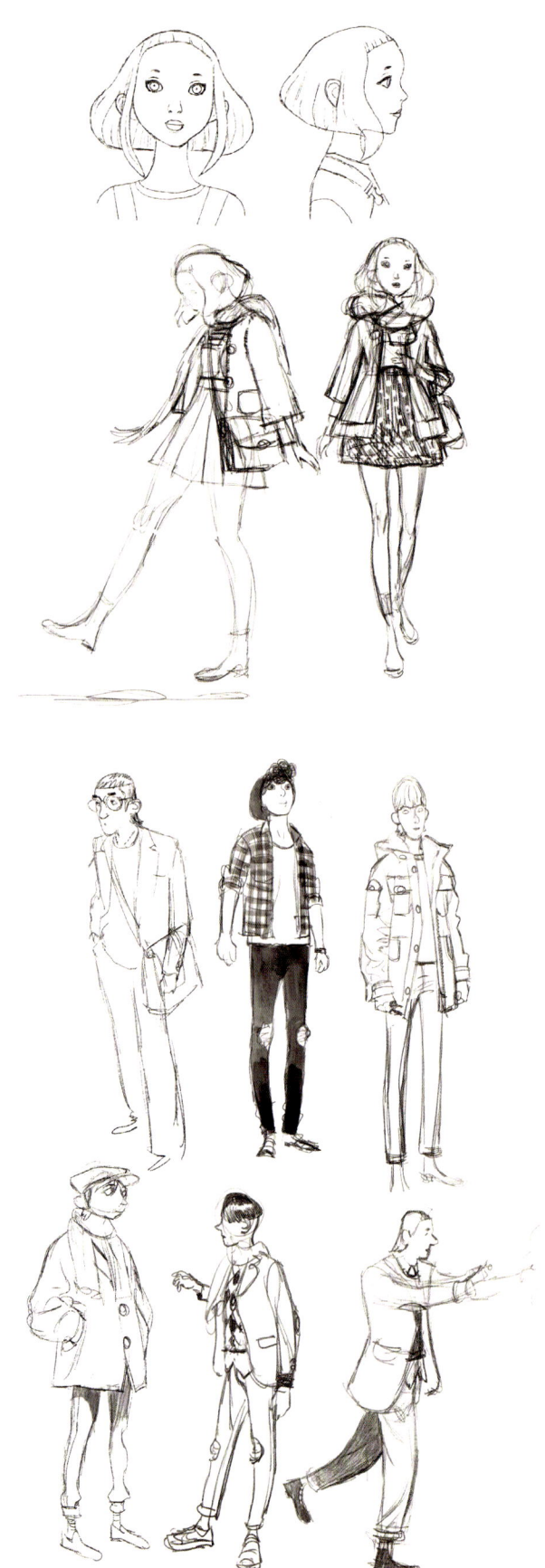

Background check

Now that you have some story ideas, it's time to sketch and explore different faces, shapes, eyes, hairstyles, expressions, and outfits. Think of this step like casting actors for a movie. Their backstory has determined their age and who the characters are, but what will they look like? You may have an idea for their faces in mind, but they aren't necessarily the most perfect fit. You need to imagine each character in action, dressing up, and acting according to your story. Keep sketching until you have at least two or three good options.

Gradually, you'll get closer to how you want your characters to look and have some solid sketches to work from. This is an energizing moment, so push every aspect a bit further. Create a few more sketches trying to diversify the proportions, head shape, hairstyle, and colours.

This page (left): I think of my characters as actors in a movie

This page (right): Every aspect of a character helps tell their story

First impressions

We have our actors, so let's get to know them better. I like to think of my design process as meeting someone for the first time – you want to know as much as possible about the person, to see their smile, all their other expressions and reactions, and how they dress and move. You need to be able to draw each character's face from different angles, understand how tall they are, what kind of physique they have, their posture, attitude, and even their gait. I don't have the space to show you everything, but you get the gist! Work through all of this and you can finally say hello to your characters – 'nice to meet you!'

Choosing the story

The casting is done, we've narrowed down the possibilities for each character, so let's circle back around to the story. After exploring both narratives, I decide to discard the ghost concept, even though I was really fond of it. I found I kept drawing girls with black circles around their eyes that had a sad, melancholic vibe, which isn't what I'm going for. Don't get too attached to an idea – even if you really like it, it doesn't mean it's the right one. The 'little moments' idea seems like a better fit for this tutorial, so I decide to move ahead with this concept.

Forming faces

It's time to focus on the face. Your character has to be relatable to your audience. Drawing expressions is key – they inject life into your designs. Personally, I don't always push broad facial expressions and instead focus on smaller, micro expressions – those subtle movements in the eyes, eyebrows, or lips that still convey more than enough emotion.

This page (left): While I liked my ghost idea, the faces seemed too sad

This page (right): Subtle facial expressions can work better than broad ones

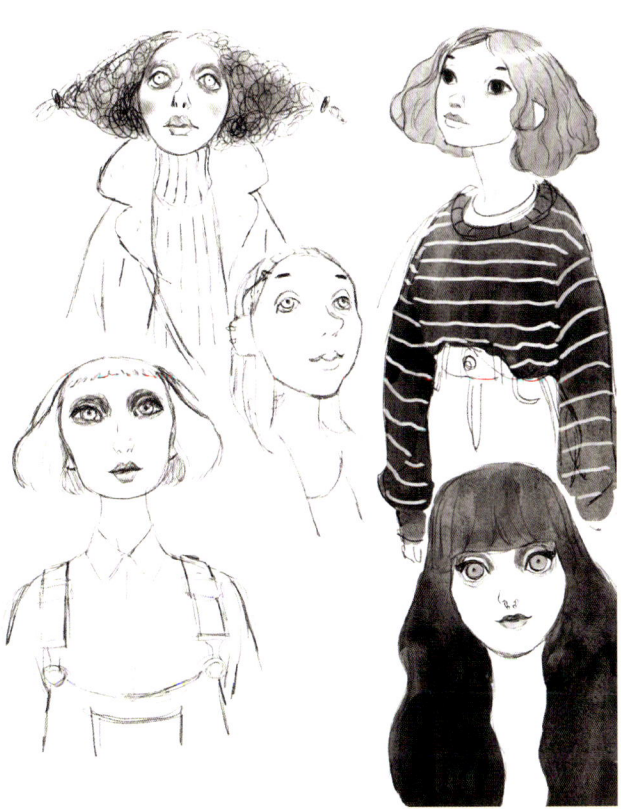

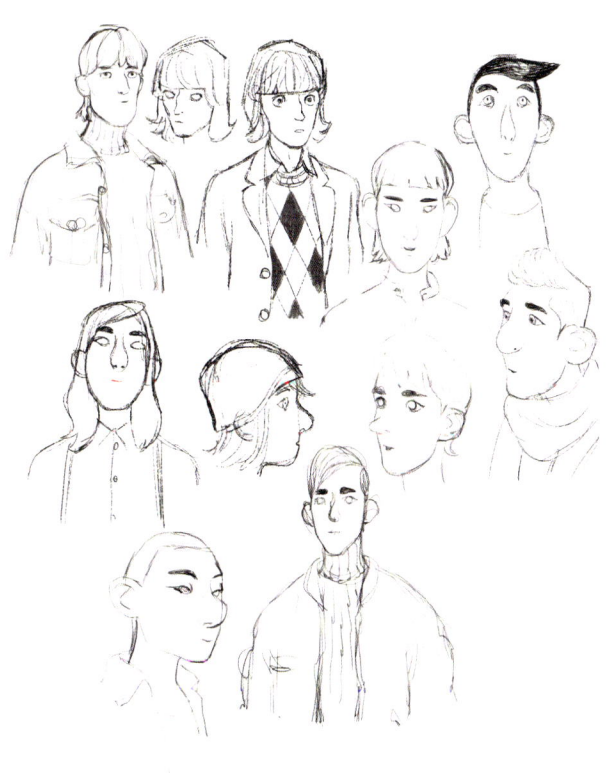

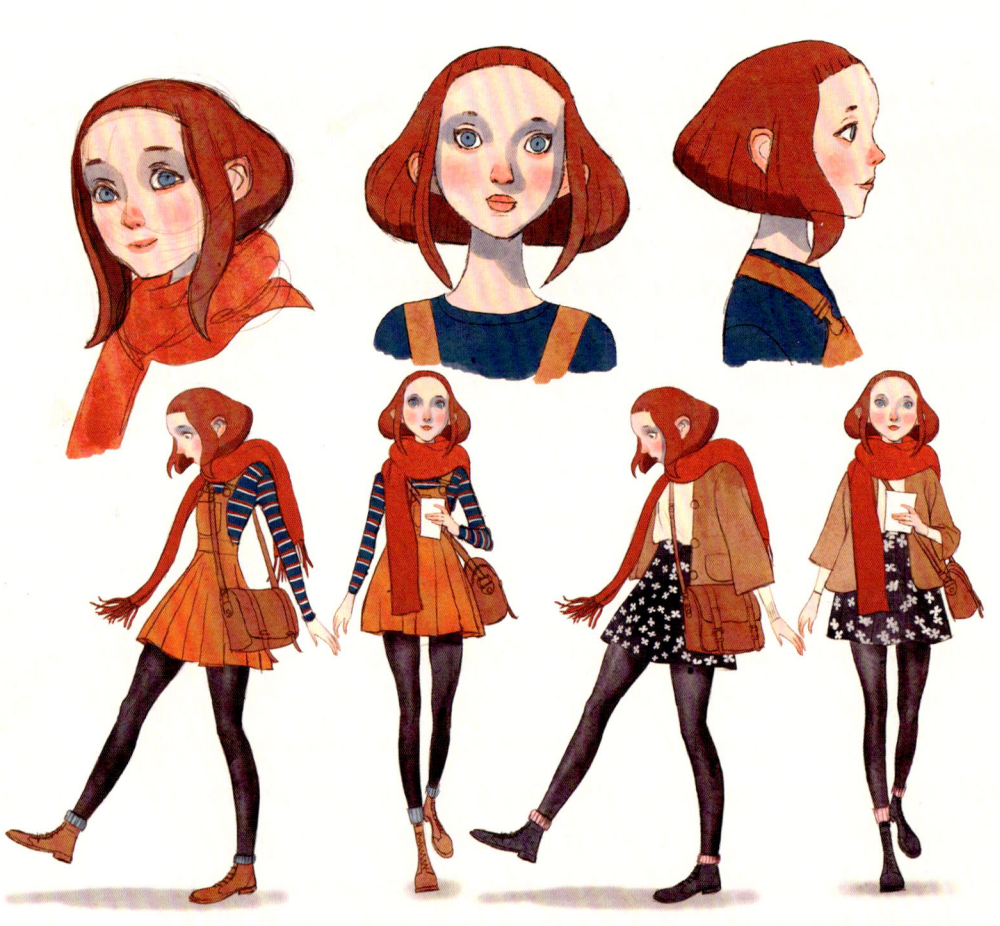

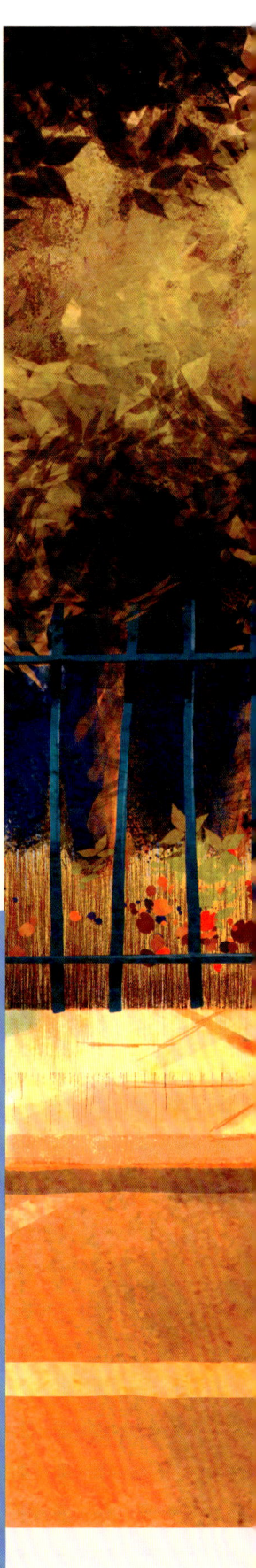

The colour puzzle

Now we can add colour. Everyone has a different approach and process. I tend to think about colours from all the way back at the early sketch stage, but that doesn't mean I'm stuck with that first idea of a colour palette. Every colour choice should not be based solely on aesthetics, but also on the mood of the story you want to tell. Think about colours like pieces of a puzzle – you need the right pieces to complete the whole image. Colours interact with one another to create a moment, a mood, and to bring your scene to life.

A romantic moment

The design stage is now complete. You have your two characters, but they can't be just drawings. To feel real, characters need to be part of a story. I choose an isolated bus stop for the background because I want the attention on our couple. I use autumn colours to give a warm feeling, but I try to express the idea of a cold day with their outfits. In the posture of the girl, we can see she's avoiding the boy – her head is slightly tilted and turned the other way, while her expression, even if it isn't exaggerated, shows she's upset. The boy respects her feelings by keeping some distance, but tries to approach her with a simple gesture, giving her a hot drink with a shy smile. The important part is they love each other – we know that because she's still there and she didn't move further away from him. While you've been reading this, they've probably kissed and made up, and caught the bus together.

This page: Adding colour to the character design

Opposite page: Capturing a moment of romance

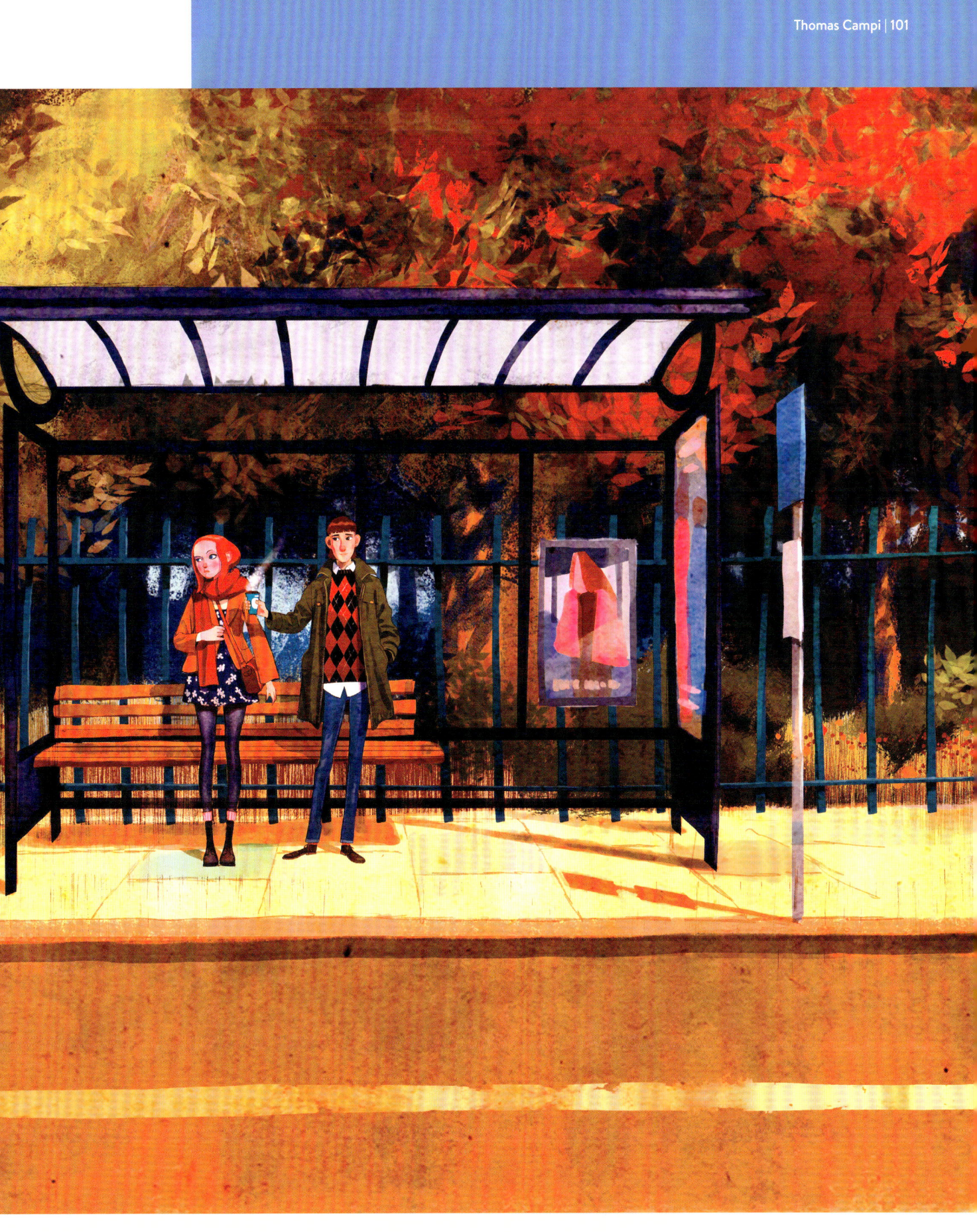

Final image © Thomas Campi

CONTRIBUTORS

ISABELLA AGOSTI
Freelance Illustrator
isabellaagosti.com

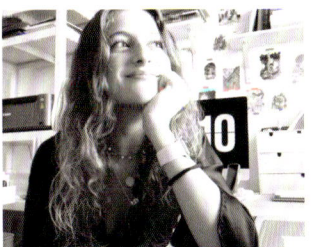

Isabella is a computer science engineer from Italy who has always been passionate about drawing and ultimately made it her freelance job.

YAROSLAVA APOLLONOVA
Freelance Illustrator
odnatamyara.com

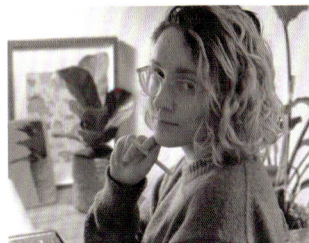

Yara is a freelance illustrator and character designer who lives in Germany. She is currently writing and illustrating her debut picture book.

THOMAS CAMPI
Art Director
thomascampi.com

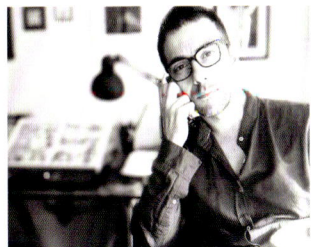

Thomas is a comic artist, currently working on a graphic novel for Dargaud. He also works at Flying Bark Productions on an animated TV series.

TRUDI CASTLE
Associate Art Director
trudiart.com

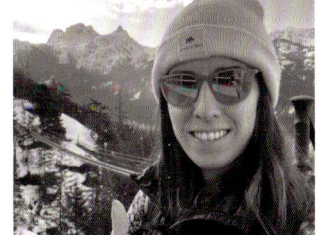

Trudi is a concept artist and illustrator, who has been working in video games for almost 20 years. She loves coffee, donuts, hiking, and, of course, gaming!

JACKIE DROUJKO
Character Designer at Disney TV
jackiedroujko.com

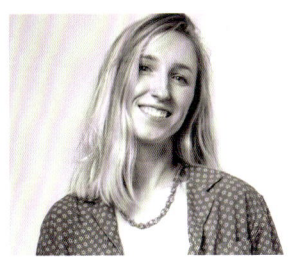

Jackie is a character designer and filmmaker based in Vancouver. She creates simple, appealing designs that communicate compelling stories.

KEVIN HONG
Freelance Illustrator
kevinhong.com

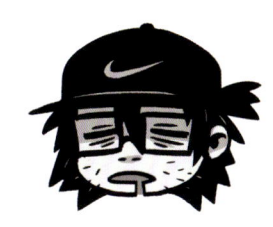

Kevin is a New York-based Korean-American illustrator working in publishing, comics, games, and animation.

JULIA KÖRNER
Illustrator & Character Designer
dyru.de

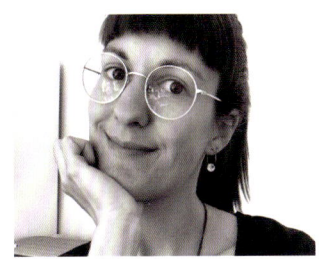

Julia is an illustrator working mostly in the video game and animation industries. She creates whimsical characters and worlds full of magic.

LIDIA MORALES
Character Designer
lidiamoralesart.com

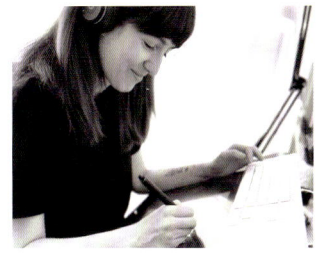

Lidia is a character designer and visual-development artist. She loves telling stories through character design and writing fantastic tales.

MAOR SHARVIT
Art Director
maorsharvitart.com

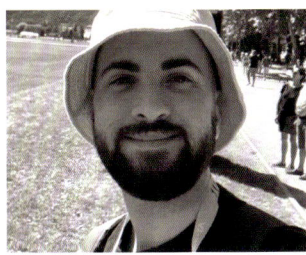

Born and raised in Israel, Maor has always loved drawing characters and has worked at Cartoon Saloon, Nexus, and Dwarf. He currently lives in Paris.

NOOR SOFI
Visual Developer
noorsofiart.com

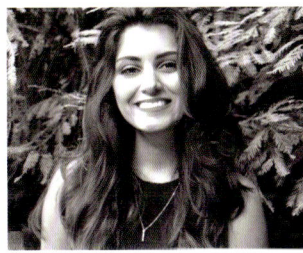

Noor is an illustrator who has worked in animation and publishing. She is inspired by colour, light, and capturing life's sweetest moments.

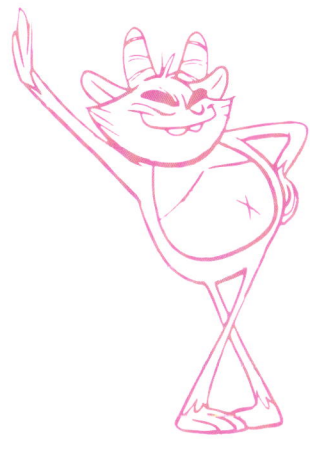

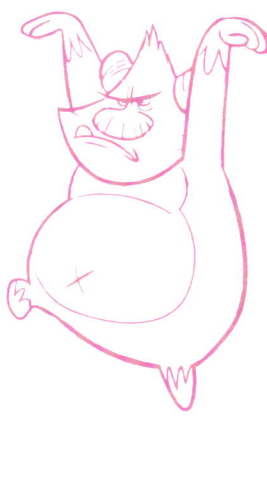

FUR
BY LORENZO ETHERINGTON

BY SIMPLY **SPACING** THE TUFTS *DIFFERENTLY* IN THE **OUTLINE** OF THE FUR, YOU CAN CREATE **TONS** OF **VARIATIONS.**

SHORT TUFTS EVENLY SPACED

MEDIUM ABOVE, LONG BELOW

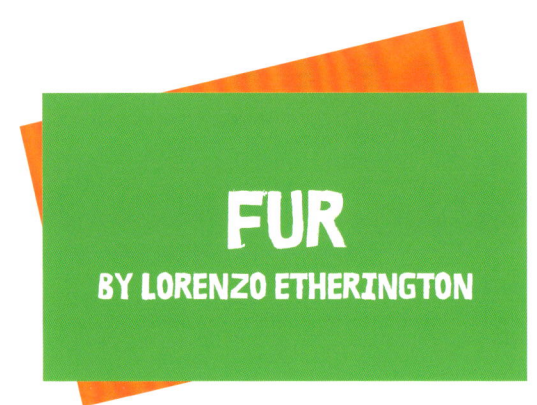

SMALL, FAIRLY EVEN GROUPINGS

LOOSE HAIRS

SMALL, MEDIUM, LARGE

A **MORE STYLISED LOOK** TO YOUR FUR CAN BE ACHIEVED BY **STRIPPING AWAY THE DETAIL** AND RETAINING JUST THE **OUTLINES** OF THE **TUFTS.**

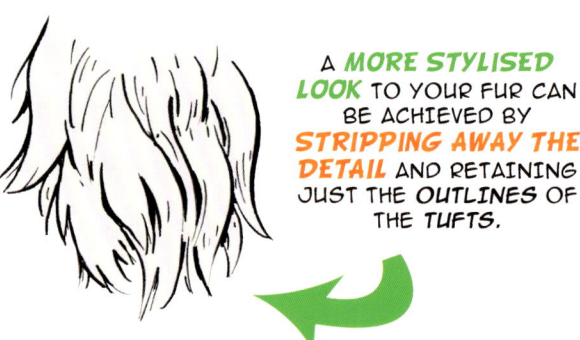

KEEPING WITH A STYLISED APPROACH, LET'S LOOK AT SOME WAYS TO **SUGGEST FUR** ON OUR **CHARACTER DESIGNS.**

BY CONSIDERING THE **SPACING, FORM** AND **SIZE** OF THE FUR, AS WELL AS THE **DIRECTION CHANGES,** YOU CAN CREATE FUR IN **YOUR STYLE.**

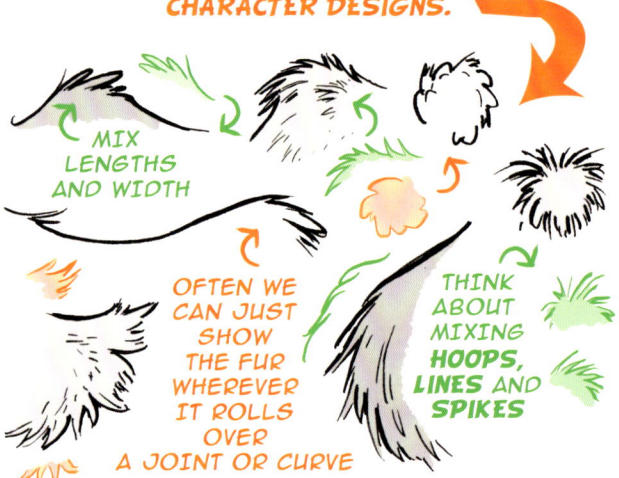

MIX LENGTHS AND WIDTH

OFTEN WE CAN JUST SHOW THE FUR WHEREVER IT ROLLS OVER A JOINT OR CURVE

THINK ABOUT MIXING **HOOPS, LINES** AND **SPIKES**

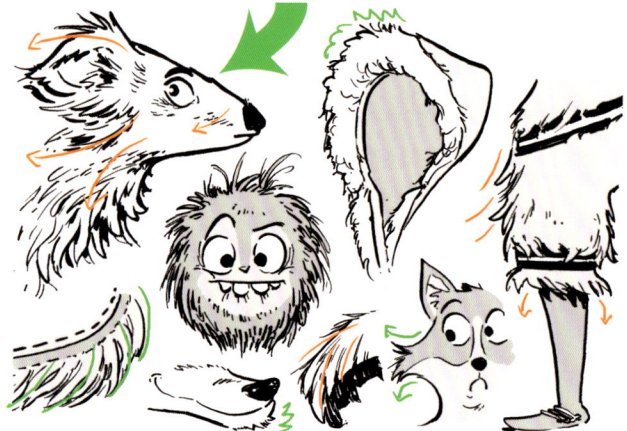